In the Snare of
the Fowler

In the Snare of
the Fowler

✦

Lured by the Charms of Small Town Life

Dale Patterson

iUniverse, Inc.
New York Lincoln Shanghai

In the Snare of the Fowler
Lured by the Charms of Small Town Life

iUniverse books may be ordered through booksellers or by contacting:

iUniverse
2021 Pine Lake Road, Suite 100
Lincoln, NE 68512
www.iuniverse.com
1-800-Authors (1-800-288-4677)

Because of the dynamic nature of the Internet, any Web addresses or links contained in this book may have changed since publication and may no longer be valid.

The views expressed in this work are solely those of the author and do not necessarily reflect the views of the publisher, and the publisher hereby disclaims any responsibility for them.

ISBN: 978-0-595-45381-8 (pbk)
ISBN: 978-0-595-89693-6 (ebk)

Printed in the United States of America

Contents

FOREWORD

The town was known only as an annoyance on my way to and from Chicago and college. It has a stoplight. The many times that light interrupted me in my haste to and from college, it never crossed my mind that someday I would be caught in its snare. I'd sit at the red fuming, catch a glance at the shabby old buildings, pity the folk who had little to do but watch the gallons and dollars register on the pump at the Amoco. I also said, "Thank God I never had to live in such a nowhere place." The green sent me on my way, but my way, years later, led me back just there. I suppose it took an act of God to bring me to that dot on the map, but living a bit down the street from that lone stoplight, I quickly was caught in the snare of this little town. I was the Presbyterian minister; that is what brought me there. But it was my years there with a most wonderful people-lovely people, ugly people, farmers, widows, bankers, babies-their love trapped me.

Being a minister, I was welcomed into the community almost immediately *ex officio*. Yet I was still an outsider, and the people's guard was up. Strangers have to prove themselves trustworthy. That trust opens doors to see what cannot be witnessed by outsiders. By great privilege, many of the people in that community trusted me and let me in to see what I would have missed had I stayed as a stranger.

In writing this book, I use the first person and third person voices, because that's the way it was for me. Sometimes I was in the middle of the people; their stories and mine intersected. In the first person, I lived the story with the people, places and events, as myself, yet, to be sure, never inseparable from my role as a clergyperson. Doing funerals and leading worship services, that's no great problem. People expect me to act like a cleric when I wear the minister's hat. But the rub comes when playing golf, hosting a beauty pageant, walking through the grocery store, or having a coffee at the local watering hole. There are times when the stories are inseparable from my vocation. The third person tells other people's stories where I am an observer. But even as an observer there is no getting away from the fact that I look at the world through the glasses of the Christian faith and my vocation. Nevertheless, first person or third, these stories combine to paint a picture of a fading facet of our twenty-first century world—small town America is less and less the rule, and more and more a novelty.

I write *In the Snare* not only to reminisce, but to invite strangers to glimpse such a lifestyle and to grasp the beauty of small town living. Ministers are voyeurs. Part of our job is to snoop about the world in which we dwell to help us all better understand the hopes, happiness and heartaches of our life situation. The reader will be the judge of the success of this endeavor.

The cover photo through the miracle of computer technology deliberately is blurred. The actual photograph comes from the very downtown wherein these stories take place. We filter-blurred it to mask the identity, and maybe make it more generic, typical of ten thousand downtowns in small town USA. The buildings are old, products of the 1930s, 40s, and have been recycled through multiple usages. If you sat at the stoplight and looked into town, the vista, the colors, the architecture offer little to attract one to come on in. The sparkling strip malls, and hustle and bustle of urban life are non-existent. Little in the picture would seduce one to say, "This looks like a great place with cool people." And you would be wrong. These stories not only speak of our human commonalities, but also of the beauty and delight of the people and community. People are the great asset. I am convinced such is true in most Zip Codes, small town or big city.

The stoplight is on red in the cover-shot, and deliberately exaggerated. "Beyond the stoplight" serves as an antiphon, like a refrain in a song. You have to stop, come into the town, to catch the wonder and the beauty. Hurrying on and the town, like most all small towns, will look like a gray, drab place, another mistaken conclusion. The reader is invited to stop at the light, and turn in to savor the color and fun of small town America.

The chapters function as the framework for the stories. Celebrations through Olympians, places, men, women, sports, and their sad times—these are the means by which I was captured in the snare. In hosting people at my home for dinners and entertaining routinely, I told these stories off the cuff, and my guests routinely laughed, sometimes even cried, but many times they encouraged me to "write them down," to share with others. As the stories came to my mind, I have done so. This is how the book came to pass.

In the Snare of the Fowler—Charmed by the Lure of Small Town Life. That is exactly what happened to me as I turned in at the stoplight and was more than charmed by my tenure amongst my friends in that community. I am increasingly convinced that my experience transcends the particular town. If you turn stop and then turn in, you too may not only be charmed, but find yourself in the snare.

The Psalmist cries out to God entrapped by the fowler's snare. I too cry out, but not a lament, instead, a love song. Life just beyond the stoplight, that is turning to the right or left, as opposed to just passing through, that life was not known to my urban roots, my suburban oblivion. The town was a little farm town in Indiana, but it could have been on the Eastern plains of Colorado, the prairies of Kansas, or the sleepy delta cotton fields of Mississippi. Love songs tell of the focal points, the highlights of two lover's courtship. And so does this love song.

"Surely he will save you from the fowler's snare"

—Psalm 91:3

CELEBRATIONS

Life beyond the stoplight made no attempt to compete with theme parks, big city symphonies, or the Super Bowl in New Orleans. But once I went beyond the stoplight, I found the town lived between celebrations, happy that the last one was over, eager for the next one to come.

"Reverend, tell the fellas that the pancakes are too thick. No one likes their pancakes wet on the inside."

"Thanks, Harley, I'll let the guys know," I said. Harley was not the food critic for the *Benton Review*. He was just a retired farmer, member of my church, and a dissatisfied customer at The Rotary Club Pancake Breakfast, a retired farmer who liked his pancakes well done.

The Pancake Breakfast began weeks before with planning discussions at the Wednesday night Rotary meeting. Ted, the President, confirmed that Steve was in charge of supplies, and the grills, Rob was in charge of setup and cleanup. It was held on Saturday morning in the community shelter at the Town Park, the weekend of the Fourth of July. Always has been, always will be.

Saturday came, usually hazy, dripping, the sun rising on another hot, sticky Indiana morning. But the big, silver, West Bend percolators already were gurgling and hissing their brew. Boiling coffee's whiff mixed with the sizzle of sausage links on the grill.

"Hey, I don't think this grill is getting hot enough. We'll be all day cooking hotcakes on these, if we don't get 'em hotter," an anonymous Rotarian hollered.

"Do you smell gas? Steve, Steve," Smitty shouted over the growing confusion at the community shelter. "Hey setup man! Stevie. Was anybody smart enough to tighten these gas fittings. Smells like we're about to go up in a puff of blue flame."

Steve, a bank teller, when not the commandant of the pancake breakfast, wished Smitty would shut up. "If you think they're leakin' go get some liquid soap and drip it on the fittings. Then look for bubbles. Otherwise, get cooking."

"Where the hell am I gonna get soap?" Smitty was nearly mutinous. "Anyway, where's the pancake batter?"

Pancake batter is a science, if not an art form. The Rotarians left such high responsibility as batter to the dentist. "Harold, where's the batter?" Smitty passed the buck.

Harold was unaffected, "It's not ready. It's too lumpy, and I'm afraid some of the lumps are flies, but give me a minute and we'll have it just right."

"Okay, Betty Crocker. We can sell the flies in the pancakes as protein enrichment, or blueberry pancakes." Smitty never gave up needling anyone who opened the door for harassment.

Behind The Rotary Club's not-so-well-oiled kitchen crew, stood the ever-faithful Rotary Auxiliary, a.k.a. wives of Rotarians, who could help with the coffee, pancake batter, or other such sexually-linked domestic duties. Most of the men in Fowler were not enlightened in the skills of domestic duties such as kitchen work. Not only were their wives, for the most part, glad of this ineptitude, but they were secure in such a stereotyped world. Through it all, a look of terror painted their faces when their inept husbands donned an apron. So they hovered over the proceedings nearly as closely as the flies.

The doors opened at seven for breakfast, but farmers and rural folk, many of them, consider seven o'clock brunch, not breakfast. So the line pressed the door at six thirty before a pancake inventory accumulated. Every year it was the same. We never could get ahead, "Need more pancakes," above the laughter, and the press of the hungry patrons. "Keep your pants on. We're making 'em as fast as we can."

"This damn grill still isn't hot enough," protested Smitty. Grill Two was hot, but as Kate Stokely expertly observed, "It's not well-seasoned. Therefore it sticks awful."

"Spray some of that stuff in the can there, or slop some oil on it," Smitty was always quick with advice. Yet in spite of the confusion, controversy, and the flies, throughout the four hours of each Pancake Breakfast, the ragtag bunch of good-natured volunteer restaurateurs would feed three hundred to five hundred hungry mouths. Most did not complain, and all paid the three bucks. You do the math.

"You put too much oil on there, and Harley will be complaining about greasy pancakes." Grill Two Chef, Jerry, knew Harley's food critic history. But Smitty, argumentative as ever, said, "Oh, Harley don't give a rip about grease. He just don't like 'em wet in the middle."

Man on the moon, Space Shuttle launched and safely returned, such accomplishments pale in comparison to the logistical demands of the Rotary Breakfast. It is a science to warm Log Cabin syrup, keep it warmed, and distributed across all the picnic tables covered with white sheets of butcher paper. A few kettles simmered, each warmed a half dozen syrup bottles. Syrup should be served like baby formula, just a drop on the inside wrist is the proper gauge. If it feels warm on the wrist, but not too hot, it is just right! Added to the technical demands of warm syrup was keeping the coffee served, orange juice topped off in the white Styrofoam cups, and sausage seconds plopped on the plates of carnivorous rural diners. For a bunch of farmers, insurance salesmen, and a dentist, this was no small accomplishment.

The community shelter looked like an abandoned army barracks. White clapboard sides, sheet metal roof, with windows of plywood on hinges that opened to let the air flow freely. Inside stood four long rows of picnic tables that spanned the fifty yards of what would be our restaurant for the morning. As the breakfast progressed flies took delight in sampling syrup spilled on the butcher paper table cloths, as well as congregating in no small number on the many tubs of margarine dispersed throughout the makeshift dining room. Along with the flies, the corn-belt has a resident we knew as the corn bug. Corn bugs are black specks the size of a pea that float over from the adjacent corn fields, and seem to prosper best while dwelling in the midst of that thin film of perspiration on any Hoosier in summer on a steamy morning. Flies, corn bugs, Rotarians, and Hoosiers, they all flocked for pancakes on Fourth of July morning.

The customers were diverse, as diverse as white folk in rural American can be. In one cluster, apron-clad Rotarians served more coffee, sausage and pancakes to the clutch of widows gathered in one corner of the shelter. Elsewhere, young families buttered and syruped pancakes, as parents cut into bite size chunks the soggy golden delicacy. "Timmy, close your mouth when you chew," the hairdresser disciplined while chatting with a girlfriend across the table. "And after we finish here, I'll pick you up and we'll go to town, to the Mall, Ayres, and maybe go to Arni's for a salad," she continued. "Timmy, what did I tell you? I don't want to see your food as you chew. It's gross. Do you understand, young man?" The more serious talk took place amongst the group of venture capitalists, also known as retired farmers. "If it don't rain right quick now as the corn's tasseling, we'll be up a creek." Harley was not only an expert on the niceties of pancake production, but also understood the complicated fiscal parameters of corn production, and its effects on the cost of a bushel of corn. "By God, no rain and corn may go to $2.50 even three bucks a bushel. But we won't have none to sell," he concluded. A resounding chorus of "Yeaps," affirmed Harley's analysis.

As cleanup approached, the line of hungry pancake eaters dwindled to a trickle, so the crew became more sophomoric. You don't know what a thrill it is to see the town dentist throw a pancake at the elementary school principal. "Sawbones, put that pancake down. Don't you even think about throwing that pancake at me," said the principal, even as he opened a bottle of syrup to defend himself.

"Harold, if you come another step further I'll get that Presbyterian Elmer Gantry to baptize you in Log Cabin." Such a threat ended the dentist's venture into violence.

"Hey, Smitty, when's your tee time?"

"One o'three. It'll be hotter than hell by then," Smitty answered. Smitty rapidly was losing interest in sausage, pancakes, and Rotarian responsibility. He was already transitioning to defend his title against Puff in the Benton County Country Club's Firecracker Open, held every Fourth of July.

"Okay, Rob, get your boys doing the cleanup. I'm off to defend my title," Smitty left no occasion unused to needle his fellow Rotarians. "Damn, there's syrup everywhere."

Actually The Rotary Pancake Breakfast was part of one great extravaganza, the town Fourth of July Celebration, held each year at the town park. The town park was five to ten acres on the outskirts of town. To one side of the park, a stand of big, old, oak trees made shade from the hot, July sun. The middle of the park shared the shelter and the town public swimming pool. The other side of the park opened for a softball field. Bordering the entire top of the park was a pond, actually a reclaimed clay pit. The entire park spanned maybe six hundred yards. This provided the setting of the Fourth of July Celebration.

The celebration amounted to a series of special events: a gospel sing, children's competitions, three on three basketball shootout, and concluded with the finale, the fireworks. Throughout it all was the self-proclaimed, World Famous Flea Market, and a host of culinary delights served at various booths.

Friday afternoon the gypsies arrived at the park in their motor homes. They weren't really gypsies, but nomads who ply their wares from one flea market to the next. Each motor home or van unpacked under the big oaks, opened folding metal tables, and spread their wares. They draped flickering Italian lights over each table area, and set about to earn their fortune. Some sold various antiques, Mason Jars, Ball Jars. The next merchant peddled tiny dolls and soda pop bottles. Antique guns were a big hit with American Legionnaires and the VFW locals.

As I strolled through the market, I found it most amusing, first, as to what people had the nerve to sell, but second, what people would buy. One old guy sold nothing but buttons, bottle caps and belt buckles. That was it, and he was doing a booming business. Grace Johnson, one of my Presbyterians, supplemented her income from working at the Nursing Home, "Serving meals to the old folk," as she liked to say. Grace was in her late eighties herself. But during the flea market she made a killing. Grace found an untapped niche in the environmental novelty market. During the cold gray winters she wove together bread loaf wrappers in the shape of a doormat. Actually she told me she crocheted them. Grace would ask her neighbors and family to save their Wonder Bread, Dolly Madison, Kroger, and Pepperidge Farm plastic bread wrappers, and there she was in the park over the Fourth asking five bucks a piece. She had just a few days to sell off her winter-built inventory. As I visited houses across the county, often I'd see there on the doorstep Grace's handiwork. I wondered if I were stepping on my own Wonder Bread bags.

Interspersed throughout the tables of junkware being pawned, I discovered the best reason to roam through the flea market: the food. Standard fare included the Christian Church's Hamburger Fry, which paled in comparison to the Hot Dog and Grilled Sausages hucksterd by the Knights of Columbus from Sacred Heart Catholic Church. Rumors perennially circulated that the K of C petitioned the town fathers to sell Beer 'n Brats at the Celebration, but were always turned down. These rumors most often were reiterated by soft-spoken Methodists or Baptists, "Catholics, you know!" But my favorites, the three I never missed come every Fourth Celebration, were Blue Snow Cones, Funnel Cakes, and Corn Dogs. The Boy Scouts shaved ice and plopped it in a cone shaped Dixie cup, and splattered syrup on that ball-topped cone of icy delight. Fifty cents got you Orange, Root Beer, Grape, Cherry, or Blue. Yes, blue, no one knew what flavor it was, so everyone just asked for ol' blue. The first and following slurps and chews of ice were heaven. The inevitable followed, a blue streak drip on my white Izod golf shirt, and those telltale blue-stained lips. It was worth it.

No sooner had I quenched my thirst, and it was time to go to the American Legion's Corn Dog booth. I cannot imagine any real American not savoring this treat, but one time I met a person who had never heard of a corn dog. I suggested that her passport be revoked, then told the unfortunate that a corn dog was a fine hot dog on a stick, dipped in a thick, seasoned batter of corn meal, then fried in hot oil. When golden brown, and slightly cooled, dressed with a little mustard or ketchup, and a few bites later, bon appetite! Chase that with a Diet Coke, and a refreshing burp, and one might be ready for dessert.

Dessert was provided by Farm Bureau Co-op: funnel cakes. Though I am not sure of the secret recipe, I suspect it is little more than pancake batter drizzled from a funnel into hot oil, fried a little bit, and then drained. When done, it looks sort of like a golden brown, but mangled waffle. Lesser funnel cakes enthusiasts plop strawberries, or chocolate syrup, even blueberries on top. I am a purist; dredge the funnel cake in powdered sugar, and then savor. If one planned the Fourth Celebration carefully, this menu could be repeated three to four times during the weekend celebration, easy.

Actually life hardly got any better than to have a blue snow cone in one's hand, sit on the grass come Saturday dusk, and listen to the mixed chorus of the various churches at the gospel sing. "Jesus Paid It All," never was so moving as with a blue snow cone buzz.

Throughout the weekend the Three on Three basketball tournament continued, but the outcome normally was the same. A few thirty year olds vainly hoped to capture the trophy, but always were finally walloped by the ringers: last year's graduated seniors from the high school who could not get on the team at Purdue or Indiana.

I never understood why the children's games were scheduled for two on Sunday afternoon. A hotter or stickier time for competition with parents required to watch could not have been found. The children's olympiad included the three-legged race. Usually in this event, two children race about fifty yards and back, each with a common leg tied together or sharing a potato sack. This actually is a race to be won by the tortoise. The hare, represented by pre-pubescent, but already macho ten year old boys with names like, Butch and Luke, will always lose to the soft-spoken, prissy, little girls, usually with names like Jennifer and Rachel, the tortoise. Butch and Luke blister from the starting line, but their machismo will be their doom. Shortly the hare, Luke and Butch, stumble as the prisses walk on by to victory. The next two events require more dexterity: the water balloon toss, and the egg toss. Basically the same event, but greater penalties for the losers of the egg toss. Partners line up in two parallel lines several feet apart. A water balloon is tossed to the other partner. If caught, and not exploded, the partners are still "alive." Each surviving partner takes a step or two back, and the balloon is tossed back again. This continues until just one pair remains. The losers normally are splattered with water. Better water though, than egg. It was only after playing this game for years that I realized its sadistic nature, everyone loses, no one wins. Because sooner or later, every pair gets creamed with an egg or water balloon. The game obviously was the entertainment brainchild of parents. It was one of the rare occasions when parents delighted to see their children smeared with egg yolk, or soaked to the gills.

Yet no where in America does a Fourth Celebration end without a Fireworks Extravaganza. The Fowler Celebration was no exception. But it almost was. Every year it was nip and tuck in the town budget whether there would be adequate funding to pay for aerial bombs, and golden sparkle bursts. And though the rumor in the depth of winter always prevailed that the fireworks had been cancelled, every Fourth, some fund, some well-heeled financier, was tapped, and the Fireworks began.

As dusk on the evening of the Fourth fell, the park crowded with blankets covered with families and grandmas and grandpas sitting nearby on folding chairs or chaise lounges. Smitty and Chuck and their families roasted marshmallows on a little Hibachi grill they got at K-Mart. In violation of city ordinances, they along with a few other rascals, sipped cool ones they pulled from their Coleman coolers in the trunks of their cars. Darkness descended, and it appeared as though most everyone had left, but their voices remained. The smell of Deep Woods Off mixed with Indiana humidity, and Hoosier perspiration, with an occasional waft of smoke from a Marlboro.

Teenage boys, called "hooligans," or "street urchins," by the town's elderly, entertained themselves in the interim firing bottle rockets at one another. Sometimes they caused the rapid crackle and machine gun popping of a packet of burning lady fingers which littered the silence. But through it all was the din of little children excitedly whispering to their parents, "Mommy, when is it gonna start?"

Ironic as it may seem, a few of the Fowler Volunteer Firemen served as assistants to the hired firework and incendiary specialists. Shortly after dark, the Fire Chief and crew located across the town pond, gave the word to begin. A thud, a hiss, and the first rocket screeched into the Hoosier sky. It was a golden fireburst with an aerial bomb chaser. In rapid fire, the first thirty seconds of the twenty minute volley whetted the appetite of the throngs for more sparkle, more booms, more colors. The crowd was insatiable; the incendiary specialists could not load and fire fast enough.

The narration was provided by the crowd itself. There was no need for an emcee. Each explosion was echoed by the "Oohs" of the crowds spread out across the park. Fathers spoke words of expertise to their little children after each new explosion, "Honey, that boom is called an aerial bomb." The barrage continued with the appropriate accompaniment, as the finale approached. The last minute lighted the sky with a continuous volley of explosions, sparkling, smoke, and the grand finale. Across the lake a twelve foot display erupted into red, white and blue light; Ol' Glory in a constitutionally-approved fire. Had John Phillip Sousa been there with his band to play "Stars and Stripes Forever," the citizenry would have risen in one accord to sing with patriotic fervor. But lacking that, we all applauded, and in satisfaction concluded, "That was very nice. I think even better than last year. I guess it's time to go home." And it was.

Another Fourth of July Celebration for the record books.

"Hi, Ernie. How ya doin'?" "Ernie. Ernie, Over here," the parade bystander emphatically waved, trying to get Ernie's attention. When Ernie finally connected the face with the voice that repeatedly hailed him, his face lit with a joy that flowed from his toes to his toothy grin. On the side of the robin's egg blue EZ GO golf cart was a poster board on which was written in bold black marker, "Little League Parade Grand Marshall, and #1 Fan," followed by even larger letters, the "E" in bright green, the "R" in iridescent red, the "N" royal blue, the "I" in sunshine yellow, and the "E" again in green, "ERNIE." The proud Grand Marshall rode in the golf cart following the Ford Police Cruiser of the Fowler Police Department. Of course, in keeping with parade protocol, every flashing light on the police car was lighted or flashing, accented with an occasional screech of the electronic siren. The Fowler Little League Parade majestically marched down the main drag, Fifth Street, heading east from the stoplight proceeding to the Court House, turning north to congregate at the Little League diamond. Had we arrived at the Hall of Fame in Cooperstown or at Yankee Stadium, it would have been no greater celebration than the mid-season Little League Parade and Carnival.

I have learned since that in the big city, often Little League baseball catches the attention of parents and participants, but much of the community remains oblivious to the games, the competition, and the hoopla associated with youth baseball. In Fowler, to be sure, parents and participants were at the center of the youth baseball hype, but most of the town invested in the fun and anxiety of Little League Baseball as well. The Parade and Carnival were proof of that thesis; the whole town turned out, whether due to volition or compulsion. After all, on a June mid-week evening in rural Hoosierland, apart from watching the Cubs on TV, or having a cold one on the front porch, there were not all that many options. Why not watch your child, or your neighbor's child indulge in the thrill of victory or the agony of defeat?

The Parade was always scheduled at the mid-point of the Little League season, normally about eight of sixteen games completed. The police car led the entourage down Fifth Street. I suspect the police officer, in this case, Art, when in the training academy was taught how to lead a parade. He probably fantasized about escorting the President of the United States down Fifth Avenue in New York City. But if you are a cop in Fowler, Indiana, Fifth Street will have to do. Escorting the Little League Parade, and the occasional funeral was about the only escort responsibility the police ever had to perform.

Art would speak through the P.A. system of his cruiser, "Ma'am, Ma'am, you'll have to get that baby stroller back on to the curb, we'd hate for anyone to hurt that little baby." The compliant citizen-mother obeyed immediately.

Ernie, the Grand Marshall, followed in the golf cart chauffeured by the head umpire and President of the Little League, Steve, also a bank teller, and Rotarian Pancake Potentate. Ernie was famous throughout town, but much-loved by all those who spend their nights at the ballpark. Today we would say that Ernie suffered a mental impairment. Then and prior, those around him and who loved him said, "Ernie is just not quite right," but he loved baseball. He loved the Chicago Cubs whom he adored by way of the radio listening to Lou Boudreau call the games on WGN. He never missed a game. But neither did he miss a game of Little League. He loved the Little League as much as the Cubs. He cheered every team, every player. His box seat at the Little League ballpark was not a luxury suite, but a folding chair right behind home plate. He watched through the chain link backstop while listening to the Cubs on the radio broadcast from the boom-box sitting next to his chair.

He cheered every batter. With a slur of speech as the next hitter dug in the batter's box, Ernie would encourage her or him, it was a co-ed league, "C'mmmooonnn, g-g-ge-ge-get a, a, hhhhit!" His next encouragement was for the pitcher, the shortstop or catcher, "Plaaayyy good deeeefense!" I guess the truth that Ernie was not quite right, meant he was not normal, not the normal fan, but he was the most considerate. Such a tradition usually earned Ernie the honor of being dubbed the Grand Marshall of the Little League Parade.

The parade itself was made up of each of the teams marching down the middle of Fifth Street, team by team, in uniform. First, came all the T-Ball teams, then came the Minor League teams. The Minor League teams' uniforms consisted of a colored t-shirt, and a matching baseball cap. Across the chest of each t-shirt was printed the team name, such as Dodgers, Cubs, Padres. Following the Minor League teams came the Major League teams. The Major League teams wore official uniforms, the likeness of the real Major League team uniforms. Each team marched in the reverse order of the current standings. That is, the team in sixth place, marched first, then fifth, marched second, and so forth. Parade protocol is not to be belittled. The current first place team got to ride on the fire truck. This amounted to no small motivation to win, to go for first place. Because all little leaguers hoped they could ride on the fire truck in the colossal Little League Parade.

The galleries that watched the parade, many seated in lawn chairs along Fifth Street, were composed of the townsfolk, not just the baseball parents. It was truly an all-town event. Each of the coaches of the teams were given a bag of candy, Tootsie rolls, Smarties, and the like. The players grabbed a handful of the candy, and tossed their treats at the adoring spectators along the parade route.

Behind the Grand Marshall trailed another five or six golf carts, the first carrying the reigning Little League Queen, followed by the candidates vying for the prestigious title of the next Little League Queen. The Queen and her accompanying court, most normally, were the little sisters of current Little League players.

Being the Queen of the Little League, or even a candidate for the next queen is no trivial title. As each of these young girls paraded toward the ballpark, they all knew for one of them, the one lucky enough to be named the next queen, that her life would be forever and indelibly marked with honor. And she would be summoned from her humdrum of normalcy one year from then to reign over that parade again in the position of distinction, in the first golf cart, the reigning Fowler Little League Queen. That honor was just a matter of minutes in the future.

Each of the Major League teams in the Little League elected one of their little sisters to be the team's candidate for that year's queen. Most of the candidates were not polished in beauty pageants or talent pageants, after all, they were usually only about six years old. Swimsuit competition, therefore, was no controversy. The candidates each wore, I guess, what would approximate an evening gown. Long frilly dresses, hair curled, some up, some down, but after each girl arrived at the ballpark, she was escorted by her older brother, or sister from the golf cart limousine onto the field, just behind the pitcher's mound. On the mound a flower draped trellis covered a white wrought iron queen's throne, on which the reigning queen was seated. The competition was about to begin.

The emcee, The Reverend Darrell Smith from down at First Christian Church, introduced the candidates, then the judges.

The judges: Rob, the pharmacist, a Presbyterian, Jenny, on the Little League Auxiliary Board, also a Presbyterian, and Garnet, another Little League mom, but a Methodist. Darrell must have consulted the Miss America Book of Vapid Questions for the sole question of the competition. But as most of the candidates were only six, their ability to wax philosophic was somewhat limited.

"Honey," Darrell asked, "What do you want to do when you grow up and why?"

Someone's little sister, Renee, was the first to respond. All feared that the pressure would overwhelm her, but Renee finally whispered, "A mommy."

But that wasn't good enough for the emcee. "Why do you want to be a mommy, honey?"

"Ummm, because." On such answers, and the overly subjective cuteness factor, the expert panel of judges would have to select the next queen.

My daughter was next. She was only four, but she started a groundswell of career choices. "Leslie, what you wanna do?"

She pondered the question, "A nurse. I want to be a nurse."

"Why do you want to be a nurse, Les'?"

Her cogent answer was to slamdunk her grasp on the queen title, "Because I want to help people." Great for a four year old, huh?

The next four candidates followed the groundswell of nursing enthusiasm, all because they also wanted to help people and five minutes later, my daughter was crowned the next Little League Queen. Any murmuring from the disgruntled families of the other candidates whining about two out of three Presbyterian judges was quickly ignored, and we celebrated in the honor and glory of the queen's triumph.

Now that the Queen had been chosen, the Little League carnival could begin. This was a carnival only in the most Spartan sense. The food was the standard Little League concession stand fare: candy bars, popcorn, hot dogs and a variety of different sodas, or as they say in that part of the country, "pop."

In addition to food there were a variety of carnival events or competitions. Little Leaguers played Home Run Derby against their mothers. Ten year old boys are almost as big a braggarts as their fathers when it comes to a desire to humiliate their mothers. But it was sweet revenge when the hairdresser, Diane, caught her son's, Timmy's, self-proclaimed awesome fastball, and launched it over the left field fence. Her performance even quieted a few of the more machismo fathers.

Rundown. Have you ever played rundown? That was a carnival event too. The parents alternated playing catch between first and second base. The object is for one of the Little Leaguers to run to the opposite base, while his/her parents throw and catch the ball as it passes back and forth between the bases. If the parents managed to catch their child in between the bases, then a rundown ensued; the parent with the ball chases the runner to tag the runner out. Though the game had certain aerobic advantages, the greatest delight was watching the kids play with their parents.

Each of the coaches of the teams had to do time at the sponge throwing pit. Sponge throwing amounted to little more than payback time. A coach stood behind a cutout sheet of plywood. Painted on the plywood was a caricature of a fat slob of a baseball coach, with a hole where the head should be. Each coach stood behind the plywood for his/her time of "duty," and various players from the league, their team and the opponent's teams, each paid a dime to have the privilege of standing ten feet in front of the coach of their choosing, pulling a sopping wet sponge from a bucket, and hurling it into the puss of the coach on duty. I was a coach, and at the time, my team was in first place. Plenty of my players desired to let me have it, and they did. But it was a bit disconcerting when other team's players paid dime after dime to cream the Oriole's coach, Reverend Patterson, in the face with a soaking sponge.

Through it all, with hot dogs and cotton candy, sponges in the face, and queens being crowned, a good time again was had by all.

"Ya comin' to the fish fry?"

"Fish fry? Well, yeah, I guess. When is it?"

"When is a fish fry in a mostly-Catholic town? Friday night!" So went many conversations on the streets during those days of the Benton County Fair. All celebrations in Fowler paled in comparison to the Benton County Fair. Not only did it mark the end of Summer, being in mid-August, but it brought not just the town together, but the whole county. Even though the fair had already been on for several days, it was the Fish Fry served by all the local service organizations, the Rotary, the Kiwanis, the Lion's Club, and even the Knights of Columbus, cooperated to put on a feed for the folk of the county. The cooks, however, were a bunch dubiously-named, the Jonah Club. Had Julia Child cooked, it would have drawn no more notoriety than the Jonah Club. Their fish fries were famous across Northern Indiana. It was the Jonah Club Fish Fry that really kicked off the Fair.

The menu was simple: fried fish, French fries, slaw, white bread slices, and iced tea or lemonade.

Junior Mason, no more of a food critic than Harley, bedeviled the Jonah Club chefs, "I never seen no square fish in the ocean that you could cut in four by four chunks." Junior referred to the fish. The fish came frozen in fifty pound blocks. Sort of like a block of ice, except it's not water, but fish. Landlubber farmers speculated that it was haddock, or cod, or even a little halibut. "You know it might be a combination of whitefish. Oh, I don't know what the hell it is. But with a cold brew it sure eats good." Beer was forbidden on the fairgrounds, but careful observers noticed a buzz amongst the Jonah Club fish fryers that could not be explained by a swarm of bees.

The blocks of frozen fish were cut with hacksaws into four by four squares. Each of the squares maybe were two feet long. Then that square was put on a meat slicer, just like the ones down at the IGA. The slicer was set for about an inch and a half, maybe two inches thick. That four by four by inch and a half square was tossed into a batter, then fried in hot fat for a few minutes. It was "All you could eat" at the fish fry. Pile on a serving of French fries, creamy cole slaw, and it was a gourmet treat. The service club tent was jammed with customers that Friday night from five o'clock until closing time, about ten. The smell of the fish fry filled not just the tent, but wafted over the fair all that night.

At some point, the Queen of the Benton County Fair made her appearance at the dinner. She ate a respectable, but not too indulgent portion of fish; her job was to look pretty, smile, and get ready for the Queen competition at the upcoming Indiana State Fair just after Labor Day.

The County Fair Queen pageant, actually was a festival within the larger fair celebration. "Reverend Patterson?" I took the phone call maybe a month or so before the fair was to begin. "Yes, this is Mr. Patterson, How may I help you?"

"My name is Pauline Fugitt. I am the chairman of the County Fair Queen Pageant Committee. Your name was suggested by the Fair Steering Committee to be the Master of Ceremonies for the Queen Pageant."

"Is that so?"

"Yes, sir, or Reverend. I go to Sacred Heart. Should I call you 'Mr.' or 'Sir,' or 'Reverend?' We call our pastor, 'father.' Should I call you 'father?'"

"No, 'Dale,' would be just fine."

"Oh, I can't do that. I'll just call you 'Mr. Patterson.' Is that all right?"

"Yes, Pauline. That'll be fine."

"Well, Mr. Patterson, the emcee sort of is the host of the pageant on the opening evening of the fair, that'd be on Wednesday night of the fair week. But also, you'd need to spend the day, that Wednesday, with the judges interviewing the girls, uh, the contestants, and observing the judging process, though you're not a judge. Do you think you could do us this big favor? Some of the folk on the Steering Committee thought you'd do a great job. Please help us out."

"Pauline, I'd be glad to do it. Thank you for asking."

That was how I came to be front and center the opening night of the Benton County Fair at the Queen Pageant. Actually it began with a luncheon at the cafeteria of one of the local elementary schools that Wednesday. The judges were there: a school principal for an adjoining county school, an Assistant Football Coach at Purdue, just twenty five miles south of Fowler, an officer from a little bank in a little town just across the state line over in Illinois, and a hairdresser from Contempo Expressions, the chic place for a coif; it too on the Purdue campus. In retrospect, the influence of hairdressers in Fowler seemed beyond all proportion that I was accustomed to in other communities in which I have lived.

The judges, the contestants, and I ate a light lunch. I do not remember enjoying the meal. I am sure the contestants were much too tense to savor the petit fours filled with chicken salad, because the interview portion of the contest was about to begin.

Each of the contestants, all young women, either seniors in high school, or maybe freshmen or sophomores in college, entered the room. They wore business suits-some variation of a dark wrap-around skirt, a matching jacket, silk blouse, some shade of stockings, and coordinated pumps or heels. Each contestant in her time entered the room. I greeted her and escorted her to a comfortable chair positioned at the open end of a U-shaped arrangement of tables. The judges sat around the U, each with a manila folder containing the contestants' dossiers, a pencil, a legal pad, and a pitcher of water with a glass. The pitchers reminded me of the coffee pitchers you may have used if you have ever been to I-Hop.

"Good afternoon, my name is Sally Percazzi. I live in Boswell. I am Senior at BC (Translate, Benton Central High School). I hope to attend IU (Translate, Indiana University) where I will major in Elementary Education. I have two little brothers, Mikey, a sophomore at BC, and Tommy, a sixth grader at Boswell Elementary. My mother is a …" So began the interview process.

Questions came from observations in each of their dossiers like, "Sally, what do you hope to accomplish as an Elementary Education teacher?" "Why IU?" or, "Tell us what it has been like growing up with two little brothers." Each interview lasted about half an hour. Six contestants later the interviews were over. Everybody took a break, and we were to reassemble at the fair grounds for the beauty and talent portion of the competition which was to begin at eight o'clock.

The six contestants: Sally, Michelle, Pepper, Heather, Paula, and Joanie. The first three, all high school seniors, the latter three, college frosh. All their parents had to be proud. These six girls were a great advertisement for raising children of character, intelligence and beauty, even amidst soybeans and cornstalks; all healthy American girls. The Beach Boys sung about them wishing they all were California girls.

That evening upon reconvening, they drew straws as to who would go first. The next event: talent competition. Michelle drew the first slot; she played Pachelbel's Canon on a console piano on stage. Though I was not a judge, she was the best talent, even though she was one of the two Presbyterians in the pageant; my opinion about talent is unarguable. Sally followed; she was a baton twirler. She twirled to the disco rage of the day, "YMCA," sung by the Village People on tape accompaniment. However, Sally was handicapped. On one of her tosses, the pageant held in the fair pavilion, little more than a barn with bleachers, the baton clanked a rafter. The judges conferred, and decided that the ground rules for this competition must afford Sally a special allowance. I concurred. After all it was no responsibility of Sally that she could throw and catch her twirling baton thirty feet in the air, even though the barn only allowed sixteen feet. Though I am sure Sally was not penalized by this problem, actually she was not that good.

Heather, not a redhead, but a bottle blonde, performed a dramatic reading; she recited Tennyson's, "Crossing the Bar." Not being a judge, I thought it an inappropriate selection for a nineteen year old to contemplate her death, "I hope to see my Pilot face-to-face. When I cross the bar." In any case speaking of death, killed her chances at winning the talent portion. Paula and Joanie provided the pageant clichés: an accordion solo playing "Lady of Spain," and a ventriloquist with a Charlie McCarthy clone, respectively.

Pepper, the second Presbyterian in the competition, ended with a sultry torch song, Gershwin's, "Someone to Watch Over Me." Presbyterians surely captured a One-Two sweep in the Talent Phase.

Then the competition became difficult for everyone, contestants, audience, especially parents, and even me. The difficulty was the swim suit and evening gown competition. Without violating my ordination vows, or being indiscreet, a few of these girls found it difficult to do good things for a swimming suit. In other words, it was not likely that *Sports Illustrated* was going to invite them to pose. Yet a few of the contestants made it difficult for their parents, because they saw their sweet, healthy daughters parade before a thousand leers in the bleachers, and their daughters looked entirely too much like they would fit just fine between the covers of *SI*. My difficulty was with the latter as well. I am a minister, a husband and a father. It was entirely inappropriate to leer with the masses.

The Evening Gown portion provided only a slight relief from the difficulty. Those contestants who struggled with a swimsuit seemed somewhat less disadvantaged by an evening gown. Yet those girls who looked stunning in a swimsuit dazzled the judges, the crowd, and me in evening gowns as well.

My difficulty, my anxiety, increased with every minute waiting for the judges' decision. I had to fill empty time. "Be funny. Be charming," the Pageant Committee warned me this was the hard part of my responsibility: entertaining one thousand in the audience while the judges tabulated the results. "You'll do just fine." I did not do just fine. I fumbled. I resorted to insulting Methodists, Catholics, even Presbyterians. My wittiness evaporated, and my anxiety grew every passing moment. I knew who was going to win, and the thought of pinning that "Miss Benton County" banner on Pepper terrified me.

Of course, she would win. She stole the interview portion of the competition. She was so chatty, gregarious; she won it when asked what she wanted to do with her Communications degree she hoped to earn at IU. "I want to be the next Jane Pauley," she giggled with the cute answer, and I was sure she would capture the interview portion. Her torch song at least kept her in second, and in all candor, her presentation in an evening gown and swimsuit reminded me of a woman competing against little girls.

When the hairdresser judge gave me the envelope my terror approached the threshold. I opened the linen envelope. My fears were only confirmed. "The Runner Up for this year's Benton County Fair Queen is Michelle Christensen." The Presbyterians took One, Two indeed. Was I in a fix! "This year's Benton County Fair Queen is Miss Pepper Banks."

After a few moments of screams, my horror was fulfilled. Pauline Fugitt, the one who corralled me into what would accomplish my defrocking, placed in my hands the royal blue banner with the gold lettering on it reading, "Miss Benton County Fair." "Mr. Patterson, pin it on her."

It was then that I prayed someone else had won. It actually was all my problem, not at all fair to Pepper. She was obviously the winner. The problem was me. Pepper wore a black, low-cut evening gown with tiny spaghetti straps across her beautifully-tanned shoulders. It was the spaghetti straps that constituted the problem. Underneath those straps was cleavage that any American boy only dreamed of. I had to fasten two safety pins on those straps, maintain my composure, keep my status as Minister of the Gospel, not offend any of my parishioners with my fumbling, or lose my wife in the process. I am sure my wife, sitting there in the first row, did not understand the pathetic angst I exuded when I my pitifully gazed at her.

I turned to Pepper. For a girl of eighteen, it surprised me that she knew my situation; she discerned the anxiety that vexed me: a pitiful thirty five year old man, caught in the vice grip of respectable decorum, and lesser animal passions. "It's alright, Dale. Just take the safety pins and put them here and here," she motioned to the very area of my anatomical concern. She giggled, "C'mon. Just pin them here." How embarrassing to be comforted by my own parishioner! With a few more giggles, I managed to affix the first pin to the strap with only minimal flesh contact. But the second was more of a challenge. I dare not close my eyes, or I would impale her, but I dare not keep my eyes open, or my failing discretion would wane completely. "There, I think that'll do." I turned her over to Pauline who crowned her, and Pepper commenced her reign.

What a comfort it was to see her at the Fish Fry in a business suit. What a comfort it was to me to know I would never volunteer for such a hellish assignment again. The Queen's entrance to the fish fry proved a convenient transition to the next venue at the fair.

Day after day, the fair was a series of events. The 4H Building housed the craft and cooking entries. Therein one night the pie contest would be held, followed by the cake contest. Audrey Jenkins not only was the cleverest tax accountant and bookkeeper in Fowler, but her Strawberry-Rhubarb pie was a perennial shoe-in to win Best Fruit Pie. Tables throughout the 4H barn were covered with pies, cakes, cookies, jellies, canned green beans; it was a regular culinary smorgasbord. All had ribbons, the green, "Participant," spoke of less than best. Blue marked the best, and blue with a pin was "Best of Kind." Audrey's Strawberry-Rhubarb was not just the best strawberry-rhubarb, but the best of kind, "Best Fruit Pie."

Another portion of the 4H Building contained the tables with the paintings, oil, water, charcoal, sculpture, but also the crafts such as quilts, knitting, crocheting, needlepoint and the like. Though I admired the detail and skill associated with these crafts, I prefer cooking to craftsmanship.

If you walked straight out of the 4H Building, you walked into the farm implement portion of the fair. All the farm implement dealers had their wares on display, with no less polish and pride than a Mercedes or Cadillac dealer. "Grrrrr, rum, rum, rum," a little boy on a big green John Deere tractor furiously twisted the wheel back and forth more like he was steering a Penske racer around Indy's oval, than passing up and down the furrows of a corn field. I tried not to let him know I overheard his motor noises. If I had the gumption to climb up on one of those tractors or combines, I would have made motor noises too. Pardon my chauvinism, but little boys make the best motor noises. I am sure it is a genetic thing. Girls are sensitive, more intuitive, I will concede. But listen to little boys on tractors at a country fair; they sound just like the real thing. At least they think they do.

Beyond the farm implements is the Midway. Carnies invite you to toss quarters on a plate in order to win prizes: in those days, Smurf dolls for one's girlfriend, or daughter. The range of games of skill includes such classics as ring toss, and the baseball thrown at the milk bottles. Everyone concedes, "They're rigged," but we squander our quarters nevertheless. Beyond the games of chance are rides. For the conservative are the classic Merry-Go-Round, and the Kiddie Train. The next level of challenge includes the Ferris Wheel, The Scrambler, and Tilt-A-Whirl. Being only a county fair, that was the limit of thrill rides available.

One evening as I meandered through the rides I witnessed a frantic mother. She was screaming at her bewildered husband outside of the House of Mirrors and Terrors. As best as I could reconstruct, the terrors were quite benign. But still too much for a four year old. Apparently a seven year old brother took his four year old brother, hand in hand, into the House of Mirrors and Terrors; it is a one-way trip. No sooner had they entered and the bewilderment of all the walls being mirrors, and the gentle terror of a burst of air blasting up the four year old's leg proved too much for the tyke's composure. He started screaming. A protective mother caught earshot of her little cub's screaming, and she shouted to the seven year old from outside of The House of Mirrors and Terrors, "Andy, bring Scotty out of there. Hurry, honey."

She turned to her befuddled husband, "Get in there and help Andy. Scotty's frightened. Hurry up. Go on!" Sorry buffoon, the father obeyed his wife's command, approached the Carnie, "Hey, bud, I've got to get my little boy out of there."

"That'll be fifty cents, bub."

"Fifty cents. I don't wanna go in here; I just wanna get my little boy."

"Sorry, bub, fifty cents."

The wife, greatly annoyed at her husband's economy, shouted, "Honey, pay him the fifty cents and get Scotty. Hurry." Can't you hear him. He's terrified."

Moments later, the father rescued trembling Scotty. Evidently it was indeed The House of Mirrors and Terrors.

Saturday night marked one of the much-loved highlights of the country fair: the Local Celebrity Amateur Demolition Derby. What a thrill it proved to be to see the town marshal smash a '67 Bonneville into the County Judge's '73 BelAir Station Wagon. The blue smoke from the tailpipes, and the steamy cloud of mist from the smashed radiators provided the perfume for the fun event.

If you have never witnessed a demolition derby, you have missed a high watermark of American culture. Rusted out autos, heaps, are gathered in a coliseum, in this case, the livestock exhibition pavilion, and they race across at one another, deliberately forcing collisions, one car upon another. The goal being to smash your opponent's chariot, a.k.a., old clunker, until it is undriveable. The last heap moving wins. Principals from the high school, the county elementary schools, and the Superintendent were featured in a heat. The Lawyer's Heat was followed by the Banker's, then the Insurance Sales Agents dueled the County Road crew. The last heat was the winners of each of the preliminary heats.

Rotarian Ted Ryan, Fowler Elementary School Principal, took it all. But his car was a ringer. "The fix is always in these little towns," murmured a losing contestant who had lost touch with the spirit of playful competition. But Ted's heap was a classic demolition derby champion, a '65, Checker Cab. If it could survive real life in Chicago, surely it would overcome the Benton County Fair Demolition Derby. It did. And Ted won.

Sunday dusk marked the end of the Fair. Closing ceremonies amounted to joint religious services, in this case, all Christian, the County Fair Vespers service. Ecumenism, even among Christians, was never put to such a test as this. The service was to be about an hour long, held in the Fair Pavilion, the same place as the Queen pageant. A combined county church choir opened with a medley of hymns. This in itself strained the Christian graces of everyone. What hymns? Pentecostal? Catholic charismatic? Lutheran's insisted on, "A Mighty Fortress," while the Baptists pressed the case for some number emphasizing being washed in the blood, and making personal decisions for Christ. We Presbyterians, like our sisters and brothers down at First Methodist, ended up filling the role of placating everyone.

Yet through it all, no matter who was the guest preacher or speaker, the celebration of these fine people worshipping their Lord, reminded everyone, that there was no place they would rather live than Benton County, USA. They thanked God for good kids, good schools, clean streets, and good health. They repented of pettiness, and rivalry. For the time being, they meant it. And for the time thereafter, for the most part, those folk kept those promises.

How fitting that those celebrations ended with what they confessed was the bedrock of all their celebrations: that God had given them all one another, and a land in which to live, and to raise up another generation to do the same thing again.

They taught me something about celebrations that the Superbowl and Mardi Gras fail to grasp. They really know how to celebrate. They really know how to party.

FUNERALS

While the town was celebrating, it always was aware of death all around it. Passing through at the stoplight, it was apparent that a pall of death hung over Fowler. What was not apparent was how life goes on in the face of death. Our contemporary culture lives in denial of morbidity and mortality. They would do well to venture into town beyond the stoplight. There they may overcome denial, and learn about life, life lived in the face of death.

"You need to sign for this package," said Don, the UPS man. He knew just where to find me, not at the church, not at 9:30 o'clock in the morning. 9:30 each weekday morning found a bunch of us at the Dairy Barn, drinking coffee, talking about news, the latest jokes, and gossip. Don put a brown paper-wrapped box, about the size of a shoebox, in the middle of the table in front of the four of us. On the box were my name, and the address of the church. The return address was somewhat cryptic. It simply read, "Johnson FH. 6th & Stuart St. Bradenton, FL." After signing for the box, Don went on his way. I picked up the package; it was heavier than I expected.

My interest in the unknown contents of the heavy parcel was equaled by my coffee-drinking companions. Chuck, the manager of the Lumber Yard, Smitty, and Henry McElroy, a golfing farmer friend of ours. "I wonder what it is? I've never heard of Johnson FH, and I don't know anyone in Bradenton."

Smitty, not one who tolerated delayed gratification, was frustrated with my contemplation, "Hell, stop guessing. Open it. Let's find out."

A cold gust of early spring wind further delayed opening the package, but brought with it a revelation. "Oh, I see you got the package already, Reverend." It was Harley. Harley was in his work clothes: overalls, insulated overalls at that, and an Asgrow Soybean seed baseball cap, but this one had earflaps, not fashionable, but warm, and while pancakes were important to Harley, fashion was not. Harley Winton, a retired farmer, a Presbyterian elder, member of the American Legion, and superintendent of the Fowler Cemetery, at least the Protestant side.

"Do you know something about this, Harley?"

"Yeap. Sorry, Reverend. I meant to call you about this last night. You know being in charge of the cemetery, I got a phone call yesterday from some funeral home down in Florida."

"FH," now was understood, as was a dawning horror on the faces of my coffee clutch partners.

"Yeap, Reverend, the funeral director there in Florida told me that a box was being shipped to Fowler for burial. He told me it was an urn with the ashes of some fellow who used to live around here years ago, Vernell Painter, I think is the guy's name. Are you free to bury him? He's there in the box."

About that time the growing dread on my buddies' faces transformed into action. "Well, I gotta get back to the yard, there's an order due in," claimed Chuck.

Henry, simultaneously echoed, "I gotta go pick up some rocks in one of my fields before I disk it next week. See ya!"

Smitty failed to offer an explanation. He leaped from the table, and headed out the door.

Harley, not given to humor, enjoyed the macabre evidently, "I guess the box with the stiff did your buddies in." And so it did.

"I was thinkin' we'd plant this poor guy this morning. Do you have some time?"

"I guess so, Harley. When? What do you think we should do?" I had not been trained in mail order funerals at seminary. This was a first.

"Here's the way I figure it," Harley outlined his strategy. "I'll go on out to the cemetery, and dig a proper hole for this over there in the pauper section." Being as the Fowler Cemetery was also the county cemetery, a portion of it was reserved for indigents. Further, as Harley was the superintendent of the cemetery, and I was his pastor, that meant I was the designated "indigent minister." "You do whatever preparation is necessary and I'll meet you out there in a half hour or an hour or so. Does that suit you, Reverend?"

"That'll be fine, Harley. Let me get my Bible, and I suppose ol' Vernell here merits me putting on my funeral suit. I'll be out there in a bit," I said. With that Harley was off to the graveyard. I was left with the box, now abandoned at the Dairy Barn, except for Peggy, the proprietor.

"Dale, did I overhear you right? That's some cremated guy you got there?"

"Yeah. It was a bit of a surprise to me as well. I guess I'll go bury him."

"That sounds like a good idea. He kind a hurt my coffee business this morning," Peggy concluded.

I put Vernell under my arms and got in my car, now a hearse, and headed for home. My wife questioned me upon my unexpected mid-morning arrival, "What'd you get there?"

"Don't ask. I've got to change."

"Change? Change for what? Can I open this? Who do you know in Bradenton, Florida?" she asked.

"Don't touch it. Let me change. Then I'll explain." She let me.

"Hon', Harley wants me to do a graveside service. That box is full of some guy's ashes who died down in Florida last week. I'm gonna meet Harley out at the cemetery now, and bury this guy."

My wife, fine pastor's wife she is, was not nearly as phased by a stiff on the kitchen table as were my coffee drinking companions.

"What's his name?"

"Vernell Painter, quite a name, huh?"

"Painter?" my wife tried to identify him further. "I don't remember anyone around here named 'Painter.' Do you?"

"No, hon'. I don't. But I've got to get out there and meet Harley."

My wife became concerned about interment protocol. "Who's going to be there? What are you going to do?"

"I don't really know what I'm going to do. I guess Harley and I will read a little scripture, say a prayer and that'll be it. I gotta go. Bye, honey," and I left, again with Vernell under my arm.

As I drove the five minutes out to the cemetery, I planned the graveside service in my mind. As I pulled through the entrance to the Protestant side of the cemetery, Harley was there, just as if he were a Marine Corps Honor Guard. As I got out of the car, I picked up the package, still with the UPS labels affixed, and walked over to the gravesite. I noticed Harley waived no honor, even for a pauper. The Asgrow seed hat was reverently held at his side.

"Reverend, I hope this is alright." I noticed a posthole digger there on the ground beside a neat pile of beautiful Benton County black dirt, and a piece of drainage tile. "I was afraid there'd still be frost and this'd be a bugger to dig, but it wasn't." Harley donned his hat again and continued, "I dug this down about four or five feet. I expect that'll do. But I didn't know what to do about the hole collapsing after we buried him. Damn funeral home would charge us a couple hundred bucks for a concrete sleeve for this urn. Hell, I went over to the lumber yard and got a couple of pieces of this eight inch tile. That'll work just fine, don't you think?"

"That was a great idea, Harley." I handed the box to him.

"Are you ready, Reverend? I'll put Mr. Painter in the hole now if that's okay." I nodded for him to proceed. After Harley knelt down with Mr. Painter in his right hand, he reverently lowered him as far as his arm would reach down the hole, then let go. The soft thud told us that Vernell had arrived at his final resting place. Harley rose up again, faced me, took off his hat, and nodded to me that it was time for me to begin.

Though I felt a little silly doing a two-person interment, Harley's reverence encouraged me to do this properly. I reminded the two of us why we were there, read a passage about the resurrection from 1 Corinthians 15, then, read what I was sure was Mr. Painter's favorite psalm, Psalm 23. After a prayer of committal, I ended with a soft, "Ah-men," which in good Presbyterian liturgical fashion was echoed by the Presbyterian cemetery superintendent, Harley Winton.

Vernell Painter had died in Florida, alone, a pauper. He was home again, back amidst his roots to rest in peace.

Vernell Painter, R.I.P. I prayed he did, so did Harley.

As I pulled up outside of the tiny little two bedroom, white clapboard bungalow, I could hear the television blaring, "Holy Cow, Sandberg really got a hold of that one. That puts the Cubs up one to nothing." The voice was Harry Carey, Cubs announcer. The house was Ila's. Her windows were all open it being a hot, humid summer day. Ila was not actually hard of hearing, especially for a woman in her late eighties. Like my fraternity brothers of years before, she just liked to turn it up loud.

I rapped on the door of the little noisy house, peered in, and saw Ila amble to greet me. A huge smile covered her face, and as she fumbled to open the door, her husky voice said, "Reverend." I loved Ila the first time I met her. This was merely a continuation of my affair with this woman, but it was a call colored by a morbid concern.

Ila had been long-retired. Her infamy was told me by her loved ones. "Ila? Ila? Oh, you mean General Patton. Pastor, you met her way too late. She's mellowed a bit from the good ol' days." Ila was not the Mayor, Sheriff, Legislator, or Judge. She was much more powerful and influential than any of those. Ila had been the telephone operator for years. The stories I heard! Dave Jenkins just laughed when he told me, "… Course, even I was just a kid, but Ila was a pistol. She really ran the county. If you wanted to put a call through, and Ila thought you'd talked too much, or had no business making such a call, she just wouldn't make the call. That's why they called her 'The General,' 'General Patton.'" Not knowing her as

The General, I just knew her as Ila, a parishioner, and a Cub fan. That made us kindred spirits.

Ila stood maybe five feet or so, was modestly overweight in a pleasant matronly way. Ila's smile, as always, projected through a fleshy face with pasty skin. Her smile was her rouge. She gestured me into her tiny living room, but it was decorated such that it more properly ought to be called a sitting room. Crocheted doilies were neatly draped over the backs of all the chairs, and sofas. Actually this was standard decoration for her peers, her generation, I learned in my occasional visits to all their homes. She turned the volume down on her twenty-five inch Zenith console, and after a few moments of preliminary conversation about the Cub's slump, we turned to the matter of concern.

"So you're going for surgery tomorrow. What time will that be?"

"Eight o'clock tomorrow morning at Home Hospital. They say they're going to take both of my breasts," Ila let me know the details. She continued, "Reverend, I'm eighty eight years old, I guess I don't need them anymore now."

"I suppose not," I said. "Do they think, Ila, that this will fix you up?"

"What they said, Reverend, is that I am an old woman. And they just don't know. But if I survive the surgery, that it's likely they'll get all the cancer."

Ila had beaten most of life's problem. She had known love. She had savored power. Eighty eight years old and she was still cooking for herself and watching the Cubs on television. Life was pretty good to her, but now she was up against cancer. All of our conversation that afternoon was not marked by fear, after all, for Ila, a woman her age, dying was not so much the issue, the issue was the ravage of cancer. That issue cast its pallor over and through our time together. No, it was not fear; it was a grave concern. We had a time of prayer together, and I departed, "Ila, I'll see you at the hospital tomorrow morning before they take you to surgery."

About 6:30 the next morning I passed the stoplight and headed for town, as they say. Being a small town, the people of Fowler drove the twenty-five miles for goods and services not available there, and had to use Lafayette as the source of those other things, hospitals in this case. The half hour drive delivered me at the hospital, and I went to Ila's room just in time to hear the anesthesiologists say to her, "Mrs. Sides, with a person of your age, and the nature of this surgery, while I am convinced everything will go just fine, the biggest risk for you is simply surviving the surgery and anesthesia." She nodded, not so much as if the doctor had startled her, or frightened her, just matter-of-fact. Then she signed the releases and he left.

Being a minister, a Christian pastor, I confess that while on no occasion do I wish ill on any of my parishioners, that when I pray for them, the nature of my calling is that there is some distance between that person being prayed for and me. I suppose it is an emotional safety barrier to protect me. Yet as the doctor left, and Ila's family and friends backed away from her side, I was caught with my safety net gone. I do not know why, but my love and concern for Ila transcended professional care; this was a personal matter for me. Selfishness overwhelmed me. Ila must not suffer, and Ila must not die. I loved Ila. That love clouded my professionalism.

"Well, Ila, you all ready?" I asked. "I guess, seeing as they're about to wheel you down to surgery, maybe we ought to have a word of prayer." The nurses and attendants already had started to wheel her out of the room; I had to assert myself, "Please, could we just have another minute?" Reluctantly they paused. Standing next to the gurney, I grabbed Ila's shriveled hand, yet was startled by her firm grip. Looking at her face, still with that wonderful smile, I saw the pale blue shower cap on her head, and began to pray. I hardly could get the words out as I interceded for God's healing, comfort and encouragement. All the time I struggled to pray, to do my duty, Ila's grip on my hand comforted me; her squeeze on my fingers was the assurance of a mother to one of her children.

"Amen." Tears ran down my cheeks. What a boob I was. Here I am paid to bring the comfort of Christ to ones such as Ila, and I am the struggling one. My embarrassment came to a head, as she pulled me closer to her. It was then that I met The General. That gravelly voice with the assurance of Moses comforted me, "Reverend. Everything is gonna be all right. Don't you be afraid now, Reverend. It's going to be okay. Do you understand?" I pitifully nodded. They rolled her away, as I sniveled a bit more. My handkerchief was out, and I was forced back into the professional mode as I turned to Ila's family and friends.

Often I have thought about what Ila meant when she reminded me, "It's going to be okay." Since I have concluded, live or die, it was okay with her, but it would not have been with me, or those who loved her. As it turned out, Ila was right.

"Dale, I'm calling to ask you a special favor for us. You know ever since Tommy's accident, we've had to make several adjustments. While his therapy and rehabilitation are coming along just great, he probably can't play in the Major League this summer during Little League. Seeing as you know his situation, and he likes you, I wonder if you think he could play on your team this season?"

The phone call and the question came from a concerned mother, Adrienne Naylor. With spring coming her concern for her son's baseball future prompted her special request. The special request came due to another one of life's tragedies that randomly visits various households. The previous Fall Tommy's tragedy ravaged the Naylor household.

Tommy Naylor, even at twelve, portended to be the classic country boy. Already he was head and shoulders larger than his classmates, stockier too. Every time Tommy walked amongst his elders, someone embarrassed him, "Boy, you're gonna be as big as an ox." He only answered with a big smile that turned his fleshy cheeks a tinge of red. The dimples angled well against his blond crew cut look. "By God, you're gonna outstrip your old man," another voice added. Actually that would be no small accomplishment. Tommy's dad, Dave, stood six feet four, and had to weigh two hundred fifty pounds. Yet he was all country boy too: gentle, shy, soft-spoken, quick to smile, eager to help. Not only was Tommy going to rival his dad's stature, he appeared destined to clone Dave's nature as well. Tommy came from good stock as they said in these parts, and had all the makings to continue that good blood line, which is what made his tragedy all the more a heartache, not just for the Naylor's, but for the town as well.

Farm folk raise their children on different schedules than city folk. While it seems that they are sheltered a bit from the urgency to grow up socially compared to city kids, ironically, they drive cars, trucks and tractors when still babies, or so it seems. It came as quite a shock to me the first time I saw one of my farm family's twelve year old boy sitting as if a midget in the cab of a huge, $100,000 combine bringing in soybeans. Such responsibilities, such freedoms is what precipitated the grave change in the Naylor household.

That fall previous to Adrienne's phone call, Tommy was doing what was work for him, which for most city twelve year old would have been a treat. He'd been out harvesting rocks. Benton County, Indiana, part of the farm belt too far north for anything like spring wheat, the only crop harvested in Benton County, Indiana, in the spring was rocks. With the spring thaw, that previous winter's frost in the ground forced rocks up to the surface of the soil. Most of those rocks were small, maybe the size of a baseball. Some, though, were doozies, weighing several hundred pounds, and the size of a bale of hay. Dave and Tommy had gone out to one of their fields after Tommy came home from school to do a little rock harvesting. Having done so, Tommy, for some unexplained reason rode back home sitting on the tailgate of his dad's Chevy pickup. He loved to dangle his feet over the blacktop, and watch the road race by underneath his feet. Not many city boys have enjoyed sitting in the back of a pickup truck with the crisp spring air racing through their hair. It was that occasion that with just the right bump in the road, Tommy bounded off the back of the truck. With the bounce, his head smashed into the asphalt. Tommy would never be the same.

"Dale, I thought you'd like to know so your folk there at First Presbyterian can pray. They just took Tommy Naylor to Children's Hospital in Indianapolis on CareFlight. It seems he fell off his dad's truck and hit his head. The damage was to his head, his brain. Early word is not very good. 'Thought you oughta know," said the minister from First Methodist, the Naylor's pastor.

"Thanks, Pete, for letting us know. We'll pass the word around and get to prayer," I said. The word on Tommy for a long time was not very good. First, it was will he live, but it improved to a different word, how will he live? Weeks in Intensive Care gave way to months of physical therapy, and by early winter Tommy came home to stay.

"How would he live?" was still the question everyone asked. Yet all it took was a visit with him one on one. The smile was still there, the spirit still vital, the character unchanged. The only thing that changed appeared to be a touch of paralysis on one side. It gave him a limp, the loss dexterity in his left arm and hand, and it slurred his speech just a bit. But everyone noted, "Why Tommy, you're doin' just fine. Mighty fine!"

He was doing mighty fine, but not so fine as he could pick up where he left off as a fine Little League star come the summer. That's why Adrienne called me.

Adrienne said, "It makes Dave and me real sad. He does so want to play on his team, the Dodgers. But even Tommy's concerned that he'll get horribly frustrated trying to play in the Majors. That' why we thought maybe he'd be better off in the Minors, playing for your Orioles. It wouldn't be such a challenge. He still could have fun. He does so love to play baseball. And if that sounds okay, we'd really appreciate it,"

"Adrienne, I think it'll work out just fine." With that Tommy became my third baseman. Our first practice it became clear that he wanted to be treated like everybody else. My coaching strategy was, "Do your best, and do what I tell you, and we'll have a good time, and win some ball games as well."

"Tommy, I know it's hard for you to get down for those grounders. But you've gotta do it, or I'll have to get somebody who can." Such cajoling and he usually managed to get it right. Playing the field with one hand is no small challenge, but it can be done, Tommy proved it. Yet practice was one thing; how would he do in a game?

Not many grounders came his way in that first game, but still he had to bat. The Orioles were pre-season favorites to win the league, and we would need

Tommy to do his duty. We couldn't carry any dead weight and win the pennant. So his batting test came early, and it came with some importance. His first few at bats were non-eventful and unsuccessful. But it was the bottom of the sixth, the last inning, and Cody, our ace pitcher was on second with two outs when Tommy came to the bat. I asked Steve, the ump, for a timeout.

"Tommy, look for a good pitch, and after you cream it, run your tail off for first. If you run it out, Cody'll make it home. We win, and you're the hero."

"Okay, Reverend Patterson," always polite, and always smiling, he stepped into the batter's box. Actually my concern was not how he was to run, it was smacking the ball. But I tried to manipulate him with my confidence that he'd hit it for sure, and that running was the problem.

With part of his upper body still just a bit frozen, he swung the bat such that not just his arms, and shoulders turned, but his whole body pivoted as if on an axle through his head down through one of his legs. That swing would do, if he could just put the bat on the ball.

I looked up in the stands. First, I glimpsed Number One Fan, Ernie, cheering everyone on, all the time listening to the Cubs playing a nightcap against Cincinnati. Just behind them were tonight's real Number One Fans, Dave and Adrienne. I'd bet anything that I caught them holding hands and praying together, just for a moment.

The first pitch was all that was needed. Tommy pivoted and the bat followed. It wasn't a blistering liner, or a homer, just stroked well enough to scoot between first and second into right field. Tommy got his season's first RBI. He'd get some more. As Cody stepped on home plate, Tommy Naylor completed a major course of physical and emotional therapy.

Not only did Tommy get to be hero for the night, he answered the burning question, "How would he live?" He would live just fine, and he was glad to be alive. He made us all glad to be alive as well.

Big city life reminds its residents of its terrors: muggings, gang wars, and burglary. Life beyond the stoplight proved a contrast: front doors unlocked, keys left in cars and wallets too. Yet we learned that even Fowler had its terrors.

"Oh, no, a fire." Living just one hundred yards from the volunteer fire department siren, we always knew when there was a fire. When the windows were open on a summer night, we lived so close that we could hear the motor come to life that whirled the siren to its blaring shriek. This night not only did we hear the roar of the siren, the din of the motors on the fire trucks, but shouting voices in the alley adjacent to our house.

"Hon', that sounds like Smitty," I said to my wife. Jumping up from my bed, I went to the bedroom window facing the alley, and my suspicions were confirmed.

"Take that hose over to the hydrant, and hook it to the truck." Though I confirmed that the voice was Smitty's, the thought of Smitty as one of the firefighters protecting me, and my community proved a bit bewildering. Smitty was good at telling the latest joke, lounging around the afternoon playing golf, and indulging in some sophomoric endeavor. Looking at Smitty's face, one did not see written on his forehead, "to serve and to protect". There he was nevertheless.

Our neighbor's garage was on fire. A quick glance and the appraisal was that it would be a total loss. In a matter of minutes the might of the Fowler Fire Department, volunteer fire department, doused the flames. Smitty *et.al.* did their job. The result: loss of garage, but no loss of life.

Pulling on my pants, shoes and a jacket, I thought I'd check it out. Bill Robertson, the Fire Chief, stood by the smoldering ruin which now housed a thoroughly totaled Ford pickup, a sizzled John Deere lawn tractor, and a collection of garage inventory—all pretty much wasted. The Fire Chief smoked his post-fire Marlboro. Seeing Bill at the Country Club, I would have known the proper conversation, "How's the slice?" or, "That new putter helping you?" I was a dope when it came to fire repartee. I gave it my best shot, "What happened?"

"Spontaneous combustion, I bet." The Fire Chief continued, "Probably a bunch of oily rags in the can or something. But once that sum'bitch got going it hit a few paints cans, a gas can for the lawnmower, and it was a damn hot toaster."

My only response was as equally unimaginative as my question, "Yeap." I turned to the owners. The Sanchez's didn't lose their house, or their transportation, just a broken down truck that hadn't run for a couple of months, a fancy lawnmower, and touchup paint for their kitchen, and the children's bedrooms. Other neighbors already were consoling them in their loss, "Sure glad none of you got hurt, and the fire department kept it from spreading." At three in the morning, the Sanchez's stood in the dim light emanating from the nearby fire trucks with somber smiles, and they appeared a tad bit dazed by it all, and occasionally acknowledged the condolences with a "Uh-huh," or, "Yeah, we sure are lucky." As I plodded back down the alley, heading again for bed, it occurred to me that the confused look on their faces may have represented their effort to figure out what was lucky about losing all their stuff in their garage and a lawnmower too.

"Hey, Smitty', I'm going to the next Town Board meeting, and see to it that you get kicked off the Fire Department." So went my greeting next morning at the Dairy Barn. "It's no comfort to me that a lazy galoot like you is the one responsible to protect the better citizens of this hamlet."

Unfazed by my heckling and without looking up or arguing with me, he simply answered with a weary smile and, "Shut up, Reverend, and buy me a cup of coffee."

So I did, and we quickly transitioned to our routine coffee clutch antics, not knowing that Firefighter Smitty would be back in my neighborhood much too soon.

"Pat, wake up, get the kids. The house is on fire!" In addition to shouting orders to my wife, I sat up in bed. It was the crackling and the smell that awakened me, again at three in the morning, just a few weeks after the previous inferno. The smell was the smoky, pungent reek of a bonfire, or leaves burning at the curb in the fall. The crackling was exactly as the pop of throwing another piece of oak in the fireplace. Though the noise and smell awakened me, what terrified me was the light and the heat. I sat up in bed just as I jostled my wife to save the kids, all the time, I was desperate to shake the cobwebs of deep sleep from my mind. Sitting up the heat of the fire startled me, as if I'd come too close to that bonfire. The flames leaped before my bedroom windows. Disbelief and horror engulfed me as I stumbled to action saving my family, but simultaneously pondering philosophically, "Why me?" The dancing flames outside the walls of my house lighted my bedroom with an intensity that was incredible. Seldom in my life have I known such relief as when I finally pulled the sheers away from the window, and realized it was not my house on fire, but my neighbor's. Still the heat staggered me.

My shallow relief gave way to sadness for my neighbors. The Thompson's were an elderly couple whose house was across the alley from us. The crackle of the fire gave way to the sad lament of another siren beckoning the volunteers to put out the flames of the household of a sad old couple. It must have been ten more minutes before the first fire hose sprayed onto the blaze. There was Smitty again, and a host of other ragtag angels of community mercy. It was too late, though, for the Thompson's. Fred and Irma Thompson stood much like the Sanchez's some weeks before in front of what used to be their home. In that home was the accumulation of more than fifty years of life together, husband and wife. Most of it was now gone.

Some of that life still remained, however. A mini-van screeched to a stop as close as he could come what with the fire department's blockade. Out of the car, jumped a middle-aged man, half-dressed, and he jogged down the sidewalk. Even before he got to Fred and Irma, he cried out, "I'm sorry, Momma, Pop. This is awful." The Thompson's sadly nodded in agreement. "But I'm so glad you two got out safely." Freddie, comforting his elderly mother and father in the early morning darkness, was the first obvious sign that life for the Thompson's was not all gone. Friends, as well, crowded in to offer condolences and comfort. These were not fair weather friends, but friends of an entire lifetime, more than eighty years. Those friends were there when the Thompson's daughter had scarlet fever back in '42, when hail destroyed the crop in '47, '55, and again in '62. Friends proved there was more to life than stuff in a house when Fred and Irma's other son went down in a battleship in '45 somewhere in the South Pacific. Again they were there on a smoky summer night, a constant reminder that Fred and Irma had not lost it all.

As we all watched friends and family come to be with Fred and Irma, the glow of a fire, now doused, gave way to the glow of a new day. Smitty evidently fulfilling a firefighter tradition, greeted me with his post-fire Marlboro. "Hi there, you ol' smokeeater. You doing okay?" I asked.

He was. He'd unbuckled his firecoat, and sat on the curb sitting next to me. Soot and sweat covered his cheeks and forehead, as we both watched the Thompson's greet people who loved them. This time it was Smitty who played the philosopher. "You know, Reverend, there's something about this particular fire that'll preach."

"Dale, sorry to call you so early, but you might want to get out to Welch's farm, if you can. I bet they're in terrible shape," the voice of Sam Jenkins advised me at six o'clock in the morning with a phone call. "Thanks, Sam. I'll see what I can do."

It wasn't a fire, this time, but the opposite, water, too much water. The spring rains had been more than sufficient, but not so bad that season as to prevent the farmers from preparing the fields. So by late April and early May most of the farmers were anxious to get their soybeans and corn planted. Sam's phone call came on the morning of the sixteenth of May.

Farmers have a love-hate relationship with rain. They love it when it rains just enough at just the right time. They hate it when it is the wrong amount, as in none, or too much. But that spring had been almost perfect, even to please crabby, whiny farmers. The creeks were full, the soil moist. But the night of the fifteenth changed all that. Like many spring evenings in the upper Midwest, the late afternoon brought thunderstorms. A crack of lightning, the rumble that followed would be expected to bring a quarter to a half an inch of rain in an hour. Then the skies would clear, and that would be it. That night, however, proved sadly different. Oh, it began quite the same. The lightning, the thunder, the deluge that followed, gully-washers, they call the storms around there. Yet after an hour, it did not stop. It was only after twelve hours that the faucets of heaven turned off, leaving more than ten inches of unwanted rain. Ten inches of rain in twelve hours means another funeral.

"Who was that?" my wife asked me of the early morning call.

"Sam Jenkins. He told me I might want to get out to visit with Susie and Al, if I could. Some problem with flooding, I guess. I wonder what Al meant, 'if I could?'"

I was soon to find out what he meant. Pair of blue jeans, sweatshirt, jacket and I was on my way. As I walked out to my car, I noticed the sun trying to come up. Its light was becoming more evident, but heavy thunderclouds still hovered ominously overhead. There in town, the evidence of heavy rain was all around, but no sign of flooding. The air smelled fresh and squeaky clean, but warning that more rain still could come. I drove to the stoplight and headed east, six miles, but just a few yards outside of town, I pulled to a stop.

After the rain ceased, and Noah went on deck to see what he could see, he must have witnessed a similar shocking spectacle. Yesterday I had noticed the fields, most with their seedlings painting the rich black dirt with six inch streaks of vivid green. That was all gone now, twelve hours later. As far as I could see was water, everywhere. So much water that it looked more like Lake Michigan than it did Okeefenokee Swamp. But a swamp it was. Interrupting the water were trees, power lines, and the occasional farm house and miscellaneous sheds. Many of the sheds I looked for were gone. Evidently they were entombed for the moment in Indiana's version of Davey Jones' locker.

Most of the roads that ribbon those fields are at a slightly higher elevation than the fields they cross. The effect this morning was to create rice paddies as in China, or a checkerboard of ponds.

I had seen more water before, but never on what we normally call dry land. Putting the car in gear again, I resumed my drive out to Welch's farm. Driving only a mile or so, I had to stop again. The dip in the road for a lazy creek no longer was there. Not more than a few yards before my bumper, water washed over the road as if a hose were splashing its contents onto the asphalt. But that innocent water quickly gave way to an ugly malevolence that was unprecedented to my vision. The lazy creek now looked more like muddy lava, carrying all manner of trash: milk cartons, Burger King bags, tree limbs, scrap lumber, occasionally what looked like the roof of a shed. I looked across the flooded creekbed, maybe a quarter mile, and in the middle of the road stood a cow. Floods such as these would strand livestock on the high grounds until it wasn't high enough. Then the animals would have to swim, or sink. Evidently, this cow swam, swam over to Highway 18.

"Well, I can't make it this way," I murmured to myself. "I have to go the backroads." The backroads were no different. On a normal day, the trip to Welch's farm was a straight shot east out of town. It would take ten minutes tops. Today it wasn't straight, and by the time I got there nearly two hours elapsed. The detours I attempted, one after another, ended with the view I had just left: flooded road bed with a menacing creek preventing my advance. Resorting to a detour of more than twenty miles, I looped North and East, so much so that I finally found a route that succeeded by approaching the Welch's farm from the East.

The view was still the same. Water all around, but the gravel road that led to their home functioned as a levee along the Mississippi, except the river was on both sides of the levee. There in the middle of one of the innumerable ponds stood the Welch's farmhouse.

Susie and Al had recently built a beautiful new home. The plans fulfilled made it look like a home featured in a magazine about country living. It was new, yet it looked mature, rustic. "Thank God, it's okay." I was speaking of the house. At the moment it was intact, and apparently dry. The house was on the highest ground around. Surrounding the house was a band of maybe fifteen to twenty feet of grass that melted into the water all around.

The barn out back and to the side appeared to have at least two to three feet of water in it, and his pickup was swamped to the axles, as was their mini-van.

As I pulled up in front of their house, I knew I was going to have to wade. So I parked in the middle of the road, stepped out of the car. There in the front yard the Welch's two boys, at nine o'clock in the morning, were sharing a morning swim.

Susie, just beyond the green grass in front of the porch, stood in water up to her knees. "C'mon in. The water's fine," she hailed. "I'll give you a cup of coffee, but you're gonna have to put on your waders to get here."

"I don't have any waders, or hipboots either."

"Then, pastor, you're going to get wet."

I took off my shoes, and waded in. By the time I forded the pond, and emerged again on dry land, I shook my feet, and greeted Susie with a hug.

"Isn't this the pits?" she asked. "Al's inside. He won't come out."

"Well, let's go inside," I answered. Susie's smile to greet me was one common on the face of farmers, a look of stoic resignation. Al had no smile whatsoever, just a blank acknowledgement that I was there.

"I'm surprised you could get here," he said.

"Having come twenty different ways, I'm a bit surprised too. But I made it."

The problem for the Welch's was not their home. It was safe, dry, beautiful. The problem was their livelihood. The farm amounted to little but their crops. And that year's crop, the investment in the future, at least for another year's livelihood, now was buried in water, that would recede, and turn into mud, then dry into something more like concrete. The crop was gone.

This sort of flood, if everything went well would take a month or more, before planting could replace the loss. Nothing could replace the loss on the calendar. Al's crop had already been planted for a month. As it turned out, he planted again the second week of June, but the bounty he had hoped for to makeup for previous years' setbacks washed away. This was just another setback.

When I got in my car that morning, I did not know I would do a funeral in my blue jeans and sweatshirt sitting at a kitchen table in a beautiful country house surrounded by an ocean of water. As we drank our coffee, we contemplated the future, and acknowledged another setback.

It was a funeral for the dream that this year's crop would free them from the setbacks of the past.

"You know they ran Walt Coleman out of town for hanging out here. I hear you spend a good deal of time out here too. 'Thought you oughta be warned," said Trip. "I know times have changed. That was more than twenty years ago, but I don't 'xpect they've changed that much. You seem like a nice enough guy; I just don't want you getting run off too."

"Thanks a lot, Trip. I appreciate your concern. I guess what will be will be," I answered Trip Harrelson's warning fatalistically.

I had seen Trip Harrelson's name on the Inactive Rolls of the church. Coincidentally, he'd been inactive for more than twenty years. Though I had been in town for a year or so already, it was at a wedding reception at the country club, that I first met him. That warning, our first conversation, was at the bar. My wife and I had just come into the club following the wedding of which I had officiated. Now it was time for the party. Sauntering up to the bar, I ordered a bourbon and water for me, and a vodka and OJ for my wife. That's when I met Trip. He waited for a drink for spouse and self as well. Only now is it evident that a drink would be the alpha and omega of our friendship.

"Reverend, I'm Trip Harrelson. I'm one of your flock, but I haven't been to church for more than twenty years. That was a real fine wedding you did. Can I buy you a drink?"

"Trip. I've heard about you, and yeah, I've seen your name on the rolls. Glad we finally met," I answered.

"People in town, the old timers like me, say you remind them of Walt Coleman. You know they run Walt Coleman out of town ..."

My introduction to Trip Harrelson was to be a warning. Pastor Walt Coleman had preceded me by more than twenty years and four pastors. For the late 1950s, Coleman may have been a bit too racy, even for progressive Presbyterians.

One of the perks of being the pastor of First Presbyterian was a membership at the local country club, Benton County Country Club. The unwritten and unspoken expectation was that the pastor would play an occasional round of golf and behave discreetly on rare visits to the club. Pastor Coleman, evidently, went far beyond these limits of appropriate decorum. Not only did he play golf several times a week during season, but it was not at all uncommon for him to be seen frequenting the club, most notably, the Horseshoe Bar.

The Horseshoe Bar was mostly the domain of the hardcore country club patrons. An outsider could tell who the regulars were. As a routine patron approached the Horseshoe Bar, the bartender would put their drink, be it a Budweiser, Scotch 'n Soda, or black coffee before him without even asking. Evidently Walt Coleman was on that list of the Horseshoe Hardcore. For that and other questionable indiscretions, Pastor Coleman parted company with his flock.

Though I had no inkling that I was heading down my predecessor's trail of indiscretion, Trip's first words to me were such a warning.

I saw Trip several more times during the reception party, each time in the proximity of the bar. While our conversation was cordial, it never dawned on me that in some strange way I had re-evangelized Trip while ordering drinks.

The next morning, Sunday morning, robed and ready to lead the saints in worship, I paraded into the sanctuary of the church. While mingling and greeting the various worshippers, there was Trip, and sitting next to him in the pew, Erla, his wife.

Harley could hardly contain himself, "Well I'll be damned," he whispered in my ear, "Trip Harrelson's in church. He hasn't been here for years."

"That's what I've heard. I met him yesterday out at the club. We were at a wedding reception. Harley, rejoice and be glad," I exhorted my disbelieving elder.

But all Harley could do was mutter to himself, "I'll be damned."

That wasn't the last time the Harrelson's came to church either. Overnight they became regulars. I'd visit them occasionally in their home. It was on one of those occasions that Trip began to call me, "Doc."

"Trip, I don't have a doctorate."

He didn't care. "You're a doctor of souls," he'd laugh. Never again did he call me, "Dale," or "Reverend, or anything else, just "Doc."

He greeted me on the phone, "Hey, Doc, Erla's got to go in for some surgery on her woman parts tomorrow. Could you come over and pray with us. She's sort a scared." I did.

Occasions such as these built the bonds of friendship. But so did a greeting at the hardware store, or Lane's Liquor store on a Friday afternoon, each of us picking up a weekend six pack. "Hi, Doc." So it went.

A few years after that first conversation at the club, I answered the phone one afternoon, "Doc, my ol' ticker's acting up. The doctor says I need a pacemaker. First thing tomorrow morning, I'm going into Lafayette to the hospital to have one installed. They say it's no big deal. But you know Erla. She's in a fuss. Could you come over here and calm her down or something?"

"Sure, Trip, I'll be there in a bit." But when I got there, it wasn't just Erla who was in a fuss. Trip himself was more anxious than normal as well. But I spent a bit of time with the two, and things calmed down. On leaving I said, "I'll see you two at the hospital tomorrow morning before the surgery."

Early next morning, after driving to the hospital and doing as I said, I had a brief word of prayer with the family, and they rolled Trip Harrelson off for his routine pacemaker placement.

Dave, his eldest son, whom I had come to know through various events including his remarriage, said, "Dale, I'll give you a call at the church later this morning, and let you know how it all turned out. Thanks a lot for being here with Pop."

So I left. Two hours later, I was back at the church in my study when my secretary interrupted me. "Dale, it's Don Harrelson on the phone. He sounds really upset."

"Don, what's up," I answered. What followed was the sound of sniffling, and hesitation when finally he stuttered, Pop, Pop, Pop's, Pop's dead. Damn it, he died."

No seminary education or life education prepares you to respond to such a shock. "What? Dead? What happened?" I asked.

Amidst more stammering he continued, "They don't know what the hell happened. One doctor came to me; he seemed just a stunned as all of us. They said he must have been sicker than anybody knew. His heart just gave up."

"Gosh, I'm sorry, Don. What's going on with your Mom?"

"Don't ask. She's a zombie, just sitting here stone silent gazing around. I'll be bringing her home in a bit. If you can, I know she'd appreciate you stopping by."

I ended the call with, "Don, call me when you get home, and I'll get right over there."

The next several days went like most days of grief associated with funerals. Loved ones, friends, family stopping by the Harrelson house, then all the town stops by the funeral home for a visit, and next the funeral at the church, but this funeral was a first for me. Normally, after the funeral at the church, we would head out to the cemetery for the interment. Following that, we were to go back to the church for a luncheon provided for the family by the ladies of the church. But this was not a normal funeral. I was about to witness the Harrelson family initiate a new sacrament.

On the surface, the process flowed the day of the funeral in the typical sequence. The procession from the church to the cemetery went as planned. Harley greeted the hearse and ushered the other cars as near as possible to the gravesite. Being close was good that day. It was a cold, misty, spring day. The wind whipped across the prairie so that everyone was glad to get as close as possible to the canvas shelter that protected the grave. I completed the interment service, and most everybody hurried quickly back to their cars to return for the lunch at the church. But Don Harrelson grabbed me as I headed to my car, "Dale, after everyone leaves, me, my brother, sister and Mom, are gonna do something special. I think Pop would want you here. Will ya stick around a few more minutes?"

"Sure, Don, what's up?"

"I'll show you in a bit," was all he'd say.

A few minutes turned into a quarter of an hour, as we waited for the funeral director and Harley to lower Trip's bronze-enameled casket into the ground. Prior to shoveling the dirt, however, the grave diggers paused and walked away. It was just the Harrelson's and me. "Dale, we're gonna do something special that we'd think Pop would want you here for," Don began. While talking he took a lush purple cloth out of a cardboard box he was holding. As he pulled back the cloth, it was apparent that the cloth was a bag with a draw string on one end. It was the dressing around a bottle of thirty year old scotch whiskey.

"We're gonna drink a toast to Pop. Do you care to share it with us?" Don asked. The family was anxious. While Don appeared confident, his words betrayed a concern that he would offend me, or that this ritual would be construed by me to be in bad taste. Far be it for me to stand in the way of sacramental initiation.

It was my turn to stutter, "No. No, nah. I'd be honored."

All this time, Don's other brother, who also had a lush purple cloth bag, began to release the drawstring which revealed five crystal whiskey glasses. After my concurrence each of us was handed a glass. Meanwhile Erla sat expressionless in one of the folding chairs adjacent to the open grave, yet she took her glass in hand when offered. Don reverently opened the bottle of whiskey and carefully poured a finger or two into each glass. We all waited for one another.

The eldest son, Don, was designated the honor of the toast. I cannot remember his exact words. But I recall they were neither witty, nor contrived, just honest, something like, "Pop, You were a hell of a man. We'll miss you. The people who loved you most are here to say goodbye. I love you, Dad." He paused a moment, and ended, "Goodbye."

A few moments later, Trip Harrelson gave me my last shock. Don, finishing his benediction, took the crystal glass, and threw it, smashing it on the casket. In rapid succession, his brother, sister and finally Erla followed, and they looked to me. Something in my economy resisted destroying fine crystal, but I overcame my conservatism, and flung the Waterford. It too exploded on the bronze-enamel.

It was then that the first tears regarding Trip came to my eyes. When I looked up at Erla, there were no tears, just a soft smile.

Trip Harrelson was gone. We met over a drink and said goodbye over a drink. Yet Trip's prophecy, his warning was wrong. That afternoon I wrote Walt Coleman, by that time a retired Presbyterian minister, a note. I told him of Trip's death, and how much ol' Trip had cared for Pastor Coleman, and how Trip had come back to church, through a meeting at a bar. I also told him of the new sacrament the Harrelson's had ushered into Presbyterian theology. The note ended, "Mr. Coleman, I think Trip would want you to drink him a toast as well. Gotta go now. I have a date with the Horseshoe Bar. Thought you'd like to know, the old bartender there says I sit in your chair."

Trip Harrelson was wrong. They didn't run me off. But they did welcome Trip back. As Harley said, "I'll be damned." Trip wasn't.

"Dale, Would you be willing to give an invocation at the Commencement Exercises at BC this year?" Carol Westerman the School Board President asked on the phone. After checking my calendar, "Sure, Carol, I'd be glad to do that."

Commencement at Benton Central High School, the county school, was another one of the celebrations, a highlight of the year for those living beyond the stop-light.

Fowler was largest of four or five towns in the county. In the mid-60s they consolidated the tiny town high schools into one larger county high school, BC. County kids went to one of the grade schools either near their local town, Boswell, Oxford, Otterbein or Fowler, or they rode the bus from their farm to the nearest grade school. However, once one was a middle-schooler it was off to BC. Six years later, came the day of graduation, and ironically, not only an end, but a beginning, a commencement to the next stage of life.

A platform, a stage, placed at one end of the basketball arena, created the only place large enough to hold the audience and participants of BC graduation exercises. The basketball arena, the gym, was a circular dome, so that with the platform offset, it had the effect of turning the arena into a semi-circular amphitheater.

The third Saturday of May at noon was the appointed hour. I arrived at the high school about 11:30 and was ushered into a locker room to be briefed as to my responsibilities. Yet as I got out of my car, and headed inside, I noticed quite a crowd already had gathered. Not just the graduates, but grandmas, grampas, aunts, uncles, cousins, and sisters and brothers.

While a considerable number of BC's graduates went on to college, most did not. A BC diploma marked the end of their formal education. This truth dawned on me, and I noted a delight and joy in the eyes of the proud moms and dads as they made their way into the arena. For most of these parents, it was their commencement as well. Tommy or Susie, soon would leave the nest. Some would go to a business college, some to the beauty college in Fort Wayne, or down to Indianapolis. Others would go to work at the John Deere dealer's repair shops, fixing combines and tractors. Others went to a job as a teller at a large bank in a distant city. But the emphasis was on going, not staying.

Promptly at noon, the School Board led our entourage onto the platform. Following the School Board came the Superintendent of Schools, and the Commencement speaker. This year's speaker was the Lieutenant Governor of the State. As we climbed the steps onto the platform, I overheard the School Board President exhort the honored guest, "Please, Mr. Governor, keep your comments to the agreed upon twenty minutes, or this thing 'll drag on forever." The High School Principal paused at the bottom step, and motioned for me to proceed up to the platform and take my assigned seat.

It was only after I took my seat that I paused to look up at the gathered audience. The gym was nearly full. Several thousand faces focused their attention on the platform.

The principal proceeded directly to the podium and began the reverent but joyful occasion. "Friends, families, ladies and gentlemen, in behalf of the School Board of Benton County School District, and the faculty and staff of Benton Central High School I welcome you to these Commencement Exercises. Would you all please rise now for the procession of our graduates?" On that cue not only did the audience stand, but the Band Director motioned the BC Concert Band to bring their instruments to the playing position. "One, two, three, four," he whispered and waved his baton. The band began to play one of many repetitions of "Pomp and Circumstance March." Led by the President of the Senior Class, the parade of graduates filed one by one onto the basketball floor, in front of the platform and then into their seats. The green ribbon of graduates processed for more than five minutes. When the last graduate, I believe her name was Kelly Zieman, came to her chair, in one accord the graduates took their seat, and spontaneously, the audience broke out in a dignified applause. The genteel atmosphere was only littered with an occasional catcall, or "Way to go, Henry," "It's a miracle, Bobby." Allowing decorum to be reestablished, the principal introduced me, and in prayer I invoked God's presence at this civil occasion.

Each graduate wore a forest green academic robe, gown, and donned a mortar board on his or her head of the same color. Tassels. Ahh, tassels, this was a matter of no small significance. Most wore a white tassel, but a few of the three hundred and fifty graduates, wore a bright gold tassel. This signified their membership in the academic elite, The National Honor Society. All the tassels, though, white or gold, were fixed on the right side of each graduate's forehead.

It was only then that it first occurred to me that not only was I an officiant at a reverent celebration, but also a funeral. While there was an air of festivity, even pomp and circumstance, a sadness began to permeate the occasion. The transition day, this commencement carried with it an unspoken morbidity.

With the "Amen," of my prayer, the principal began his remarks, his exhortation to the graduating class. His conclusion also served as an introduction to the Lieutenant Governor. With the obligatory opening humor, his honor confined himself to the statutory twenty minutes. It was a non-partisan exercise in Hoosier blessing, and parental admonishment, but then it was over. The principal introduced the salutatorian of that year's class, Cassie Miller. Cassie limited her references to such comments as, "I really love you guys," and "We've been well-prepared here at BC, now it's time to prove our mettle."

After proper introduction by the principal, the Valedictory address by Tony Muller, brought some nervous levity to the otherwise well-behaved proceedings. Evidently, Tony discarded his principal-approved speech in exchange for a lampoon of life at BC. I couldn't help but notice the principal's body language displayed no small discomfort with gestures of some annoyance. The audience, including myself, were left out of most of the barbs and one liners, but the graduates and faculty, for the most part, thought it to be a hoot. He made comments about the band director, and an apparent illicit romance between the Business Skills teacher (We used to call this the Typing Teacher) and the Calculus teacher. No small giggling followed some slur of the football coach, but Mr. Muller saved the last one liner for the principal himself. I missed the comment, but the students cracked up over some bawdy allusion.

With a strained smile on his face the principal rose, and thanked Tony for his academic leadership and precociousness. Then the superintendent of schools completed the ritual. The principal declared, "Mr. Superintendent. Having completed all the requirements by the State of Indiana, I declare this class ready for graduation." With that the superintendent rose and stood on the front of the platform in front of a large stack of diplomas. Then the graduates rose and the green ribbon of graduates proceeded, one by one onto the stage. When in front of the superintendent, each was handed a diploma and granted a handshake and a, "Congratulations," and proceeded back to their seats from A to Z. When Kelly Zieman, diploma in hand, returned to her seat, the principal said, "Graduates, you may move your tassels." With that all the tassels were shifted from the right side of their foreheads to the left. It was a symbolic gesture of completion.

But it was more than that. The funeral was nearly over. Small town America is slowly dying. It is a slow relentless death. High School graduation is an ominous reminder of the morbidity and mortality of a way of life. Nearly everyone there knew this truth though it remained unspoken. America for more than one hundred fifty years has made an unswerving beeline away from rural, from the farming way of life to an urban setting, a city way of life. The farm and neighboring farm towns can no longer support its own progeny. Only a few are needed to carry on. The rest must move on.

As the graduates recessed from the arena, most would just keep on going, never to come back to their hometown, except for a visit. As they left the arena, it was to go to graduation parties, but also to the wake of a way of life.

"Arlis ministered to me as well. He helped with a putting tip. Now you ask, 'How could a man, whom I never played golf with, who never even played golf, give me a golf tip?' Good question. Admittedly it was in a round about way. Let me explain."

So went an excerpt from my sermon at the funeral for Arlis Bennett. The first time I met Arlis Bennett, was also the only time I met him; it was at his hospital bed; his death bed.

Being new in the town, new to my flock, I deliberately perused the rolls of the church, a good number I had yet to see on any given Sunday in worship. Arlis was one of those I had yet to meet. Meeting Arlis in Sunday worship was not going to happen. His little wife, though, was there nearly every Sunday. Alma Bennett, a prim and proper little woman looked like she could have been a retired school teacher or librarian. In her early eighties, I suppose, when we first met, she greeted me, "Pleased to meet you, Reverend," and then peculiarly, "Don't expect to see my husband, Arlis in church. He rarely comes." "Rarely" was interpreted to me by a few of the thirty-eight widows in the church to mean, "Almost never," or, "I don't even remember the last time that man came to church. Why he's too busy tooting his own horn to listen to anyone else, even you, pastor."

Whenever the Bennett's came up in conversation at the Dairy Barn, or any-where else, fondly, kindly they would speak of Alma. She was the sweet, soft-spo-ken, grandmother, no one would expect anything of but the best of motives and social graces. Not so, when speaking of Arlis. Though I had yet to meet him, with the gossip-laden references to him, a personality profile emerged of a crotchety old geezer, a curmudgeon of the highest order. Arlis' profile was of a tough old cob that one would rather avoid than encounter.

Fortunately, I managed to avoid him. Yet evidence of his presence was all around. Whether it be seeing Alma in church, or at the Country Club. One of my very first outings for a bit of golf, I wandered out on my own, only to bump into another singleton. "Hi, I'm Lavon Bennett." I reciprocated the introduction, but one of the salts sitting in the Horseshoe Bar butted in, "You better watch out, Bennett, that's the new preacher in town."

"Preacher?" Lavon probed based on this uninvited tip. "Are you a preacher?"

"Yeah. I just was called a couple of months ago to be the pastor at the Presby-terian Church."

"Presbyterian? Hell. I'm a Presbyterian. You probably know my mom and dad, Alma and Arlis Bennett," said Lavon.

"Well, sort of. I've met your mother, but not met your father as of yet."

Lavon Bennett almost bent over laughing. When he recomposed himself he continued, "No, and you won't. You'll probably never see that old S.O.B. in a church, your church, any church."

"What about you, Lavon, do you come to church?" I asked.

With a certain bout of nervous stammering, he rallied quickly, "Actually, well, yeah. I'm a school teacher down the road in Covington. My wife and I live there and we go to First Christian Church. Mom raised me right. You ready to play golf. Need a partner?"

I accepted his change of subject. "Sure, let's play a bit." Off we left for eighteen. It was on that first day, and numerous occasions thereafter, that I went to the Lavon Bennett School of Putting. When he putt, I noticed that very first day, he went through a step by step ritual. He'd squat down on the green like most putters do, to align the upcoming stroke. Putting in the game of golf, I am told, is nothing but speed and distance. Whack the ball on the green with the correct force and in the correct direction and the ball will go in the whole. So like any golfer, during Lavon's squat on the green, he'd assay the geometry of the green, and calculate the force of the blow with the putter on the ball that would put the ball in the little cup. His squatting was not at all unique. But what he did whilst squatting I had never seen. While he hunkered down and after peering from his ball to the distant hole, he'd reach down to his golf ball, and start twisting it back and forth, sort of like he was dialing in a station on an old radio. Then, apparently, after getting it set just right, he'd rise up from his crouch, assume an orthodox putting posture, and shortly would stroke the ball. Usually the results were most gratifying. Lavon wasn't a very good golfer as a whole, but he was an above average putter. Watching this ritual repeated hole after hole, I finally could not tolerate the suspense any longer. As he crouched down again and started dialing the station, I interrupted him, "What in the world are you doing? Twisting that ball back and forth?"

He stood up and his clinic began. "Preacher, putting is nothing but speed and distance. I have yet to figure out how to come up with a system to judge speed. But I have found a way to make me more confident about what direction I'll whack it."

Holding the ball before my eyes he asked, "You see that?" What I saw was the trademark on the golf ball; it read, "Titleist." "What is that?"

I answered my tutor, "That's the trademark."

"Right," he said, and the lesson picked up momentum. "That trademark is a straight line, almost like an arrow. All I do is squat down, figure out the best I can which direction this ball needs to go. Then I put the ball down on the green, and twist it back and forth until it lines up in the direction I want to putt." Then I stand over the ball with the putter face perpendicular to that arrow on the ball, and then stroke it. I don't worry about direction. All I have to do is concentrate on speed. It's really helped my game."

Then and there, I implemented the Lavon Bennett putting tip. I have little evidence that it has helped me, but I do feel more confident. In any case, Lavon and I became friends; I humored him with my testimony as my instructor. Between Lavon, and Alma, his mother, and an occasional snide comment about Arlis' curmudgeonly ways floating in the rumor mill, this was the sum of my knowledge of Arlis Bennett. That was until Lavon called me on the phone one day.

"Dale, do you suppose you could visit my dad down to the hospital? His emphysema's been acting up. He's not doing very well."

"Sure, I'll be going to town this afternoon," I said. So my inevitable first encounter with notorious Arlis Bennett would take place at last.

The doors on the elevator opened on his floor in Pulmonary Care. After checking with the Nurses Station I proceeded to Arlis' room. On the door out-side of his room was a sign of caution, "Warning! Oxygen in use." Yet when I pushed the door aside, I thought I caught a whiff of stale tobacco smoke hanging in the air. A few sniffs and I was sure I smelled a cigarette having been recently smoked.

My mental picture of Arlis proved off target. After all, Lavon, his son, was a fairly big man, nearly six feet tall, close to two hundred pounds. Yet the man I saw in bed was hardly any bigger then his petite wife. Arlis Bennett was a pipsqueak. Though he lay in bed, I guessed he was but five feet six inches, and maybe one hundred twenty pounds or so. Eighty years, the last sixty or more, spent smoking and drinking had turned his skin to a texture like an elephant, yet it had the frail transparency that I had become accustomed to in most octogenar-ians. His head sheltered a few wisps of white hair, and there were sickly bags under his eyes. In spite of my inexperience as a pastor, I knew a very sick, if not dying person, when I saw one. My first glimpse of the much murmured, cursed, and gossiped-about Arlis Bennett was a disappointment. He did not appear to be much of a threat, nor capable of waging much of a fight at the moment. IV's fed him some sort of medicine, and two clear nylon hoses snaked down into each nostril.

"Are you Mr. Bennett? Arlis Bennett?"

After a phlegmy cough he raised himself just a bit and with the annoyance of interruption on his face he answered, "Yeah. Who are you?"

"Arlis, I'm your pastor, Dale Patterson. Your son said maybe I oughta stop by and visit with you a bit."

A partial smile enlightened his weathered and sickly face, and he became more cordial. Coughing a bit more he added, "That was real nice. Alma's speaks kindly of you. She said you seemed to be a nice young boy."

"That was kind of her, Arlis. I thought I might just drop by, and chat a bit with you." After a nervous pause I asked, "Anything on your mind? Anything you'd like to chat about? And by the way, have you been smoking?"

Amazing as it seems, it's hard to fathom the power some of our habits have over us. Arlis was gasping for air, his lungs ransacked by a lifetime of cigarette pollution, forced to supplement his body's own system by force feeding himself oxygen, yet Arlis still smoked more Camels.

"Yeah, I know it's stupid. The nurse warned me that smoking around this oxygen could set me and the whole dern hospital on fire. But I don't care. I just disconnect this hose," he pointed to the oxygen line into his nostrils, "then I light up. After I have a smoke, I just plug into the oxygen, and I'm just fine."

He continued uninterrupted for twenty minutes or so. He didn't look like much of an old dog, but there was still a good deal of bite in him. The thirty-eight widows at the Presbyterian Church were right. It didn't take him long to show me the much-discussed and infamous Arlis Bennett.

I sat in a chair at his bedside, and marveled. He carried on and on in a combination, indoctrination, lecture, diatribe of Arlis' philosophy, not just of life, but of the meaning of the universe, the nature of salvation, the significance of the Bible, the role of religion in an individual's life, the hypocrisy of the church and religious people in general, what happens to Buddhist babies who die without embracing the faith of Christ, and why the Cubs would never win the pennant let alone the Word Series. Yet as I listened to him carry on, I sensed a question mark hidden in the midst of all his poppycock.

Poppycock. Yes, that's what it was. Twenty minutes of the greatest collage of pop philosophy, *Poor Farmer's Almanac* street wisdom, and false Christian doctrine I had never, ever heard. All through it I heard him asking himself, and me, or anyone for that matter, "Is this right?"

The more I listened, the more troubled I became. "This guy is nuts," I said to myself. "For nearly eighty years he's been spouting off this baloney and no one has told him to shut up. No one has had the guts to tell him he's off his rocker. That his philosophy is no philosophy at all, just baloney."

Another voice in me argued just as vehemently. "Dale, he's just an old man. In the name of Christ, just let him be. What good will it do to get in a fight with a dying old man?"

Good. It was decided. I'd just let him be. The latter self had won.

Arlis' harangue paused with a question to me, "Well, Patterson, what do YOU think? Aren't I right?"

The civil war inside, I thought resolved, was settled in a manner surprising even to me, normally a conciliator, a placator.

"Right? Arlis." I took a breath, and with an unprecedented force I nearly shouted back at him, "No Arlis. That was the biggest pile of bull I have ever heard."

We both stopped motionless and speechless. About the time I said, "Bull," Arlis recoiled just as if I'd hit the poor old man with a right upper cut to the jaw. I just remained silently shocked for a moment more when Arlis finally broke the stalemate. "Oh." What followed was amazing, almost as if Arlis had spent his entire life looking for someone to argue with him, someone to tell him he was full of it. We both were surprised it was a Presbyterian minister who told him to button it.

"Oh. Well what do you think, Mr. Wiseguy Preacher?"

For the next five minutes or so, I share with Arlis Bennett what it meant to be a Christian, at least from a respectable orthodox Presbyterian perspective, and how I thought it differed from his heterodox hodgepodge of belief.

While I spoke to him, I noticed Arlis relax in expression; the corners of his eyes were not nearly so squinting. When I finished he simply again said, "Oh."

He coughed a bit more then said, "Pastor, Alma was right about you. You're okay. Come back and chat with me again, okay?" The annoyance on his faith of a more than half an hour ago, had given way to a friendly grin.

"Okay, Arlis. I'll see you again."

But I didn't. Arlis Bennett died three days later.

"Arlis ministered to me as well. He helped with a putting tip," I said, as I spoke to the congregation of Presbyterians, and friends and enemies of Arlis Bennett at his funeral. "Arlis Bennett gave me and you a son, Lavon Bennett. And Lavon gave me a sure fire tip to help my sorry golf game."

Of course I don't know if anyone had ever argued with Arlis before, or told him he was full of it, but we became friends, friends forever about the time I shouted at that little coughing old fool, "Bull."

When the snow wafted down that Christmas, we thought it romantic. The cozy serenity, the idyllic picture of a New England holiday evening came to mind; I looked for Clydesdale horses pulling a sleigh through the snow-covered lane, a humming chorus chanting the Budweiser theme. Yet the snow only lasted a bit, an inch or so. The sky cleared and the Canadian Norther imposed an icebox grip that would last more than a week. Added to that, thirty mile per hour gusts picked up the snow and the drifting began. As I walked across from my house, the Presbyterian Manse, to the church to put the last touches on the Christmas Eve Candlelight Service, I suspected things were going down hill. Still it was Christmas, so I repressed the obvious signs, and thought it time for a cup of coffee.

By 9:30 that morning, two days before Christmas, the temperature had slipped into the mid-teens, destined for below zero. Walking into the Dairy Barn for a coffee and donut with my coffee-drinking fraternity, we griped about the coming frigid weather and shared our plans.

"Hey, Peggy, you got any of that stuff to put in my gas tank so my diesel fuel won't freeze up?" asked Smitty. Peggy nodded affirmatively, and he continued, "Those diesels are all right except for when it gets so darn cold. Then they're just a heap of metal."

Others told of Christmas trips on which they were about to depart, or who was coming to visit them. With another frigid blast from the open door, Shorty Shamburger made his arrival. A minor curse, pulling off his gloves, and a smile warmed us all, "How the hell are you guys? Snow's pretty much closed Highway Eighteen already."

This was the problem. Just a little snow stirred up by twenty to thirty mile per hour winds, spelled doom for prairie roads. The wind shoveled the snow off the flat fields, and dumped it along all the roads. The beams along the highways and county roads served as moats, troughs to guard the snow and force its accumulation on the only thoroughfare across the county. Thus in only a few hours the roads in and out of town could be sealed shut with just a little snow and a few gusts of wind. The County Highway Department ventured out into the developing blizzard with their yellow dump trucks with snowplow on the front and salt in the hopper, but the task was futile. They had twenty or thirty trucks, and hundreds of miles of highway to keep clear. This blizzard would have required several hundred trucks.

Yet, we continued to ignore the indications of coming hardships and persevered with holiday plans. "Playing any golf today, Smitty'?" asked Shorty.

"No, I don't have any of those orange balls. Plus I played awful back on Halloween," which was the last time he had played. "I guess I'll watch Anne cook pies and wrap presents. Then I'll have a couple of cold ones and watch ESPN." Smitty possessed modest ambition.

Shorty continued his inquiry one by one until he interviewed me, "Patterson. What are you doing? You gonna come to Sacred Heart and meet Jesus?" My

Catholic comrades were always interceding, concerned for my eternal security, trapped in the throes of Protestant rebellion.

"No, Shorty. I'll just be doing my thing at the church, and we have a bunch of family coming in. My wife's parents will be up from Lafayette, my mom and dad with my grandmother from Pennsylvania, my brother-in-law, and one of my sisters will be in from Chicago. It'll be a great time."

"Geesh. It sounds like the whole fam damily." Shorty concluded. "Merry Christmas," and he was off again into the cold.

Eugene, the town sheriff announced about then, "I just heard on my scanner that they're about to close 52." US 52 was the main route between Chicago and Indianapolis with Fowler in between.

Thus began the Christmas holiday blizzard that would kill plans of many in that part of the world. My brother-in-law was the first one due in that night about six o'clock at O'Hare Field in Chicago. Uncle Tom was the hero of my little boys, and they insisted on going with me into the blizzard for the one hundred mile trip to pick him up at the airport. By three o'clock, as I drove out of town north toward Chicago, I thought myself a fool for going at all. Periodically the highway was a whiteout. A whiteout is to blowing snow in the prairie as fog is to the mountain passes around the world. For both, visibility is not bad, it is zero; the road disappears. I lied to my boys when they asked me with no small concern, "Dad, can you see the road?"

"Sure, boys, I just look down at the side of the highway. It's a piece of cake." With such comfort they beamed smiles that betrayed the truth; their smiles said,

"Boy, our dad is an awesome driver."

I murmured, "Your dad is a fool." But the last thirty miles inside the city were clear; away from the prairies one never would have known there was a problem. Little did I know twelve hours later that would portend still another foolish decision.

Uncle Tom's six o'clock flight did not make it in from Boston until ten o'clock. By that time the boys were both asleep in my lap waiting in the United Airlines lounge. Like youngster somnambulists, they escorted their Uncle Tom back to our car. The arctic grip clamped tighter. A bank thermometer not far from the airport indicated eight degrees below zero. Still the city sheltered us from reality, but as soon as we returned to the country highway the whiteout continued, this time in the dark with the thermometer headed for twenty-four below.

When I stopped for gas and a cup of coffee, the frigid gale froze the lining of my nostrils instantly. I had no gloves capable of protecting me from such a frosty blast. As we resumed our trek for the remaining sixty miles it was midnight. The four lane Highway 52 amounted to two pair of ruts in opposite directions. More and more I saw the shoulder littered with abandoned cars-frozen to death, at least inactivity. Others slid down into the ditch. The red glare of burning flares brought me to a stop. A tractor trailer was parked in the middle of the highway. Rolling the window down a crack, I asked the unfortunate trailer jockey, "Hey buddy. Need any help?"

"No. The darn diesel fuels turned to jelly. I've called a wrecker. He should be here in a few more minutes." Diesel fuel turns to Jell-O around zero. This diesel was the first of many more I would witness in the next miles having been rendered useless. Carefully I pulled around the semi, plowing a new path until I returned to the comfort and familiarity of the ruts marking Highway 52.

Travel seldom frightens me. My little boys were sound asleep wrapped in sleeping bags in the back seat. It was so cold the heater could barely keep up. Looking at them safe in the car, I thought to double my efforts to drive safely. To be in the ditch at one o'clock in the morning in the middle of the prairie and twenty-four below spelled doom. And it was not their fault that their father was dumb enough to let them come along.

My vigilance paid off, and by two that Christmas Eve morning we pulled up at home.

The next scheduled to arrive were my parents and my octogenarian grandmother who set out the twenty-third from Pittsburgh and made it to Western Ohio. About one o'clock Christmas Eve afternoon, the phone rang. "Dad, where are you?" I asked.

"We're in Indianapolis. What's all the fuss? I know it's cold, but the State Police say the highway's closed up your way. What's going on?" dad asked.

"Dad. You better stay put and try to make it tomorrow when this wind dies down. There's blizzard conditions here. No one can make it in. The roads have blown closed. Especially with grandma. You better stay put." I exhorted him.

"Well, we'll see. I'll let you know what we're gonna do. Bye," was all he said. He hung up on me. I noted it was one o'clock.

I gave the same advice to my sister in Chicago that morning about ten o'clock. "Michelle, you and Dan just stay put. I'd try to come tomorrow if I were you."

"Well, I'm not you. As soon as I get this pie out of the oven, we'll be on our way. We should be there by two."

"No, Michelle. Listen to me. It's not worth it. Last night at two o'clock I barely made it back. And it's been blowing even more since then." Ignoring my counsel, my sister, like her father, hung up on me too.

"Reverend?" Harley greeted me on the phone.

He continued seeking my counsel, but apparently the decision, he assumed, had been made. "You're not planning on having Christmas Eve Services are you? It sure would be awful to have people try to make it in to church tonight and get stuck or worse."

"Harley, I've been thinking we ought to cancel services. 'Suppose the elders ought to call the church families and tell 'em to stay at home." And so the decision to kill the high holy day of Christian worship, Christmas Eve services, was made in a moment.

Harley was pleased, and he told me, "I'll call the elders and get them to call around."

"Thank you, Harley, and Merry Christmas to you and Martha." It was finished.

But the family gathering, in spite of difficulties continued. By three o'clock that Christmas Eve afternoon, if you looked out the window of our big house, looking upward through the thin white veil of drifting snow, you could see clear, blue sky. Yet looking at ground level it reminded me of travelogues of Antarctica. White tornados of snow blinded the vision with periodic moments of visibility which allowed a clear view of the street, maybe a hundred yards or more.

I was on the lookout for Michelle and Dan, an hour overdue from Chicago. Continuing to gaze into the white glare, my concern for them grew by the moment, only to be interrupted by the surprise of the entire ordeal. On a beautiful summer day; it takes two hours to drive from Indianapolis to Fowler. My father had done what seemed impossible. As I saw his silver Buick Park Avenue with Pennsylvania plates pull up along the curb in the midst of the white blur, I gaped incredulously. It was three o'clock. Dad had made it around State Police barriers, across highways few had even ventured to traverse that day in the same time it would take on a July Sunday afternoon drive. My parents and my grandma stepped into the blizzard and trudged up the steps into the warmth, safety and fellowship of our gathering family.

I wondered if my sister and her husband would share the same good fortune.

After greetings, hugs, and bragging on dad's intrepid blizzard accomplishments, mom added, "I'm so glad we made it. We'll be able to go to the Christmas Eve services. They'll be lovely, I'm sure."

My mother always was eager to see her clergy son do his ministerial duties. Still I had to burst her bubble. "Mom, due to the blizzard, we thought it best to cancel the services. I'm sorry, but there won't be anything going on tonight but what celebration we have together." The disappointment painted her face; since

planning this trip, the high point was the family gathering in the pews to celebrate the birth of the Savior together, like old times. This would have been a rare
dream for us, but it was not to be.

Still other concerns overshadowed such disappointments. Four, five, six
o'clock, still no sign of my sister and her husband. Darkness again descended
while the wind kept up its incessant howl. Worry and fear infected us all. It was
hard to be celebratory with the uncertainty of my sister's safety.

The ring of the phone interrupted our fears. "Dale, we're okay," it was
Michelle; she was sniffling, and her voice filled with emotion. "We went around
the barriers at Kentland just as it was getting dark. We couldn't see a thing, and
we got stuck. The car just smashed into a drift and it would go no further. This
drama was told in between controlled sobs. We're okay. It was so cold. A police
car found us about a half hour later, and brought us to the Kentland Elementary
School. We'll spend the night here. But our car's buried."

They had made it to within ten miles of our town. "Michelle, if that police-
man hadn't got you, you'd have frozen to death. Thank God you're safe." I interrupted.

"I know. We're glad to be safe, but darn it," she broke down with a small fit of
weeping. "We're so close. I can't believe we didn't make it," she said.

"We'll come get you in the morning. But I've got another idea. Let me call
some friends of mine up there in Kentland. They'll take you in for the night. You
can stay there, shower, clean up, be with them. That'll be much better than a
gym. I'll have 'em come get you."

And so it was that my sister and her husband were rescued twice in several
hours. Once from a snowdrift, and twice, from the Red Cross temporary motel in
a grade school gym.

We went to bed that night, not worshipping at the Christmas Eve Candlelight
Service, but snug in our beds. All night I pondered if we'd make it up to Kentland to rescue my sister.

The brightness of the morning awakened me, yet so did the silence. For the
first time in several days, the air was still. The silence was deafening. Ambling to
the window, I gazed out through the ice crystals on the window pane to behold a
glistening white surface, and a blue sky as shiny and gorgeous as any spring morning. Still the temperature was more than twenty below.

Everyone was still sleeping, so I thought, as I squeaked down the staircase to
put on a pot of coffee. My father already was in the kitchen. His morning greeting was terse, "Let's try to go get your sister." Ten minutes later we stepped out
into the icepack, started the car, and headed north to Kentland. While it was

bone-chilling, so that the moisture in one's nostrils frosted with the first inhale of this intensely crisp air, all signs as we turned north at the stoplight for Kentland, foretold an easy and safe trip.

Dad's Park Avenue sped beyond the speed limit up the beige concrete ribbon called US 52. Snow was everywhere, except on the highway. The wind had plowed the highway clean, except for an occasional dusting here and there on the pavement. Five miles north of town, halfway, still all seemed well until the highway bent a bit to the right to parallel a railroad track that was about eight to ten feet above the road. Suddenly the concrete disappeared. It seemed obvious that the last four miles of the road into Kentland, all paralleling the railroad, were covered with eight to ten feet of snow. There was no way we were going any further. But others were. The Highway Department had large bulldozers and payloaders already digging a path into the mountain of snow. As dad turned back south for the comfort of our house, he concluded, "Maybe this'll be cleared by noon."

As Christmas Eve had been colored by our grief over the storm difficulties and my sister's troubles in completing her holiday rendezvous, so that morning, watching our little ones open their Christmas loot was still joyous, but not quite as carefree and crazy had everyone been there. But the grief was about to give way to partying.

As I jumped up to answer the ringing phone, I noticed the clock struck eleven o'clock in the morning. It was my sister, "Dale, the police said the highway's open to one lane each way. You'll have to come get us, because our car's buried still." I interrupted, "Michelle, dad and I'll be up there in fifteen minutes." We were.

Our return trip to Fowler, having liberated my sister and her husband from the hospitality of my friends there, was paused only to dig through the snow a bit to find their car. We drove to the spot where the car was submerged in the drift. All we could see was a chrome strip on the driver's side door, along the roof line. I brought a shovel. So we dug for a few minutes and opened the door and the trunk. We pulled the Christmas presents, a frozen honey-baked ham, Christmas Dinner, and a case of frozen beer from the car and transferred them to our warm south-bound car.

As Michelle and Dan stepped into the house to be greeted, hugged, and teased, our temporary grief gave way to an unabashed family celebration. True, my mother didn't get to have her family in the pews together on Christmas Eve, but as my grandma in her quivering voice, summoned us all, the generations around the table, to give thanks to the Lord on that Christmas Day, any disappointment was forgotten, having been washed away by tears of joy. And oh, scraped away by ice flakes still on the honey-baked ham.

"What you doin' for Decoration?" I was asked. Not just me, but it was a common greeting as the bittersweet holiday approached. "Decoration," as many old-timers called it, was more formally, "Decoration Day," still more commonly, "Memorial Day." Yet in the Midwest, it's not uncommon to hear it simply labeled, decoration. As in, "What you doin' for Decoration?"

I suppose, though I am not sure, it earned its named for the activity that marks the annual observance each late May. People, survivors, spouses and families set out every Decoration Day for the cemeteries across the prairie, pause a moment to grieve a bit more for the deceased loved one, and in doing so, they place a bouquet of flowers, a spray of carnations or the like, near the grave's headstone. In this manner they decorate the place of the dead. Theology aside, it is a reverent and often, loving occasion, a mini-re-funeral.

Memorial Day, Decoration Day, above all is a military holiday as well. I remember as a teenage boy visiting Arlington National Cemetery in suburban Washington D.C. being so impressed by the reverence and pomp all around, above all at the Tomb of the Unknown Soldier—The crack soldiers keeping watching over this hallowed place of military and civic honor. Those thoughts returned to me years later as I was part of the pageantry of Memorial Day Observances at the Benton County Cemetery-The Protestant Side.

The Commander of the local American Legion post, Junior Mason, also the county auctioneer, accosted me in the lobby of the bank about a week before Decoration. "Pastor, it's the Presbyterians' year to officiate at the Memorial Day Observances. Could you be out there Monday morning just a little before ten, say a few words in respect about the deceased veterans, and have a prayer before the Honor Guard salutes our fallen comrades?"

The Protestant ministers rotated this responsibility: one year the Methodist, then the Baptist, and so forth. That year it was my turn. The cemeteries not only represented ecclesiastical rivalry in town, the Catholic side and the Protestant side, but when it came to veterans' organizations, there were two choices as well. The VFW, Veterans of Foreign Wars, competed with the American Legion. Never clear of the source and rationale of this tribal rivalry, I chose to stay out of it. Yet when Memorial Day observances came, the two rivals buried the hatchet, and cooperated in the solemn festivities.

I drove out to the cemetery that Memorial Day Monday morning. The previous day's hoopla still made me a bit dopey: Memorial Day weekend is a three day event. Usually picnics, trips to the lake, baseball games, and so forth. In Indiana, however, Sunday marks the greatest spectacle in racing, The Indianapolis 500. I preached a short sermon, and pronounced a rapid benediction, paused for a few perfunctory handshakes and greetings, and jogged home to listen to the race. Hoosiers often spend that Sunday listening to the radio, grilling chicken, or burgers, playing catch in the yard, even tossing a few horseshoes. All the time, though, one ear listens to find out if A.J. Foyt could win another race, or Mario Andretti could cast out the demons of bad luck and win his second race. It wasn't to be. The lord of the Brickyard during the eighties and nineties, Roger Penske, and his team won still another race driven by Fittipaldi.

Pulling into the cemetery I still grieved that A.J. or Mario hadn't made it happen that year. Yet turning into the cemetery, I was disappointed; Harley Winton was no where to be seen. I couldn't remember coming to the Benton County Cemetery and not have Harley greet me. Gazing across and through the gravestones toward a gathering of people, I picked him out, and in doing so it explained why he did not greet me. Harley was part of the VFW Honor guard; he was in full dress uniform. He was standing at ease in a line of six others representing the Veterans of Foreign Wars. Facing them was the Honor Guard from the American Legion. The Legionnaires also wore full dress attire. A space of nearly twenty feet separated the parallel honor guards. At the head of their respective rank was a flower-draped trellis with spring flowers, and a small podium stood under the trellis. This evidently was the place for the orations, and my prayers.

Stepping out of my car, it was only about fifty yards of cushioned grass to be traversed before Commander Junior Mason greeted me. "Pastor, we'll be getting under way here in just a few minutes." He handed me a typed sheet indicating the order of service, and Junior added, "You do the Invocation, later a few comments about our lost loved ones. It'll conclude with your Benediction, a twenty-one gun salute, and then Jim Mercer's girl's gonna play Taps. That'll be it. Okay?"

"Sure, Junior; I got it." The Commander went about his business, and I gazed around me. Several hundred folk, mostly senior citizens, pressed around the trellis to form a theater effect. All around us the gravestones proclaimed their ancestors. Most of the names were familiar: Winton, Jenkins, Ownby, Walker, Mason, Shamburger, Wilson, Beecham. But looking at the Honor guards, an observation and a question came to mind to the point of no small distraction.

The observation was their uniforms didn't fit. On their heads each donned a khaki colored hat or cap. I don't know what you call them. Soldiers around the world in various armies wear them; they remind me of the sort of hat your butcher wears as he serves you bologna at the meat counter. Each of the Oscar Meyer soldier hats had an official insignia on it designating their branch of services and rank. Most of the hats fit, but some rested on top of naked scalps; years before they covered jet-black hair. Now there was little hair, and none of it jet-black.

Beneath the head came the Honor Guard's dress blouse. Years before these virile soldiers had broad shoulders. Now what was broad was supported by their belt and a shiny brass buckle on those belts brought focus to each soldier's pear-shaped figures.

I suspect that parade inspection before the Top Brass in Germany in the forties or Korea in the fifties to have missing buttons would earn a demerit, if not K.P. Several of these fellows, though, had lost buttons, producing gaps just above their bellies, and on one I saw a protruding navel, a second, a B.V.D. undershirt. While they looked a bit more shabby than when they left boot camp years ago, the pride of serving their beloved country still burned in their hearts. That sort of pride polished away any blemishes in their outward appearance.

The question was: How can fourteen fellows fire a twenty-one salute? Each of the seven veterans from their respective organization carried a field rifle and live ammunition. It was clear they expected to fire those guns. I began to fret to myself, "How can fourteen guns fire a twenty-one gun salute." My question would just have to wait, but my concern did not abate.

"Honor Guard, Attention," Commander Mason sounded just like the Honor Guard officer at Arlington National Cemetery. The snap, the spit and polish of Arlington, the well-drilled precision was a bit more muddled, however, in Benton County, USA. The slap of a precision drill team was more a fumbling of well-intentioned farmers, auctioneers, and fuel oil deliverymen, so that in the span of several seconds, the clatter of rifles to shoulders, a few whispers, "Oh, crap!," and fourteen men, veterans of the greatest Armed Forces the world has ever seen, stood eye to eye, ready to steward this reverent occasion.

I was invited by Junior to offer that morning's invocation. Following that came the most solemn and splendid element of the morning. Each of the two organizations, the Veterans of Foreign Wars, and the American Legion, respectively, slowly, and solemnly announced the names of the soldiers of the county who had died serving their country. For the tiny county in the middle of nowhere, the list was startlingly long.

Each name was cited, including rank, and in what action said soldier died. It was then that I forgot about over-stressed uniforms and remembered the gravity and beauty of this day. The names kept coming. "Seaman Thomas A. Harold,

US Army Air Corps, WWII," the brother of a retired farmer, and landowner. "Private John R. Lester, US Army, Korea," the twin brother of the Amoco Gas station owner, the station right next to the stoplight. "Ensign Donald Donley, US Navy, WWII," a murmur swept the crowd. The murmur clarified, "Donley's are catholic," I overheard. It was scandalous. Then I heard a whispered, "No, Donald, was old man Donley's son who married that Jewish girl, don't you remember. He had to quit the church. Poor thing got shot down over Leyte Gulf, out there in the Pacific." Such murmured whispers seemed to quiet and address the scandal. "Lance Corporal Junior Mason, II. USMC, Vietnam." I was caught off guard. "I didn't know that," I said to myself. Immediately I caught myself staring at Commander Junior Mason, auctioneer, town giver of good cheer, and veteran. He maintained the carriage of an officer. Junior, himself, had been a Captain in the Korean conflict. While his demeanor was that of a disciplined soldier, his eyes welled up to overflowing, as a discreet tear ran down the wrinkled skin of this seventy year old.

Not too much longer and the list of those to be honored came to an end. My comments were trivial in light of what I had just heard. What can you say that is profound and helpful regarding the loss of one in service to his country? I mumbled a bit about the sovereignty of God, the grief that heals the believer, and our resolve not to let the dead's contribution to their progeny be in vain. I closed with the benediction, and my nagging question was resolved.

I learned later of the compromise that solved the twenty-one gun salute. Usually, I am told, twenty-one gun salutes, the highest honor for fired salutes, are fired by an honor guard of seven each firing three volleys. The compromise was each team of seven would fire three volleys, supposedly for their own respective veterans. It still sounded like a forty-two gun salute to me.

"Honor Guard. Present Arms," shouted Commander Mason; he was thoroughly recomposed. Still it sounded to me like they always say, "Present H-h-harms."

Next the orders came more rapidly. "Ready." At first it seemed to me like the precision or Arlington was closer than I had expected. But as Junior re-shouted, "Ready." Smiles broke over some faces, others were horrified. Three of the soldiers could not get the bolts on their field rifles to put a shell in the firing chamber. Eleven soldiers stood with rifles held vertically before their breasts, ready for the next command. Three hunched over fiddling with the bolts on their rifles. The clicking of machinery, the rifles, kept up for several seconds. Occasionally one of the old soldiers gasped, "Damn it. I'll get it here in a second." As the embarrassment continued, all but one was ready. Junior could wait no more,

"Aim." With that thirteen rifles, all held at various angles, pointed safely away from the crowd toward the Hoosier May sky.

I remember Honor Guards elsewhere. When the command "Fire," was given, all the guns fired as one. That was not the case here. There was one huge, "Bang," followed by lesser, individual, "bang---bang-bang---bang-bang bang." Precision was not the forte of the combined Legion-VFW Honor Guard.

The next two volleys went much as the first. Through it all thirteen guns fired. Darrell Gillmer, VFW Honor Guard Member, Vietnam Veteran, and Benton County Country Club Greenskeeper, could never get his rifle to fire. He was nearly in tears when he realized his chance to fire the rifle had past. Darrell took no end of harassment in the days to come. Off color comments were the talk of the Horseshoe Bar out at the club, about Darrell never being able to fire when it counted. In spite of his failure, he took the good-natured ribbing quite well. In fact, the story became the stuff of legend. In years following the Catholics scheduled their observance so as not to conflict, thereby hoping for a repeat performance. But it never happened.

When Commander Mason said his third, "Fire," we all had just witnessed our first thirty-nine gun salute. For all the fumbling, and the fact that only thirteen guns were ever fired, the honor was no less, the love for the departed, and love of country only kindled more.

Sunny Mercer, a member of the BC High School Band was drafted to play Taps. Evidently no one in either veteran's group could blow a bugle. But Sunny could, and when she finished, the Memorial Day celebration was complete.

The lost sons, fathers, brothers, cousins, uncles—they had been remembered, and their offering was now assured not to have been in vain. Had a wing of fighter jets thundered overhead, it would have added nothing to the reverence and honor accorded them by the families and fourteen veterans with butcher hats on their heads, and bulging blouses at their belts. Rest in peace, those who paid such a high price so that we can picnic, listen to a race, and say the Pledge of Allegiance every last weekend of May.

Disappointment and death seemed to be much of life beyond the stoplight. Stoics just plod on as if automatons. Not so in Benton County USA. They grieve, they cry, they hold one another, console one another. Then when the sun rises they march on to enjoy another day-with a firm but gentle grin on their face.

WATERING HOLES

Life in much of the world revolves around eating and drinking. When visiting the inhabitants of small villages in China amidst the Himalayan foothills, being with the people means sitting down at table dining with them, eating their exotic, often repulsive entrees. I visited a tiny tribal village in extreme Southern Mexico along the Guatemalan border. No sooner than we arrived and the hospitality of the people nearly forced us to sup with them. We could not speak their language for they spoke neither English nor Spanish; so we spoke the language of food and drink. We learn about one another speaking this peculiar language. What is true in quaint mountain villages in the mountains of China or Mexico is true of the plains of Indiana as well. Driving through town on Highway 52 one learns little. Travelling beyond the stoplight, though, and braving a visit to the various watering holes, the snack shops and dining emporiums, one can learn much. And most there speak some form of English.

Turning to the right at the stoplight, and a jog to the left, there by Lester's Amoco, go a block north, and the visitor comes to a point of entry, entry that is, to life as it is in Fowler. The Chocolate Shop does not require an immersion too deep into the life of the town. In much of America it would be called the Tastee Freeze, or Dairy Queen. The Chocolate Shop was the closest equivalent that Fowler had to any fast food restaurant. While it had a diverse menu, its primary focus was frozen custard specialties: ice cream cones, milk shakes, sundaes and the like.

It was a suitable point of entry to life in Fowler, because it only required pulling up front, strolling up to the window, and ordering a shake, or whatever, and then returning to the shelter of one's car to continue on beyond town. But such a visit would miss much of the color of life surrounding The Chocolate Shop.

"Hey, The Chocolate Shop's open. Let's go get a cone after practice," so said a Little Leaguer to a teammate prior to a practice at one of the practice diamonds several blocks from the point of their snacking plans. The Chocolate Shop was not a year-round establishment. I don't know why. I guess the thought of eating some ice cream product served through a cubbyhole window, and eating on picnic tables in a twenty-four below zero gale does not bode well for profit and loss statements-better to close for Winter. So usually it closed from about November 1st until May 1st.

With Little League practices in Indiana in the beginning of May, the temperature could be thirty-five degrees as well as seventy-five. But when young boys have practiced catching grounders for an hour or so, and the novelty of ice cream cones being served again after a winter-long famine of same, and fifty cents burning in their pockets, as soon as the coach says, "Practice is over," they zoom on their Huffy's or Schwinn's the several blocks to savor that frozen chocolate custard delight called a cone. It doesn't matter that it's still so cold at night, and the dripping of mid-Summer heat is not the problem. The problem is hypothermia from being twice frozen-a frosty Hoosier evening, and a freezing Hoosier ice cream cone. Yet there is no complaining. The taste of that chocolate ice cream treat first touching the ten year old kid's palate atones for any external temperature discomforts.

Usually, however, by Memorial Day, most days and nights are Hoosier hot 'n sticky-perfect for trips to The Chocolate Shop. The quintessential visit to The Chocolate Shop comes on hot summer nights. Winds blow during the winter and spring on the prairie, but usually when it gets sultry, hot and sticky on a June, July, or August night, the prairie is becalmed. The absence of howling winds is replaced by the screeching drone of locusts, cicadas, tree frogs and katydids. Some folk in that region call these noisemakers, hot bugs.

The Chocolate Shop was little more than a shack containing a few frozen custard machines, soda machines, deep fryer, and a griddle. On the back of The Shop it merged into a small house where the proprietors lived. On the business side of the shop was a gravel parking lot which accommodated five or six cars and forty-six bicycles. Stepping out of the car one ambled up to the glass storefront with two windows, cubbyholes. Each of those cubbyholes had glass that slid to the side so an employee, usually a BC High School girl, could bow over and say, "What can I get ya?" Splattered all over the glass was what passed as the menu. A sheet of paper pictured an ice cream cone and with marker was written, "Small, $.85, Medium, $1.25, Large, $1.55, Jumbo, $1.95." Others advertised slurpees, sundaes, hamburgers, coney dogs, and an Indiana favorite, tenderloin sandwich. Along with this always expanding list of entrees were the obligatory french fries, fried mushrooms, and on and on. The emphasis was on frozen something, or fried whatever. The customer, like the employee order-taker, would bend over and say, "I'll have a burger with everything, fries, and a chocolate shake." Five minutes or so later the girl would shout out through the window, "Burger with everything, fries and shake." Pay for the order and the customers, if not desiring to eat in the front seat of the car, would walk a few steps to the lean-to next to the windows, also known as the dining area. This makeshift dining room sheltered two picnic tables. Those tables amounted to layers upon layers of gray enamel covering last season's carvings of various initials, and telephone numbers. Such memos were carved as "J.P. loves D.G." enclosed in a heart. Or the more scandalous, "Call 287-4539 for a good time." On top of this makeshift cultural table cloth were a host of drippings, laminated pickle relish, a dollop of ketchup, and the ever present stickiness of smeared ice cream products.

Such was the Chocolate Shop. On my first visit a local town mother had bicycled from her nearby home with her two year old daughter in the affixed toddler seat on the back of the bike. As I sat waiting for my burger, the young mother had just taken delivery on what appeared to be a chocolate shake. The two-year old had not mastered the sophisticated skills of drinking through a straw. So the young mother tipped the shake up over the little blonde's cherubic face. With the tip, a huge glop of cold ice cream plastered the baby's face. Shocked, the little girl didn't know to laugh or cry. When the mother broke out giggling at her baby's mishap, the baptized toddler thought it something to laugh about as well. A few licks and she continued to savor the shake.

Such scenes were repeated many times in a day at The Chocolate Shop.

If a day in Fowler often ended with a hot fudge sundae at The Chocolate Shop, few days could start better than a trucker's platter breakfast at The Fillin' Station. I-65 usurped US 52's dominance as the main north-south route in that part of the world. With the decline of US 52, came the demise of its highway culture as well: motels dwindled and disappeared; restaurants became fewer and much farther between, and gas stations that depended solely on highway traffic evaporated as the gas each proprietor pumped. Yet a few of these services survived the transition. Survival usually required having a sufficient local clientele to make it, and finding a novelty niche. The Fillin' Station had both. Locals kept the tables filled enough and the parking spaces occupied enough so that out-of-towners were convinced that the restaurant would be worth a first time gamble. The novelty was that The Fillin's Station no longer was a gas station, as the name historically implied, but a place to fill one's belly.

Years before it was a gas station and truck stop along busy US 52, a Conoco station, as I recall. Yet it had been abandoned for ten to twenty years. The only interest the old gas station had for anyone was as a classic model, in disrepair, of a vintage 50s service station. Two islands of old gas pumps stood out front, maybe fifty yards or so off the road. The pumps were tall, skinny pillars, one painted red for regular, the other green for ethyl. On top of each of the pumps was a white glass globe that in the good ol' days was lighted at night with the Conoco logo glowing for all to see. In 1958 you would have pulled up to a pump in your '57 BelAir and a guy named Earl, perhaps would have asked, "Fill 'er up?" And you would have answered according to ritual, "Yeah, and check the oil, air, and do the windows for me too, please." Earl would have been pleased to do it; it was part of the deal. But such conversations were just ghosts out of the past by the time I came to life beyond the stoplight. A few years ago, however, a couple of financed-entrepreneurs took a gamble and turned the old Conoco into a restaurant; one for real Americans, like farmers and above all, truck drivers. The whole town profited from their gamble.

They closed up the service bays, leveled the floor, brought in a bunch of vintage 50s kitchen tables—the ones with nickel-plated legs and table edges and porcelain or Formica tops—added a bunch of assorted chairs, and opened an establishment. This establishment was dedicated not to filling a person's gas tank, but one's stomach. The walls of The Fillin' Station were littered with license plates from across the nation and across the years, plus gas station memorabilia: cans of oil, radiator treatment products and tire repair tools. The Fillin' Station was a hit.

It wasn't cute like memorabilia establishments in the city. Truckers don't frequent cute. Still smelling like an old gas station on the inside, it wasn't so much cute, but it made the farmers and truckers feel like they were back home, unlike the modern efficient truckstops of today, and the boring humdrum of the chain fast-food dining emporium.

The employees, waitresses and cooks, were not clean-scrubbed American high school kids, but earthy, down-to-earth folk. Sitting at the table, Vera, Molly, or a fifty-ish Irene boldly came to your table and virtually ordered your order, "What can I get you, honey? Care for some coffee?" While menus were available, it was expected, the proper protocol of the house, that you knew what you wanted, and a guy named Lou, back in the kitchen could whip it up, whatever you wanted. Whatever, provided it was real American food. That meant eggs in the morning, or maybe hotcakes; burgers, Blue Plate Special meat loaf, or tenderloin sandwich, for lunch, and something like fried chicken, roast beef, or chicken and noodles come supper time. If you really wanted a menu you probably ought not to frequent The Fillin' Station.

Breakfast was always my favorite time there. Breakfast was served twenty-four hours a day, but more typically from about five o'clock until about ten, ten-thirty in the morning. The coffee cups that Irene would drop before you were filled with a steaming, stout brew of java. The cups were a solid piece of white china-I mean solid, the walls of the cup, must have been three quarters of an inch thick-not to be lifted by the weak or arthritic. But they contained the lifeblood of the establishment. And any waitress worth her salt kept the lifeblood filled. The waitresses always had the refill pot in their hand to keep it to the brim.

"I'll have a couple over easy, toast, bacon, hash browns, and a half order of biscuits and sausage gravy on the side," a trucker would ask. Vera, unfazed answered, "That'll be just a few minutes, honey." She walked to the window, really a hole in the wall separating the kitchen from the counter with dining stools, and shouted out the order to Lou back in the kitchen. No matter how many orders Vera, Molly, and Irene shouted in to Lou, in an amazing logistical accomplishment and in a few minutes, Vera would plop your order before you, "Hon', there you go. Get ya anything else?" With that she was off to fill someone's coffee or take another order. Upon her departure, the customer, the diner, was confronted by a large china platter. The platter was made of the same stuff as the coffee cups. Each platter, especially when filled, could have been weighed on the nearby truck scales. Not only was the platter heavy, it was enormous. Those plates, more properly platters, reminded me more of what my grandma served the Thanksgiving turkey on, than any plate we used at home. And that platter was filled, filled with no space wasted on garnish like a parsley sprig, or a cutely-twisted slice of orange.

The Fillin' Station thrived on a lack of pretense and an abundance of cholesterol. So did its patrons. The patrons were another matter. Local farmers used The Fillin' Station as one of the sole places in the county were one could get a legitimate breakfast. They also came to meet their buddies and sip a little coffee.

It was one of two restaurants in town that attracted foreigners. Foreigners does not mean people from other countries or ethnic groups. Foreigners are simply people the locals don't know. Truckers, of course, were foreigners, yet if they ran that route often enough, even though they might live in Charlotte, Columbus, or Memphis, they became locals, at least to Lou, Vera, Irene, and Molly. Most city folk, foreigners as well, were too intimidated to venture into The Fillin' Station, but when they did, the patrons gaped at them as they meekly sat at a table; foreigners were the pariahs of the community, which probably explains why they'd rather patronize McDonald's or Wendy's.

Occasionally local professionals, people wearing shirts and ties would dine, or do lunch at The Fillin' Station. Wearing a tie at such an establishment also drew the customers' and the workers' attention, but if they knew the names of the tie-wearers, the professionals were welcomed. I never wore a tie to The Fillin' Station until I was sure Vera knew my name. "Save any souls, today, Reverend?" she'd ask. Such a greeting indicated I was welcome, tie or not.

Like it or not, if one's meal was eaten, the converted service station lived up to its name. No one who's been to The Fillin' Station left any way but filled, filled not just with food, but with a glimpse of an almost-extinct American way of life, a dining experience colored with personality, not just a generic meal.

"Have you been to Tommy Sanchez's restaurant yet?" inquired one of the coffee drinkers one morning at the Dairy Barn.

"What does Sanchez know about restaurants?" asked another farmer.

Completely ignoring that question one of the coffee klatch, Henry McElroy said, "Yeah. And it's one of them dern Mexican restaurants to boot."

His partner in crime, Shorty Shamburger said, "Where the hell is it? I ain't seen it."

McElroy attempted an answer but the CO-OP manager Dick Dawson cut him off, "Oh it's just off Fifth Street, downtown, just a building away from the NAPA. Anybody been there yet?"

"Hell, no," answered Shorty, "and I don't plan on it. I don't much like Mexican food, and the idea of Tommy Sanchez cooking my vittles doesn't make it anymore appealing."

And so it came to pass that tiny, provincial Fowler, had its own Mexican restaurant, at least for a while. It was a genuine Mexican restaurant, food even cooked by a genuine Mexican, in of all places rural Indiana.

"Is he a real Mexican?" asked Dick. "I thought he was from California, or SanDiego, someplace like that."

With a laugh McElroy said, with just a mild flavor of bigotry and a dose of anti-California bias, "What the hell difference does it make. California, Mexico, it's all the same." Midwestern farmers had little use for foreigners, especially when associated with California. California has captured too many of the county's kids; too many Benton County kids had moved away to the sunny, glamour of California. While Midwesterners were happy for their children's success, they still resented the fact that their babies, and grandbabies had to live so far away.

Tommy Sanchez had come to Fowler some years before. He and his pretty wife and three kids, moved into one of the old houses on Fifth Street. They seemed nice enough, yet nobody knew exactly what Tommy did for a living. His wife, everybody knew, she was busy raising three little boys; that's what she did.

But Tommy was another matter. He tended bar out at The Club now and then, then somebody would see him tending over at The Hundred Mile House. He'd be in over at Chuck Allen's lumber yard buying paint, "Yep. I'm doing a little fix up job for old lady Smith." Then he'd be selling cars down at the Ford-Chrysler-Plymouth dealer. No one could call Tommy lazy, he was always doing something to support his family, but no one could ever really figure out just what he was doing at any given time.

As for Tommy being a Mexican, it was true that his lineage was full-blooded California-Mexican, but he was American as Harry Truman. No one thought much of Tommy's racial-ethnic mix, at least not until he opened a restaurant in town.

When you think of a Mexican restaurant, do not be confused, this was nothing so ambitious as a Taco Bell, or as quaint and ethnic as those little hole-in-the-wall cafes throughout the Southwest. No, this was a tiny little restaurant space, that had already housed ten or fifteen other failed dining establishments. And Tommy attempted to be the first to make it in that cursed space. The space had housed several pizza places, a few sandwich shops, and a donut joint. But they all failed.

Tommy did little to change the space. He simply conformed to what was there. Space for a dozen diners or so, and he hung southwestern style cafe curtains in the windows. Voila! Throw in some refried beans and an enchilada, and you got your first Mexican restaurant in Fowler.

Small town folk appreciate anybody risking their money to launch a business in a struggling community. So the folk were inclined to give Tommy the benefit of the doubt, at least once, they would try a meal at Tommy's. That was the name, simple and unpretentious: Tommy's Mexican Restaurant.

The strength of Sanchez's entrepreneurial leap in the dark was he was filling a great vacuum in Benton County. There certainly were no other ethnic food competitors to challenge him, unless you think pizza is ethnic food. If you do, however, hamburgers are German food! So Tommy had an open playing field. The market, the niche, as they say in Madison Avenue marketing think tanks, the niche was not the problem. Tommy's Mexican Restaurant was plagued with two significant problems: Tommy and the food.

Let's address the food first. While locals gave Sanchez the benefit of the doubt, and for the first few days, maybe weeks, the food was tolerable, it became clear that Tommy's Restaurant was only going to be one of those places where you said, "Yeah. I ate there ... once."

A few days after I overheard the farmers blabbing about Sanchez opening a restaurant, I also heard them de-briefing about what clearly was their first and only trip to Tommy's. "Patterson, you wouldn't believe it," said Shorty Shamburger. As he said it he leaned toward me and waved his hands in my face with an animation and enthusiasm I hadn't seen in Shorty since he told this old joke about a Pirate who'd lost an eye, arm and a leg. "You wouldn't have believed it. Ol' McElroy and I pick up Dick over at the CO-OP and we stumble in that little Mexican hole-in-the-wall right about lunchtime yesterday. There's only one table left, and Tommy is the cook and the waiter. He was busier than a cow swatting flies at a manure pile. He brings us some water and brings us some menus. Ten minutes later, ten minutes later, can you believe it, he comes back and asks us if he can get us anything to drink. He said, 'I'm sorry you got here at a bad time; it's real busy.' Bad time. Bad time. Like lunch time is a bad time to order and eat lunch. You wouldn't believe it."

Shorty carried on for three or four minutes, more brutal than any food critic for *The New York Times*, or even Willard Winton. "We finally ordered," he continued, "We all ordered the same thing. A couple of chicken enchiladas and some beans. A full half hour later, a half hour later, wasn't it a half hour McElroy?" Henry McElroy confirmed Shorty's assertion with a nod and a smile. "A half hour later poor old Tommy brings out three Styrofoam plates with what I guess was enchiladas and some greasy beans. He forgot our knives and forks and ran back in the kitchen to get 'em and threw them on the table with a few paper napkins."

Such was the dining experience not just of McElroy, Dawson and Shamburger, but virtually all who paid the mandatory, "I'll give it a try," first-time visit. So the food and the service were a large part of the demise of Tommy's Mexican Restaurant. But Tommy was the other problem.

It wasn't that Tommy lacked ambition, as I've already said. What he lacked was staying power. Starting and running a restaurant, I guess, requires a lot of hard work for a long, long time. I stopped in for an early lunch a month or so after Tommy opened. Maybe it was 11:30, and the sign on the door said, "OPEN," but Tommy was no where to be found. A young girl told me, "He oughta be here in just a bit, but until then, I can't serve you anything. I think he's helping Windler put a new porch on his house." Tommy had tired of being a restaurateur. But Tommy's weariness almost perfectly coincided with Fowler's waning support for his new venture. About three months after Tommy's Mexican Restaurant, the only Mexican restaurant in those parts, opened, it closed.

A week or so after Tommy's closed, he popped into The Dairy Barn while a bunch of us were drinking coffee. "Tommy, what ya doing now," Shorty asked. "Oh, I'm selling and installing car stereos down in Lafayette.

Maybe I was wrong in my analysis. The biggest problem facing Tommy's Mexican Restaurant maybe wasn't the food.

If Tommy's was a temporary blight for county dining, Sweet Amy's was a temporary treasure. Sweet Amy's was an American cuisine establishment started by a young couple who knew good basic food, and the frills of presentation. If you look in those dining guides that rank restaurants from one star to five, five being the best, notice that they usually rank three criteria: food, service and atmosphere. Sweet Amy's would have ranked at least three's for food and service and four or more for atmosphere. Small town America, Fowler being no exception, a certain constituency beyond the stoplight, longed for a bit more gentility. Sweet Amy's provided just that.

A young couple came to town and refurbished an abandoned store downtown, added a Victorian veneer and interior, so that one felt like one entered a ginger-bread house anytime one frequented Amy's. This was a considerable upgrade over the standard Benton County restaurant decor.

It appeared that Martha Stewart was the interior consultant-everything from potpourri to flowers on the table, to little country knick knacks covering the walls. Country was the mood with American primitive paintings tastefully scattered throughout the field of vision. Eating at Sweet Amy's was like coming into to the most posh of country farm house kitchens.

The restaurant took its name from the wife of the husband-wife couple who built the restaurant. Amy, come to think of it, kind of a Martha Stewart clone, and her husband served as hosts, and one of them would usher the many diners to their tables. Shortly thereafter a waiter would bring Ball jars filled with ice water to your table, and the menus would be handed to you.

The food was not extraordinary, but good and ample in portion. Lunchtime was marked with regular menu items and the Midwestern requirement, the Blue Plate special. One day that special would be chicken and noodles, the next Yankee Pot Roast, and then Chicken Pot Pie.

Everything was served on upgraded china, and no paper napkins, but linen napkins, neatly folded, properly placed on the table, and the waiters would open them for you and place them on your lap. Such service was unprecedented for miles around. Even in town, there in Lafayette, no restaurant put the napkins in the diners' laps. More about the china: I suppose when Amy and her husband came up with the idea, she insisted on using special china plates, cups and saucers. The china was a heavier than normal kind, and it had country images glazed into every cup, plate or saucer. On some plates would be cute depictions of farm animals, cows, pigs, horses, and chickens. Likewise the same or similar characters were on all the china in an off white color and blue ink and pattern across the plates. With the decor, and the china, the atmosphere was complete.

And Sweet Amy's was a staggering success. It's run of fame and good fortune was so impressive and renown that people did the unthinkable. People in Lafayette, in the big city, came to Fowler to eat, and enjoy the gentility of Sweet Amy's. It was so popular that lunch time for most restaurants in Fowler was noon, but for Amy's it was 11:30, if you wanted to be seated immediately.

Friday and Saturday nights during the Summer people actually sat upon quaint Deacon's benches out front waiting for a table to free up inside. It was quite a hit. Locals were proud of Sweet Amy's success. For once a business out in the country rivaled or outdid the ones in Lafayette.

With word of mouth the newspapers sent their dining critics to check it out: first it was the county paper, *The Benton Review*, then the Lafayette paper. A real fuss was stirred up when the Indianapolis paper recommended Amy's as the place for a pleasant drive and a good dine.

All was going well for Sweet Amy's until the whole town was awakened by the wail of the siren in the wee small hours of the morning. It seems that an after-hour fire started in the kitchen. The fire chief, Bill, suggested it was an electrical short or something like that. But with the sunrise, Sweet Amy's was gone in rubble and smoke, and with it the town's esteem and pride.

Murmurs and ugly gossip began to be heard that it may have been arson, some sort of insurance fraud was even alleged by some. But the truth was that after the insurance settlement finally put check in hand, Amy and her husband did not rebuild in Fowler. But they did rebuild. Where else? In Lafayette where their success continued. For a year or so, though, Fowler had a touch of dining elegance and grace until it went up in smoke. Afterwards the town just made do with what they had.

If there had been a bordello in town, and there were none, I suppose it would have been out next to Street's Liquor Store. Street's certainly qualifies as one of the town's watering holes, though, to my knowledge there was no consuming going on there at the premises. It was north of town, about a half block off US 52. You'd turn right at about the spot where all the cars headed north to Chicago would see the 55 M.P.H. sign and be flooring it to resume the race to the city. But if you turned to the right, about the time all the Chicago-bound drivers were putting the pedal to the metal, the first establishment was the liquor store, Street's. I never asked why it was out on the outskirts of our little hamlet. Surely it had something to do with low real estate costs, as opposed to the need to be discreet. Too many trips, too frequently to Street's and one might get a reputation, one not desired. Putting it on the edge of town, perhaps, minimized the scandal of having a liquor store in town available, though most in town, I am convinced, would have deemed Street's as much of a necessity as the fire house, or a doctor.

Street's Liquor Store was a homey, cozy little business, compressed into three rooms, each the size of a walk-in closet in today's finer homes. Passing through the door, Dave or Jack would greet you, each customer, warmly. It was a father-son establishment, Jack the cigar-smoking, cigar-chomping king of the business, and Dave, the heir apparent to the family fortune, the Fowler liquor tycoon.

Jack, cigar in mouth, would greet you as you came through the door, maybe he'd even sit up from his Lazy Boy placed behind the counter, and turned to watch the fifteen inch TV which was always on some sporting event on ESPN. Sometimes he'd be watching college basketball, maybe Purdue or IU, or in the lesser hours, it would be Australian Rules Football, or full-contact Chess. On the wall behind Jack was the latest Coors calendar with the scantily-clad beer wench of the month, and a lifetime collection of neon beer signs tastefully, if not artistically, placed across the wall for dramatic effect. The more common signs said in red neon, "Drink the King of Beers," above a Budweiser logo, but the real collectors items were, "Tap a Big Mouth of Sterling." Some of the signs were as simple as, "Stroh's;" in bright light, others were beer drinking historians' prizes: "Falstaff," "Say Black Label, Mabel." I suppose some patrons of Street's came almost as if to the art museum to recall that first sip of Miller High-Life quaffed in the back seat of a fifty-five Chevy driving through the corn fields when they were only seventeen.

Jack's and Dave's primary responsibility was to ring the customer up when you had finished your selection, or to get the beer you wanted out of the cooler, which made up the backroom of the three rooms. Few people who came to Street's needed customer service. The Nordstrom's department store philosophy of hyper-customer service would have been squandered on most of Street's patrons. Most knew what they wanted before they came in the door. Street's was not the place to culture one's knowledge of beer, wine, or liquor. It was a place for the knowledgeable.

On the counter before the customer, in addition to the cash register was an assortment of accessories for the social or serious drinker: Beer Nuts, peanuts, jerky, a wonderful sausage delight called, Slim Jims, and the ever-present portion size of chips or pretzels. In addition one could buy openers, and bottle stops, plus primitive corkscrews.

To the right, though, as the customer entered, was the main liquor-wine emporium. The room, maybe eight by ten feet across, the three walls contained Street's inventory of wine and spirits. The left wall contained a limited selection of wines and mixers. The wine labels featured such classics as Gallo, Taylor, and Mogen David. If one's uppity wine palate demanded one of the trendy California labels, or some French vintage, it would be at least a twenty mile drive into Lafayette.

The center wall, the one facing you as you entered the main room and the wall to the right, was where the spirits, the serious drinkers' inventory was located. Like the wine wall, this wall featured All-American booze. If you wanted something called Glen_____-something, single malt Scot's whiskey (a wonderful Presbyterian addiction), or Russian vodka, you wouldn't go to Street's. But if Ol' Skullpopper was to your liking, or you thought Midwestern grain would ferment as well as any dern Russian grain, then Street's could fix you up in a shake.

Yet Street's Liquor Store was much more than a place to nurture someone's lesser passions; it, like most of the waters holes in Fowler, was a place to socialize, fraternize. It was not a place to go to hide, or to be anonymous. If you wanted anonymity you would have to drive to Lafayette again. If you wanted a bit of conversation, sports or political editorials from the Street boys, then this was just the spot.

I was a bit wary of going to Street's, my first time; anonymity appealed to me. I wasn't at all sure how the town, or my members at the church would react to the Presbyterian minister being seen frequenting Street's. But one Saturday afternoon, my thirst for a cold beer outweighed both any fear of censure, or the thought of driving nearly fifty miles round-trip just for a six pack. So I ventured over to Street's, still with a slight memory of Trip Harrelson's prophecy about running Pastor Walt Coleman out of town. Yet my thirst, my baser passion, prevailed.

As I stepped through the door, Jack, cigar on lip, greeted me, "Who the hell are you?" Just as I was about to introduce my self, Dave, his son, whom I already had met playing golf over at the club, fulfilled etiquette and completed our introduction. "Dad, this is Reverend Patterson, Dale, isn't it? He's the new preacher over at the Presbyterian Church."

Jack coughed a bit, cleared his throat, and with a gravelly, whiskey-and-cigar-smoke marinated voice, said, "Yeah. And if he hangs out too much over here, he'll be the former Presbyterian preacher." They both enjoyed Jack's biting wit at my expense, and then turned to business. Dave politely and with a warm smile asked, "What can we get you, Dale?" I told him, and after paying for my six-pack of Bud' I turned to head out the door.

No sooner then I touched the door, I saw a member of the church, Dick Dowell, headed in to make his own purchase. Dick touched the door the same moment I did from the other side. We both made eye contact at same moment. My heart sunk as I pushed open the door. Dick, apparently, experienced the same embarrassment as I did. But he didn't drop the six pack of beer; I did. Beer cans hit the pavement, and a few broke free and rolled out toward the street. "Ahh, sorry to startle you, Reverend," Dick shouted, as he scurried to collect my runaway Budweiser. He laughed as he put my beers back in my hand. "Here you go, Reverend. See you in church tomorrow." His embarrassment at frequenting such a place of ill-repute, evidently quickly evaporated as he realized, if I was coming out, his minister, he had little to fear, or be ashamed about for going in. He must have assumed I was there for some reason other than evangelism; the runaway beer cans only confirmed his assumption.

As some may have thought, my ill-advised relationship with Street's Liquor Store only grew in public awareness. On one of my Saturday frequents at Street's, Dave bamboozled me into a game of chance. I never figured out quite how the game went, but for a buck, the gambler signed his name in a spiral notebook, to enter the daily pool. And when the day was over, if your name was drawn, or your name matched some number, you won that day's pool, provided you claimed the prize within one week. Each week in *The Benton Review*, Street's would advertise the beer and wine specials of the week, and last week's winners of the daily pool, and as it said in the ad, "So c'mon in and pick up your winnings, and buy this week's special."

One Thursday, the day the new *Review* comes out, I was home for lunch eating a ham 'n cheese, and to my horror, there's my name listed with the other five winners, Monday through Saturday: "Saturday-Reverend Dale Patterson-$43." Suddenly the ham 'n cheese did not taste so good. This surely would be the test of Trip Harrelson's and Jack Street's prophecy. Surprisingly, I never heard a word about it, no ribbing, no harassing, and no de-frocking. But neither could I get up the nerve to claim my $43 within the deadline.

After the deadline, a week or so later, still not hearing a word of condemnation or needling, I went back into Street's to resupply, and Dave said, "Reverend, you blew it. You won, but you're too late to collect. You missed the deadline. You're a lucky cuss. Sign up here again, and gimme a buck. You're sure to win again."

Pondering the opportunity I declined, "Nah, Dave. I don't think so. Just please get me a six of Bud." He did, and we were still friends.

Stereotypically, Americans eat hamburgers. McDonald's Restaurants were some of the first to invade both Moscow and Beijing when the way was clear. The golden arches seem to be as much a trademark of the U.S. way of life as Old Glory and the Yankee greenback. Now while I concede that even the smallest of burgs in our country, if they have a restaurant, will have a place to get burgers and fries, yet right next to that restaurant, and next on the list of popular American entrees is pizza. Fowler was no exception. Being a Chicago native, I was a bit of a pizza snob, looking down the nose on any pizza less than a Chicago deep dish. But central Indiana has a franchise that makes its own unique recipe: Pizza King.

After Hoosier-hysteria, basketball games on Friday nights at Benton Central High School, the phone would ring off the wall at Kenton's Pizza King to order this delicacy. Out-of-towners visiting Fowler for the weekend staying with family would condescend to eat some Pizza King pizza, but after a few bites, most were converted fans.

The pizza was indeed unique, at least in that part of the country. The chains like P. Hut or P. Inn, or Little Caesar's made nothing to compare. Pizza King offered no option of crusts, just variety of toppings. The crust was light and thin by any standard. A thin layer of mildly spiced tomato sauce was lathered on next, then the cheese and the toppings. It was the crust and the toppings that made the Pizza King unique. The crust baked thin, and crispy. The toppings, however, sausage, mushroom, pepperoni and the like, were all ground into small chunks, then spread out like gravel on top of the mozzarella. It was usually messy to eat. The pepperoni and sausage always were falling off as you munched down on a tasty piece. Messy or not, it "ate real good," as they say in those parts.

Kenton's Pizza King, initially, was a carry-out joint, located around the corner from Sweet Amy's. After Amy's burned, business was so good that Pizza King expanded by rebuilding in the scorched space previously occupied by Sweet Amy's. The carry-out space connected with a window in the kitchen to a most informal dining area. The reclaimed Victorian Restaurant now became one boring room with tables and chairs scattered throughout. Added to the seating were a pool table, an air hockey game, and miscellaneous electronic arcade games. It lacked all of the charm of Sweet Amy's, but if you wanted a post-b-ball pizza, it worked quite well.

The popularity of pizza guaranteed the success of Kenton's, whereas other trendy restaurants, or poorly-run Mexican restaurants, were quickly doomed in Fowler. Likewise, due to poor demographics and the lack of an abundance of cosmopolitan influence, gourmet coffee and bagel cafes will never come to the snare of the Fowler. But after hamburgers, pizza is indeed king. Yet one concern did threaten Pizza King's future.

Things got a little tense one night at the Town Board monthly meeting. "Well I don't like the sort of kids that hang out there at Kenton's. They frighten the other children there, and I've heard they smoke, maybe drink and some of the other kids say they sell marijuana there. I think the town ought to do something about that to make sure Pizza King stays a nice family place, and doesn't turn in to a hangout for toughs." Such was the impassioned speech, complaint, made by Mrs. Wilma Bishop, Chucky Bishop's mother. Apparently Chucky had been muscled by a few of the street urchins who risked turning Kenton's into a hang-out for street toughs-Yes, even small town America has its potential gang problems. But, Wilma's petition provoked quick action.

Cyndi Lester, the Town Board President, suggested that Eugene, the Sheriff, have him or his boys pay a bit more attention to Pizza King, roust it every hour or so, to make sure kids move on. And Cyndi agreed to ask Mr. Kenton to post a "No Loitering" sign, which he did. Still Mrs. Bishop was not entirely satisfied. "Well … okay. But I don't like those arcade games. There's a pinball game there with a cartoon figure of a woman who is shamefully dressed, and she has huge breasts. No family, or child ought to see such a disgrace."

Al Krause, the town jeweler, Town Board member, suddenly gained interest, "Oh, yeah. I seen that game in there the other day. It's called "Amazon Women;" when you win a free game, the Amazon women light all up and bells go off; it does sort of get your attention."

"Wilma, we'll do as we agreed, but I don't think there's much we can do about some game called, 'Amazon Women.' If you don't like it, just don't go there," suggested Cyndi. So ended the threat to Kenton's prosperity, and Fowler's pizza supply chain.

Hamburgers, corn boils, snow cones, cold beer, and hot coffee, these are a large part of life beyond the stoplight, but don't forget the pizza.

"I'm sorry, honey, but it's so hot out there in the kitchen, I told the cook to turn off the deep fryer to cool off the place a bit. So we don't have any items on the menu that require deep frying," so went the greeting that Becky, the Benton County Country Club Manager and Hostess offered two couples one Saturday night as they prepared to enjoy a lovely evening of repartee and repast. "Here's your menus. I'll send a girl over to get your drink orders."

As the two couples seated in the dining room began their evening at quaint Benton County Country Club, they began to scan the menus. In addition to Fried Mushrooms, Fried Cheesesticks, and the most famous, French Fries, they passed on to the featured menus items. Fried Shrimp, Fried Chicken, Fried Catfish, Fried Fish-O-the-Day, Fried Frog Legs-a pattern readily became apparent. Turning the fryer off, greatly limited BCCC's menu. Dick turned to his wife, "Hell, they even fry the milk here. What's left?"

Nancy tried to quiet any embarrassment, "Oh, Dick hush. It's not Becky's fault it's so hot these past few days."

The other couple joined the discussion. Dorothy added, "You know they have plenty of broiled items, steaks, fish. Al loves the broiled scrod."

"Yeah, Dick, you can get a baked potato, and some steamed vegetables. You like that don't you?" Al attempted to placate. "What bums me out is that I had my heart set on some of that Fried Ice Cream for dessert. Have you ever tried that?"

Dick's pouting continued, "Well I sure can't tonight. Oh, I don't care that the fryer's not working. It just bugs me that Becky's first words were not, 'Hi,' or, 'How can I help you," but, the first things she says to us is what she isn't gonna do for us. That's why this club always struggles. The members always get the shaft."

So began a typical night for the members of Benton County Country Club. Not many towns as small as Fowler could boast its own private club: a golf course, dining room, banquet facility, and several bars. Yet out on the western edge of town, just beyond the town park against the press of corn and soybean fields nestled BCCC, a club, semi-private.

"Semi-private" was never really defined. It was defined by practice meaning that non-members beyond the county could play golf for a daily fee, but local non-members could only play with a member in good standing. As for use of the dining facility, only members could walk in to the bar, grill or dining room; locals could not. But as Dick previously may have pointed out, "I don't know why any non-member would want to eat here."

Such criticisms betrayed the truth of just how hard it is to make a profit, or simply break even, running a private bar and restaurant in any community, let alone, a tiny rural locale. Getting good staff, club manager, cooks, and waiters was a constant hassle. No sooner than the club hired a good manager, the cook would get mad and quit, or the bartender would steal the club blind. As has been said all too often, at BCCC, "It's always something." But like the town itself, the club survived. It survived because the members wanted it to do so. It survived by the strength of will of members to have their special place.

BCCC was a place where the county's finest could go for a drink of an evening, and not worry too much about getting in a brawl with a drunk, as was not too uncommon at the county's lesser drinking establishments. BCCC was the place where your kids had their wedding receptions or rehearsal dinners, or both. BCCC was where the parties were held: New Year's Eve, and the Fall Harvest Dance. So while it usually frustrated its members, it did fill a needed niche.

The Club itself, the facilities were adequate for the challenge. Walking into the main entrance, you walked up a short flight of stairs into the lobby which melded into the main dining room. To the left, an adequate dance floor which doubled as the banquet area, hosted large events like receptions, or all-member parties. On the opposite side of the dance floor, separated by a small half-height partition was the bar and lounge area. This lounge overlooked the green: the ninth and eighteenth greens. So a party could have a gin and tonic there at the bar, and overlook the concluding play on the green, like watching Chuck mumble while Smitty set up a bet-winning putt. But he choked, and went on to three putt. So during golfing hours, the lounge conversation usually was seasoned with golfing vignettes: putts made, shots in the pond, and the most famous of all, the 'withas'-a mainstay of any golf conversation. A 'witha' for the ignorant is a golfer's rationalization. As in, "I shot a ninety-one today, with-a eight on number seven, and with-four three putts." Downstairs from these facilities were the locker rooms, and the infamous Horseshoe Bar. Not like the Men's Grill of some clubs in other parts; chauvinism was not the forte of The Horseshoe Bar. Women were welcome as much as any, but it was for the strong of heart. The Horseshoe Bar was for the hardcore club devotee. The Dining Room or the Lounge upstairs is where a lot of the guys brought their families or wives for a night out at the club. But The Horseshoe was where one went to play a little Gin, drink a bit too much gin, and where the bawdy was a bit more frequent.

The club was much less a place to eat, as it was a sorority, fraternity, one of the two most legitimate watering holes in the county. If you wanted to set up some bets on golf or the latest line on a football or basketball game, that was not done upstairs, but reserved for the dim lighting of The Horseshoe Bar. If you wanted to eat, you could order anything on the menu upstairs, that'd be just fine. But The Horseshoe wasn't so much for eating as socializing, fraternizing, harassing and being harassed.

It took its name from the U-shaped bar at one side of the room. The other side of the room had eight cocktail tables and comfy chairs. In the afternoon, as on the bar, the tables each had a basket of "fish crackers," munchies that went along well with a beer, a coke, and the latest joke about Purdue-Indiana University rivalry, or some slur joke about wives not wanting their husbands to golf anymore.

It was late on a cold November afternoon when the Club Manager, Becky, shouted to all the guys sitting down at The Horseshoe Bar, "Hey, guys, don't wait 'til the last minute to get your tickets for the New Year's Eve Party. It's gonna be a great party. Good band, party favors, shrimp bowl, banquet table with all sorts of great food, free champagne; it's just fifty bucks per couple." While fifty dollars may have been more than reasonable for such festivities, her quote raised the ire of a few of the more surly patrons.

"Fifty dollars? Fifty dollars. That's a lot a money for a lousy band, shoe leather roast beef, and a bottle of Ripple," complained Henry McElroy.

But Becky was not intimidated, "Oh, shut up, Henry. Gimme your money, and Rosie and you'll have a great time."

Henry submitted, "Hold your horses, Bec'. You'll get your money … as usual. We'll be there." Such was the way of BCCC. Lot of murmuring and complaining, but usually the members supported such festivities.

About eight o'clock that New Year's Eve, the crowd began to gather. A few had already spent too much time and too much money at one of the bars, and were a bit too lubricated, and too gregarious, at least for only eight o'clock on New Year's Eve. Most of the dining room had been cleared to allow space for the steam tables, and quantities of hors d'oeurves, and the famous massive shrimp bowl. The menu for that evening included the assorted appetizers, crackers, cheese balls, dips, and the main courses were roast beef, ham, tastefully arranged with the appropriate accessories and condiments to make little sandwiches. It was a finger food menu, as Dorothy Beecham described it.

To meet the expected demand, and in addition to the two bars, the one in the lounge, and the one downstairs, The Horseshoe, an additional temporary saloon was constructed at the far end of the dance floor not far from the bandstand.

Ah, the band and bandstand: it was always one of those easy to forget combos. It could have been Harry Harwood and the Hodgepodge; these party bands all sound a like. But they are effective in what they do. Their music must be "party eclectic." They must play pop, country, dance music (meaning foxtrot stuff), dance music (meaning Rock 'n Roll), and dance music (meaning, in those days, Disco, like The Bee Gees, and KC and the Sunshine Band.) Any band that can do all this, which is a requirement, must of sorts, be also mediocre in any one of these specialties.

It was between nine and ten o'clock that the band struck up the melodies. The Hodgepodge began with "Red Roses for a Blue Lady," doing a pretty good mimic of Wayne Newton with a smooth transition into such timeless party hits as Humperdink's, not the classical composer, but this was a classic, "Please Release Me." Yet as the party became more lubricated, and Harry had a few more Salty Dogs, he picked up the tempo with "Hang on Sloopy," and "Light My Fire." By the time the band was playing "Boogie Wonderland," and "Soulful Strut," the hands on the old clock were pushing midnight.

Party segregation had also taken place. Upon arriving, early in the party, most were committed to be open, spending time with their spouses and other not so good friends, but by 11:30, the cliques were re-formed and more and more of the ol' boys were hanging out by The Horseshoe and more and more of the women were complaining about their husbands while sitting around their tables-party segregation.

But at about 11:45, Becky made the waiters and waitresses pass out the party hats, and while not all that many people wanted their free champagne, and fewer needed it, the champagne was poured freely to all.

"Ten, nine, eight, seven, …" The countdown to midnight had begun. The Hodgepodge stood ready for Auld Lang Syne, even as Harry counted, "three, two, one. Happy New Year. Happy New Year." With that the horns honked, confetti was tossed, kisses and passionate embraces exchanged, for the most part with one's spouse or the appropriate date, and all began to blubber, "Should old acquaintance be forgot …"

Between hot summer days at the club golfing and consorting with one's pals, and New Year's Eve, this was BCCC at it best.

Novelty stops litter or adorn the landscapes of America. The World's Largest Ball of String in one of those prairie states, The Paper House in the Smokey Mountains, The Most Colossal Stuffed Beaver in upper Wisconsin. But Fowler was not to be left out of this braggadocio. The Hundred Mile House was such a novelty, not nearly as grand, but nevertheless, its name prompted the question, the interest from passers by, the bored and curious.

The Hundred Mile House earned its name in the heyday of US 52 before the interstate highway by-passed the local color, and prompted the creation of new color. It takes traffic to inspire creativity, I suppose. The traveler, the tourist dollar whisks by one after another. The enterprising conjure up clever ideas, novelties, to tap into that fiscal mother lode. I remember driving a hundred miles across Southern Minnesota barraged by an army of signs, every five or ten miles, urging me to stop and see The Northern Pike Shak, and its collection of the largest and most impressive taxidermied pike, and to eat a pike sandwich. Each consecutive sign elaborated further on what a cultural and entertainment treat awaited my carload if we would just come to The Northern Pike Shak. Each sign added, "We serve Coke." "Eighty-three miles, Seventy-four miles ... Thirty-seven miles ... Just Nine miles ... Just Eight Hundred Yards Left." At about thirty or forty miles, I wished my children were illiterate. "Dad, Can we go to The Northern Pike Shak?" With each passing sign their lobbying intensified. And as we got out of the car, indeed it was a shack; the Coke was cold, but my kids revolted at a Pike Sandwich. "I want a Kids Meal at McDonald's." So with a Coke and we were off to the Golden Arches, but the signs seduced us, the traffic, to the novelty of it all. That's the way it used to be of The One Hundred Mile House. But now the traffic was mostly gone.

Yet the restaurant endured. The 100, as it was affectionately abbreviated, derived its name from its spot on the map. Though I am convinced that no survey ever confirmed this assertion, The 100 claimed to be exactly one hundred miles south of downtown Chicago, more specifically, the corner of State and Randolph in the Windy City's Loop, the legendary heart of Chicago. The 100 was also one hundred miles north of The Indiana Veterans Memorial on the circle in downtown Indianapolis, maybe not as legendary and famous as State and Randolph, but endeared by sentimental Hoosiers. The One Hundred Mile House at various times was a bus stop between the two cities when the buses used to run that route.

The history by this time of The 100 was more forgotten than remembered. You could even ask an occasional patron, "Why do they call this place The 100?" They were just as likely to be annoyed, "How would I know? Maybe you ought to ask the waitress."

The 100 had staying power. It was the restaurant of those who didn't belong to the club, and yet wanted to have a steak, a belt, and not get caught up in the periodic invasion of a short-lived phenomenon like Sweet Amy's. The 100 persevered through periodic changes of management, ownership, bartenders, cooks, and competition from other restaurants.

It had the flavor of a road house. The 100 was fun, though lacking any gentility or polish. It served beer, and booze. If you wanted a wine list, you better go to the city; the wine list was a jug of red, and a jug of white. The beer was served cold, draft or bottle. The liquor came not in crystal, but in clear high ball glasses, functional, but not aesthetically-affected.

The 100 came to life at weekday lunches, and Friday and Saturday nights. The restaurant was bisected, half being the barroom with a bar and a half dozen lounge tables. The more serious drinkers who wanted to eat, did so in there. The other half made the dining room.

A stroll into The 100 on a Friday night may well feature a special fish fry, but usually it meant a crammed, loud, energetic, and slightly bawdy atmosphere. Nothing "dirty" was going on, but just a lot of people packed into two small rooms, telling the latest joke, drinking a little bit too much beer, and each with a fervent commitment to having a good time.

The food was straight-up tavern fare: steaks, burgers, and fish, fried, of course. Like The Fillin' Station, your T-Bone, would be put on a platter with fries, and a vegetable side, no silly garnish to confuse you. And it was a T-Bone, nothing as uppity as a Porterhouse.

Being the locus of such All-American fare, it was also the haven of All-American tavern endeavor. Sometimes a fellow would have a few too many and his eyes would wander beyond respectful parameters upon the appeal of someone else's wife. When her husband realized such was going on, he too, having a bit too much beyond the normal blood alcohol level, engaged in pecking order head-banging. Sometimes it was little more than, "Hey, buddy, keep your eyes on your own wife." Like two mountain goats smashing foreheads, these opening shots sometimes quieted the whole affair. But sometimes it doesn't. The 100 was famous for "it doesn't." Escalation resulted in more intense language. Decorum necessitates your use of imagination to picture two farmers, or a couple of truck drivers using ever-increasing intensity in their selection of vocabulary to try to resolve this unfortunate disagreement. But sometimes it went beyond words.

"It was the funniest damn thing I've seen in years," Smitty giggled. It was Saturday morning at the lumber yard. I was in for some spackle and finishing nails, but the boys were hovering around the cash register as Smitty narrated the latest altercation at The 100. "Yeah, Peno was about half lit, when he realized that Kathy, you know that's his wife, is flirting with Billy. Hell, there was nothing to it. She was wearing a tight sweater, and Billy was interested, and not drooling too much …" Smitty broke into a paroxysm of giggling and cussing. Upon recomposing himself, he continued. "Well, when Peno figures out what's going on, he stomps over to Billy and says something like, 'You better get moving on. I don't appreciate you gaping at Kathy like ya been.' Then all hell broke loose. Of course, they were both drunk enough that they couldn't do much damage, but make pests of themselves, and interrupt other peoples' dinners. Which is exactly what happened. But as soon as ol' Hap …"

Hap was the bartender. Hap was no youngster, nor would you describe Hap Deno as petite. He was also the bouncer at The 100. Stepping between two drunk thirty-five year olds, Hap was in over his head.

Smitty continued, giggling all the time, "So ol' Hap hurries over from the bar and Peno sort a slurs at Hap, 'Get the hell out a here ol' man. This is between me and Billy.' But about that time, Billy finally gives up shouting and cussin' and let's fly with a left roundhouse toward Peno. Hell, it creamed poor ol' Hap right on his jaw, and Hap collapsed onto Remsburg's table and french fries, a steak sandwich, and a bottle of Stroh's goes flying everywhere. Now Remsburg's mad as hell, and he tries to smack them both, and Eugene (the Sheriff) runs in from the dining room shouting himself. 'Okay you drunks stop it. Not another word. Get out of here, and buy Remsburg another dinner. Now, get out of here." Smitty continued his story and was interviewed by the lumberyard gossips until they milked the story for all it was worth, and they had to return to dry-walling, or plumbing or whatever.

Such was a typical night at The 100. It was no longer a novelty, but still a good place for a beer, a steak, and a giggle.

The archetype watering hole in the country had to be The Dairy Barn. Considering its name, one would not have guessed it to be the fraternity or sorority lounge of town, or the gossip pit of the county. Not only did you have to venture into town, deep beyond the stoplight, but to savor The Dairy Barn to its fullest, one needed more than a fill-up or a gallon of milk. It was the closest thing to a 7 Eleven for thirty miles. The Dairy Barn: A combination Sunoco, custom-blend gas station, and a convenience store. But that is where the similarity to the city-genre-convenience store ended.

Whether a patron turned to the right or the left upon going through the double-door entrance made all the difference. To turn to the left was to enter a generic convenience store. A counter and cashier, with a donut case giving way to cigarette display, candy and gum, bread rack-you know what a 7 Eleven looks like. Two brightly-lighted coolers chilled sodas, and the other milk and dairy products, from whence, I assume, the story took its name.

But it was turning to the right, away from the standard fare of slurpee cups, that you stepped away from the world of "Oh thank heaven for 7 Eleven," to a world unique to rural America. To the right was the host of Bunn coffee pots, always hot, always ready to fill up a steaming Styrofoam cup, but beyond the coffee, just slightly more to the right was the lounge area, where the clubhouse began. Six tables scattered along the walls of the narrow room, each table with four chairs, constituted the context that made for the most enjoyable conversation and maximum frivolous unproductivity that any town ever witnessed.

The daily Dairy Barn fellowship ritual began early. As Kay, the proprietor, arrived, no matter if the snow was blowing, or the heat and humidity of mid-summer produced a sauna, three or four regulars were already waiting for her when she put the key in the front doors at six o'clock. They'd walk in with her, and while she was turning on the lights, and opening the cash register, they'd be saying, "Kay, you take care of your chores. We'll just put on a couple of pots of coffee here to help you out." So the day began.

The first few customers were a couple of retired farmers, and Jim, Jim, and Dave. Jim #1 was the owner of the Massey-Ferguson tractor dealership. He poured a cup and went around behind the counter and selected two donuts out of a box, even before Kay had time to put them in the donut display case. He ambled over to sit, sip and grumble about what the day held in store for him. Jim #2 was Jim #1's dad, the former owner of the dealership who supposedly retired from the business ten years before, but still was always there to help junior, who was deep in his forties, run the business. The two Jims without saying it knew that they loved one another, but the older never was entirely satisfied with how the younger was running the family business, and the younger was always glad when his dad and mom would pack up and go to Florida for the winter. Dave was Jim #1's brother-in-law, and the Parts Manager of the business to boot. They sat around the tables at 6:05 in the morning, fighting off sleep and repeating the ritual that was lived out five days a week, week after week. The Massey-Ferguson contingent would be asked by the two retired farmers how business was, "Sold any combines lately, Jim?" And Dave would smirk and laugh at once, "Yeah, back in June, June of '54." Business was never a very positive topic, and conversation would then turn to politics, grain prices, or Indiana basketball. "Dave," one of the farmers would light up to break through the yawns, "Did you hear this one? What are three hundred lawyers drowned on the bottom of the Atlantic Ocean?" Or maybe it would be a joke about Democrats, or some racial-ethnic slur. Yet after twenty minutes of this daily foreplay, Jim #1 would struggle up from his chair, pour another cup of coffee, put a buck or two on the counter, and say, "Well, I guess I better get at it." And off he went to work, and the other Jim and Dave were not far behind.

The clientele came in waves, almost as if in shifts, especially throughout the morning. Some of the farmers, Henry McElroy, Shorty Shamburger and a few others frequented The Dairy Barn three and four times a day, depending on the season. They'd be there before they went to do their chores on the farm, sometime between six and seven, then a little later in the mid-morning, around ten. The afternoon might catch them gossiping at a table around two and finally a late afternoon cup before they headed home around suppertime.

But it wasn't only men that frequented The Dairy Barn. A number of sororities met there daily as well. The exercise babes came for coffee and a donut mid-morning. And late morning, before the noontime Paul Harvey radio broadcast came on, Martha Winton, Millie Putnam and a few others took a cup and listened in on the men tell lies to one another.

In spite of the mixed company, and though on occasion the men's stories and conversation became a bit coarse, usually, they behaved modestly, for in Fowler most of the men still had some pride in being called gentlemen. Yet once in a while, proper decorum evaporated.

It was Friday morning, Chuck, the lumber yard manager and Smitty, McElroy, Shorty and I were gathered for our daily called 9:30 meeting when Smitty queried Chuck. "What's with you, buddy? You seem sort a down in the dumps? What's up?"

Chuck in vain tried to brush off Smitty's interrogation with the typical, "Ahh, nuthin." But Smitty was relentless. Finally, and in a very soft voice, revealing some embarrassment, Chuck said, "I'm going in for a vasectomy today at noon."

Smitty burst with instant emotion, "Oh, crap! You'd never see me letting any doctor cut on my cahonees. No way." Smitty was a salesman, not a pastor. But he wasn't finished either. "I knew this guy who had that done, and he swelled up to the size of …" Needless to say, Smitty's listening skills were infantile, and his encouragement to his very best friend waned for this critical occasion.

Nevertheless, Chuck did not seem too fazed by Smitty's long litany of vasectomies from hell. That morning, as he left, Chuck broke the conversation with, "The doctor says everything should be all right if I lay low for the weekend. So I guess I'll see you guys Monday. Wish me luck."

"You'll need it, sucker," was Smitty's benediction.

Monday morning, 9:30, saw the klatch reconvened minus Chuck. "I talked to him yesterday afternoon on the phone. He said he was doing okay. Maybe he had a relapse. You know that happens. Sometimes infections set in down there …" Smitty's reiteration of the possible horrors from vasectomies was interrupted by Chuck's late arrival. He strode in carefully, like he had a bad back, or he'd stepped on a piece of glass or something, but he persevered only to be interrupted incredulously by his best friend. Smitty shouted across the room for all to hear, "Hey Chuck, are you shootin' blanks?" Decorum vanished for a few moments.

My wife seldom visited The Dairy Barn. I guess she felt a little left out, and not entirely welcomed. It could have been the time she spoke out in judgment about the calendar on the wall. Late every fall, about the time deer season began somebody hung a calendar on the wall. It was usually an ammunition calendar, advertising shotgun shells from Remington, or Federal. But on the date that deer season starts in bright marker would be written, "Deer Season Begins." The corresponding day when the season ended was written, "Deer Season Ends." Every day a hunter bagged a deer, a hunter who frequented The Dairy Barn, he'd write his name on that date, and a number for how many points the buck had. The more points on the buck's antlers, the bigger, more substantial the deer, and therefore, the kill. So went the scoring system. During season, people would peek at the calendar for an update as to who recently had bagged some big game.

My wife, no great friend of hunters, but neither a rabid member of the Sierra Club, still was mildly offended at the macabre bad taste the day she did venture into The Dairy Barn. There on the calendar, the chronicle of Benton County deer-killing, was the advertisement for Remington ammunition with the picture of a big, handsome buck. Some macho comedian, and patron of The Dairy Barn, had taken a black marker and put a big X over the picture of the deer, and written, "November 27th, Billy Brown kills Bambi." Most patrons, even the ones not too bloodthirsty, thought it was a bit funny, in a sick way, but not my wife. As she entered, the calendar was pointed out to her by one of my table companions, McElroy. My wife was quick to judge, "Bambi! That's awful. And I don't think that's very funny." While there were a few more giggles, and snide comments, she poured a little cold water on the sick humor. She felt not all that interested in returning to such a gathering, and the patrons weren't all that disappointed that she was not a regular.

The lounging population dwindled throughout the day to a trickle after suppertime, when it finally closed around ten. But The Dairy Barn had served its purpose well. Living in the city, I have never discovered such a pleasant place in which to chat, gossip, debrief, hear the latest jokes, and get to know my neighbors. And I am a poorer person, and my community is a poorer place for the lack of such a place. Happy Hours in brass rail, fern littered bars in the city are no replacement. No, the city, urban life cannot fill this niche. The Dairy Barn ... It's too inefficient, unproductive. Coffee breaks at corporate headquarters are not safe havens for frivolity and getting to know our partners in this journey. Not like

The Dairy Barn, the hundreds of little watering holes just like this one through-out dwindling rural America.

It takes a bit of courage for the foreigner, the out-of-towner, to venture into these venues of food and friendship. For when you step through the door, all activity will stop as if to say, "Who's that?" But if you have the gumption to come on in, and to listen, and to watch, you'll want to be included. You won't want to miss the fun, the fraternizing, you'll want to be on the inside; you won't want to be on the outside again.

STEEL MAGNOLIAS

We live amidst the ongoing debate these days between patriarchy or matriarchy, and its influence in our culture. I was never quite sure whether the men or the women ran the town. Everybody agreed it was not the town council or the sheriff who had the power. No, sovereignty was to be decided as a battle between the sexes. Oh, I'm not talking about the government of the town, the less important matters like taxes, road repairs, and what curriculum would be used at the elementary school. Who runs the households? That was the question that occupied my attention. Militant feminists claim that America is a patriarchal system, and nothing short of a revolution on behalf of the enlightened women of the land is required to free women from the bondage of male domination. A case could have been made in Benton County that patriarchy ran rampant. The culture had the facade of male rule. Husbands would come into their castles in Fowler and say things like, "Hon,' I think it's time to buy a new car." Deferring, the wife would say, "Well, whatever you think is right, dear. Make sure you pick out one with a pretty color." While such conversations seem to indicate males running the show, I suspect that they were increasingly rare. By observation, cracks in the foundation of male hegemony, if it ever existed, were more numerous and getting deeper. Yes, the bank president was a man, but the President of the Chamber of Commerce was a woman. One of the town's more prosperous real estate offices took its name from the man, but it was obvious to all in town that the woman ran the business, not into the ground, but into success and profitability. Even The Dairy Barn was not an exclusive men's club; it was co-ed all the way.

Pondering the observations I'm still no clearer to resolving the debate as to whether it was a matriarchy or a patriarchy. But passing through the stoplight means not getting to know the men or the women. To resolve the question requires going into town, turning to the right or left at the stoplight, and invading the habitations of the folk.

Unashamedly, I borrowed the term "Steel Magnolias" from the movie of some years ago. I met the matriarchs of Fowler and found them to be pretty like the magnolia flower, sometimes with the appearance of fragility. Getting to know them, there was a strength about them, as of steel, that made the phrase "the weaker sex" an obvious lie.

Eleanor and Violet were born sisters, and well into their eighties they remained as close as when they played in the nursery as toddlers. The only interruption in their closeness was Eleanor's forty year marriage. Violet, in her mid-eighties, had yet to marry.

"Well, sis,' is Phil going to take you to town to buy a new car?" Violet asked her big sister. Violet and Eleanor were born into the Jenkins clan. But Eleanor married a Davidson, which made her Eleanor Davidson; Violet remained Violet Jenkins. Their young nephew, Phil Jenkins, a retired farmer in his mid-sixties, was the appointed one to assist his Aunt Eleanor purchase a new car. "To town," in this case, meant going, not to Lafayette, but the three blocks to McCreary Chevrolet-Oldsmobile-GMC.

Moments later, Phil stepped into his aunt's living room with an apprehension not only on his face, but in his voice as well. "Eleanor, are you sure you wanna do this? … sure you wanna buy a new car? The insurance company may not even renew your policy. I know you can afford to buy a new car, but you can't afford to drive without insurance, and what happens when they take your license away from you?"

"Oh, pooh! Phil, they're not gonna stop this old woman from driving to the grocery or to check on grain prices. And if that guy down at the body shop says my poor Cadillac isn't worth enough to fix again, then we'll just buy a new car that will be worth fixing if it gets hurt. Now let's go."

Miss Davidson was not to be put off. She was not about to be grounded, prevented from driving her car, even if she had exceeded her limit in driving indiscretions.

Violet affirmed her sister's argument, "Yes, Phil. I think it's awful that they're threatening not to let sis' drive anymore."

The threat to take Eleanor's wheels away came from the town sheriff, Eugene, her insurance company, and most of Eleanor's loved ones. Eleanor had the appearance of being a soft-spoken, demure woman of culture. Yet while she was always soft-spoken, Eleanor was used to getting her way.

Eleanor's husband was the owner of one of the grain brokerages in town. Every day he drove his car to work, and parked in the spot, just off the courthouse square, and right in front of his business. He'd be there by six-thirty every morning, so his car was always in that spot. It was his spot. So when he died, and though Eleanor sold the business, every day, after her husband's death, she would drive to the brokerage to check the prices of the various commodities in which she invested. As Phil said of his Aunt Eleanor's financial security, "Aunt Eleanor is doing okay." That was always interpreted to listeners as she could buy most of the county if she wanted it. Yet it always grated her when she pulled up to the business and someone had parked in her husband's spot, his parking place. She'd fuss and fume about it to anyone who would listen, complaining of such an affront. But there wasn't much she could do about it. At least until recently.

Not long after she passed eighty, her Germanic roots, perhaps, her Teutonic warrior blood, became more assertive in this apparently reserved little old lady. Eleanor Davidson had a rose-colored Cadillac Sedan deVille. The Toyota Corolla parked in his spot, her husband's spot, did not have a chance. That fateful morning as she drove to check the prices of her investments, something snapped inside Eleanor. Her sister inquired, but not to offend her elder sister, "Sis, what, um, are you doing? You're about to hit that car. That little red car. You're going to hit it." Eleanor ignored her sister's caution. Eleanor did not so much as hit the car, not as in a routine traffic collision, or fender-bender. She pulled in behind the little red Toyota, gently tapped the intruder's bumper, applied a bit more power from the Cadillac's V-8, and pushed the interloper out of her husband's place.

She got out of the car; walked into the office, and found out that her corn was at $2.40 per bushel, and her soybeans were about seven dollars. With her sister still dumbfounded in the front seat, Eleanor calmly sat again behind the wheel of her deVille, and went home for a tuna fish salad sandwich with her sister.

It was several hours later that Eugene got a call down at the Police Station to come over to the office, "There's been a hit and run accident." The rear end of the Corolla had been crunched considerably, scratched even more, and there were just a few tell-tale rose-colored scratches left behind. Such was the evidence. In talking to people who might have seen what happened, Eugene came up almost empty, except for Diane. Diane, whose beauty shop is adjacent to the brokerage, noticed that, "Miss Davidson's Cadillac had been parked for a bit earlier in the morning, out front. And you know, come to think of it, it did seem awfully close to that car in front of it. But surely, poor Miss Davidson didn't hit it, and drive off without telling anyone."

Eugene now had two problems. The crunched Toyota's owner was a foreigner, an out-of-towner, and this guy could care less about the niceties of small town law enforcement. "All I know is that my car was wrecked by a hit and run driver, and I want to make him pay."

Eugene answered the out-of-towner's rage with, "Sir, you just cool down a bit. Come with me over to the station. I'll get you some coffee, and I need to go visit somebody. When I get back, I think we'll have this problem solved."

"Solved? I don't want it solved. I want that!@#$%^ to pay." If Eleanor Davidson would have know that an out-of-towner had called her a!@#$%^, a common trespasser in her husband's parking spot libeled her for only taking what was rightfully hers, if she would have known that … just let it be said that any cordial resolution of this matter would have been impossible. The drive to the station house, and the cup of coffee, appeared to placate the out-of-towner, at least a bit.

"I'll be back just shortly. You sit tight sir, and we'll have this settled," and Eugene stepped out of the office heading to Eleanor's.

Upon pulling up in front of Eleanor's, Eugene was glad to see Miss Davidson's Sedan deVille parked in the driveway. He walked up the driveway, and his suspicions were confirmed as he examined the front end of Eleanor's car. It was thoroughly scratched on both the chrome of the bumper, and a few spots of the rose-colored paint had been replaced by Toyota Corolla Red.

"Eleanor, Eleanor, Oh no. Come look out the window. The sheriff's here looking at your car. What's he going to do?" Violet was terrified. Visions of her poor old sister in handcuffs filled her mind. "Eleanor, when he asks you tell them I was driving; I wrecked it. It's all my fault." Violet was not about to let the fact that she had never sat behind the wheel of a car prevent her from protecting her sister. But Violet's attempts at substitutionary atonement were rejected.

"I'll do nothing of the sort. That car was parked in my spot. I did what any person would do to defend his property." Eleanor defended herself and her actions with a defiant streak.

As Violet opened the door for Eugene, she greeted him. "Good afternoon, Sir. Is there some problem? What brings you here this beautiful day?"

Eugene answered as the consummate professional, "Miss Jenkins, I just need to visit a bit with your sister. Do you mind?"

Eleanor interrupted, "Come in. Have a seat here on the davenport. Could I have my sister get us a cup of tea?"

"No, I don't believe so. Thank you anyway. This will only take a minute." Eugene paused just a breath, and dove in. "Miss Davidson, this morning were you involved in a collision with a small car out front of your late husband's brokerage?"

Eleanor sat up a bit in her winged chair to give the appearance of more determination. "No I was not." Violet gasped in the background. Miss Davidson continued, "No I was not in a collision as you call it. This morning I pushed that car out of my dear late husband's spot. That car was trespassing in his spot. And I'm tired of that happening, so I just pushed it out of the way."

Eugene interrupted, "But Miss Davidson, you can't do that. You wrecked that person's ..."

"What do you mean I can't do that? Well, my husband parked in that spot for nearly forty years. It just sticks in my craw when I see another car in his spot. Of course, I can do that."

Eugene bent over his knees, and began rubbing his face with his hands, and occasionally scratching his head. The room was quiet as he mapped out a strategy for placating the Toyota owner, and hearing out the defiant, demure, gentle, but not always soft-spoken Eleanor Davidson.

He sat up suddenly after a minute or two of silent contemplation only interrupted by the ticking of Eleanor's mantle clock, "Miss Davidson, is Van Lindstrom your insurance man?"

Violet answered the question, "Yes," and she smiled, thinking now that maybe her elder sister was perhaps not headed for Alcatraz.

"Thanks for chatting with me, Miss Davidson, Miss Jenkins, Good day." And Eugene stood up and was gone, but headed for the insurance office of Van Lindstrom. After an explanation, Van laughed a bit, and told Eugene he would take care of everything. Eugene's day was slowly improving. Yet he still had one last obstacle to overcome, the out-of-towner.

But to Eugene's dismay, the out-of-towner was not appeased by Eugene's explanation of the behavior of an eccentric little old lady. "I don't care who it was or how sweet she is. I want to press charges. She left the scene of an accident. What kind of a town do you run here? I want to press charges."

"What do you mean you want to press charges? Charges for what?" Bill Tucker, the town prosecutor, just happened to be walking past Eugene's open office door.

"Your sheriff refuses to enforce the law."

Things once again were degenerating for Eugene as the town's chief law enforcement officer, and pastor to its usually law-abiding citizens. Eugene took Bill aside, explained the situation, and Bill ended it with, "You take care of Miss Davidson; I'll take care of this guy."

Bill turned to the irate foreigner, "Sir, would you step into my office. I think we can work this out to your satisfaction, but you must stop shouting. Come with me." A half an hour later, the out-of-towner quietly left The Prosecutor's Office, sedate and satisfied as predicted.

Eleanor's insurance repaired the out-of-towner's Toyota. Eugene paid a visit upon Miss Davidson urging her not to repeat this incident, and within a day or so of Eugene's interrupted routine, he settled down into a quieter rhythm. But it wasn't to last. Not for Eugene, not for Phil, Eleanor's nephew, or for Van, the insurance man.

Van did not laugh when Eugene informed him that Eleanor the Plow had struck again. And again. Yes, the day that Phil took his little ol' aunt to replace her Cadillac deVille, the rose-colored road warrior had shoved three cars, three times from her husband's spot. The threats from Van, the insurance man, Eugene, the town sheriff, and Phil the dutiful nephew had been ignored. Eleanor replaced her beat up deVille with an Oldsmobile '98. She was armed again.

It wasn't long after the gold metallic '98 adorned Eleanor's garage that life took a turn for the two ladies of steel, Violet and Eleanor. I have never investigated the statistics, but I suspect broken hips are a major cause of morbidity and mortality right up there with cancer and heart disease. Eleanor fell coming up the sidewalk at the church going to her Women's Circle Meeting. It was a walk, and a fall that devastated her life for nearly two years. She never had cancer, or a heart attack, but a simple broken bone almost killed her, but only almost.

As I stepped into the kitchen that evening, my wife greeted me, "Hi. How did the meeting go?" I had been away for the day at one of those necessary nuisance meetings.

"Oh, fine, another meeting, you know."

"You may not want to take off your coat. You may want to go to Lafayette to the hospital. Eleanor Davidson's fallen trying to go to the Circle Meeting this afternoon. It looks like she's broken her hip," my wife brought me up to speed.

Forty-five minutes later I was in Lafayette at the hospital. As I headed down the corridor, doting nephew Phil greeted me with a smile and a note of concern. "Thanks for coming. They've just given her the word. Broken hip. The doctor's in there right now telling her what's going to happen." I waited a bit longer and the doctor left. Phil and I came to Eleanor's bedside, and there at the foot of a bed was her faithful companion, and ever-present sibling, Violet. Violet's face was wrinkled with fretting. But the shock to me was Eleanor's face. To be sure, she was eighty-five, but every time I had seen her prior her makeup had been meticulously applied, and her hair was never mussed. This time was no exception, except that she appeared to have aged twenty years in the four hours since she fell.

Pastors are supposed to be honest, truthful, at least about theology, the things of God, and ethical matters. Yet pastors telling lies was a necessity cultured with experience when it came to even an eighty-five year old woman's vanity. "Eleanor, I'm sure sorry this happened while trying to come to a Bible Study. Hardly seems fair." Through a grimace of pain, a contrived smile forced its way to the surface of her face. "You still look great. Was that your hairdresser I just saw leave?"

Eleanor answered my half-hearted attempt to feed her vanity with a slight giggle, "No. That was my doctor. He says that tomorrow morning they'll replace my hip. It's going to be a long time until I'm back in church, and even longer before I get in trouble driving my Oldsmobile."

And so it was. The surgery went just fine. But the surgery was the easy part of the ordeal ahead. Athletes tear up their knees, and it takes them a year or so to recover. A year! Yet these athletes are in their twenties, prime condition. Eleanor was in prime health, but she was more than eighty. The recovery began with a month in the hospital, and physical therapy.

I visited her a couple times a week in the rehabilitation unit of the hospital. Every time I was there, early in the morning, or late in the afternoon, Violet was there as well. After a month in the hospital, Eleanor was transferred to a skilled care nursing home in Lafayette to continue her physical therapy. Fowler had a nursing home, but not with skilled care, no therapy.

So visits to Eleanor, by me, family, or her sister, required a sixty mile round trip, but every time, Violet was there. "Do you live here, Violet?" I joked.

"Oh, no. No, I just have Phil bring me, or somebody else. I know sis' needs me," Violet matter of factly answered.

Six months after the fall, Eleanor was released from therapy; she could be transferred to the nursing home in Fowler. Using a walker, Eleanor Davidson, stepped out of her own Olds '98, driven by her chauffeur nephew, Phil, and checked into the nursing home.

"I hate these nursing homes, pastor, but if this is where I need to be to get back to living, then that's what I need to do." Her marked Germanic defiance colored her determined declaration of purpose.

It was six months again, when she could get about well enough to go home. A full year had passed since Eleanor had fallen coming to church. Yet her progress slowed. Doctors tell me that the terror of a broken hip for a woman such as Eleanor normally was not that she would never walk again. The terror is that during the incapacity she would catch a cold, and become bedridden, then die of pneumonia. As the doctors said, "The death certificate says, 'Cause of death:

pneumonia.' But many just die being debilitated by a broken bone, most notably a broken hip."

During the next year, when I visited at Eleanor's, I was always greeted by Violet. "Eleanor's doing just fine. But she only goes out if she has to go to the doctor's."

Two years after the fall was a lovely day in Fowler. Jack Jenkins, Eleanor's great nephew, was to be married at two that afternoon. The bride and groom were in their appointed rooms preparing for their special day. But it wasn't just their special day.

About fifteen minutes before the nuptials were to begin, I saw the metallic gold '98 pull up at the curb. It stopped in the exact same spot, I was told, where two years before, Eleanor had fallen. The door opened on the passenger side. It was Violet. But I knew Phil wasn't driving. He'd already arrived to open up the church thirty minutes prior.

The driver's side door opened and a walker, not a cane touched the pavement. A white-haired head followed, perfectly coiffed. Eleanor had driven to her great nephew's wedding. Eleanor had come back to church.

I skipped down the steps and out to the curb to assist. But she rebuked me. "Stand back, pastor. I'm coming to church like I have for more than eighty years-on my own power," Eleanor said.

I looked at her face. "You look great." This time I wasn't lying.

Never had I hit a fairway three wood more than two hundred and forty yards. Smitty was in a hurry; he needed to relieve himself in the men's room in the club house. "Go ahead, and hit. Hell, you haven't hit a ball that far even in your dreams. C'mon. I have got to go." Smitty was right. I was in the thin rough way over on the right side of the Eighteenth Hole at lovely BCCC, Benton County Country Club. My drive was typical, a pathetic push-slice, leaving me nearly as far away from the green as I was on the Eighteenth Tee. We checked the yardage markers. "Two hundred forty-three to the middle," shouted Smitty to me. "Hit all you got Patterson, but do it now. I have got to go."

"Smitty, I'm not sure. The women are still putting," I argued back with him. That's when Smitty insulted me with the truth that I had never hit a fairway wood that far before. Yet even as I pulled my three wood out of the bag I was concerned. I sure didn't want to hit into those women.

"Those women," actually should be called, "The Women," a foursome of female golfers with more notoriety no country club has yet met. Only the most foolish and intrepid of male golfers ever ventured too close to, to … The

Women. Being advised to steer clear of them, avoid their wrath at all costs, haunted me as I prepared to address my ball, and send it in the proximity of them, The Women. Yet Smitty's harassment, albeit with the truth, prodded me to take up arms, and whack it toward the green. "Heck," I said to myself. "One decent shot here, chip, and two putts, and I still card a five, even with that crummy drive; maybe I can one putt and save a par."

Yet still there was The Women. Prior to that moment, I had met The Women only with a handshake. I had managed to avoid trespassing on the golf course concurrent with their presence. The Women were truly the matriarchs of BCCC. Annette DuBoise was the aristocrat; her husband was the owner of much of the county; in addition he made his fortune trading commodities. Francis Morrow not only was the female head of a large clan, prolific breeders that Catholics are, but her handicap put her as a chronic contender for club champion amongst the fairer sex. The third of four, Cyndi Lester, while a competent golfer, was there as much for comradeship and filling out the foursome, as anything else. BC, Benton Central High School's Women's basketball coach was the fourth, and the most dominant of the four when it came to golf championships. Jill Campbell's accomplishments with her girl's hoops team took back seat during the summer for it was golfing time. She took her golf seriously, most seriously, as I was soon to find out.

I was far enough away from the Eighteenth green, that I could not make out who it was that was putting at the time, but I was sure it was one of The Women. "Dale, Smitty's right. Just smack it. There's no way you're gonna hit it that far. Just swing easy. Keep your head down, and let it fly," so I whispered in my mind to myself as I prepared to take the club-the three wood, out of the light rough-as I prepared to take the club back. One last peek to check alignment, "Yeap, she's still putting. Well, here goes. Let 'er rip."

Not wanting to kill it, I swung very relaxed, "easy," as golfers say. Keeping my head down, I started my downswing, watched the club head skim through the light rough, and felt a solid click, the sort of click that means I made good contact, really good contact. Quickly, I looked up, after my follow-through, only to see the three wood of a lifetime heading just to the right of the green. As if fired from a cannon, the ball exploded off the club face on an inverse trajectory; it started off rather low, and powerfully, gracefully, gained altitude. While the ball started just to the right of the green, it had what golfers call a draw. A draw is good news for a hacker golfer like me. It means striking the ball very well. But a draw in this case was very bad news, bad news because The Women were on the green. The ball that had started just to the right of the green was drawing, just crabbing ever so slowly to the left toward The Women. Mind you, I was still more than two hundred and forty yards short of the green, so it was somewhat difficult to see what was to transpire in the next microseconds or so.

"Patterson, Oh!@#$%^; you creamed it," Smitty screamed. I had; I had creamed it. Even from this distance I knew I was about to be in an encounter with The Women. I saw the little white sphere hit earth maybe ten yards in front of the green. The ball's forward progress was halted greatly by my expertly-applied backspin, and its encounter with Benton County green grass. But the forward progress was not halted enough, not enough to save me.

"Where did it go, Smitty?" I cried.

"The damn thing rolled up on the green," laughed Smitty. Yet I could tell that while he was laughing, he knew he was a partner in impending doom.

The woman I saw putting, whom I could not as of yet identify, lacking binoculars, stood up and turned in our direction. Evidently the ball had landed some yards in front on the green, and its forward progress carried it onto the green. It rolled about another twenty or thirty feet, coming to a stop, harmlessly, gently right in the middle of the green. It sure looked harmless, and gentle to me.

The woman who turned toward us seemed to ignore my two hands thrown up into the air, the universal signal of sorrow, a *mea culpa;* any reasonable, civilized citizen would comprehend I acknowledged my silly little mistake. However, when I saw her aggressively stomp off the green, and jump onto her golf cart on a beeline toward me, I suspected she was not coming to congratulate me on my shot of a lifetime.

As the golf cart targeted me, and closed range, I began to understand what sailors on a freighter felt in the middle of the ocean when they first saw a torpedo slicing through the water to sink their ship. At about two hundred yards, maybe it was one hundred and fifty yards, I heard Smitty mutter, "Geesh, it's Jill Campbell." As my eyes focused on Coach Campbell, I took some comfort that she had not carried a club with her as she mounted the golf cart, but my consolation evaporated when I realized she was driving a ballistic golf cart whose guidance system was locked onto me. Flashing in my mind were the next headlines of *The Benton Review,* "Coach Creams Clergyman." Followed by the subtitle, "Judge Rules It Justifiable Homicide."

About ten yards in front of me, Coach Campbell dismounted the cart as it rolled to a stop just to my left. As she jumped off the cart, the verbal assault began, and I thought it maybe preferable for her to finish me with the cart, as opposed to her fists or a tongue-lashing. Jill was a woman of some stature.

"What do you think you are doing?" It began. She chose her weapon: verbal assault. Perhaps you've seen a disgruntled baseball manager storm out of the dugout and scream face to face with the umpire. Jill Campbell stood toe to toe with me, and face to face. "What do you think you are doing? I don't know who the hell you think you are pulling off that kind of stuff, and I don't care if you are some hoity-toity minister. But I've a mind to take that club out of your hand and shove it down your …" As she continued my emasculation, I made several pathetic attempts to apologize, to explain how I had just accomplished the impossible, but it was all in vain.

After the event, Smitty and I debriefed, and he uttered the utmost understatement, "Patterson, she wasn't in the mood to hear your explanation." That she was not.

While it seemed at the time to go on for fifteen minutes, I actually was only on her verbal rack for about a minute. I don't remember the full details of the accusations against me, but she insulted my mother, insinuated that the circumstances of my birth were less than honorable, suggested that she would never be visiting The Presbyterian Church as a potential church member, and worse than all others, she, being a member of the Membership Committee threatened to have my membership at BCCC revoked.

With this threat two things clarified in my mind. First, she concluded that because I was in Smitty's company I must be like Smitty, a good golfer, but also, just the sort of guy who would hit into even The Women when given the chance. Second, I had to stop the diatribe.

The wind of her fury blew all around me, but I had, in the name of masculinity, to defend myself and my gender. "Jill, hold the phone." It had been a minute or so when I finally managed to catch her somewhat out of breath. "Jill, you've got this all wrong, and while I'm sorry about hitting into you, you have to believe me it was all a big mistake."

She refueled. "You bet it was, buster. I was bent over putting that ball, and I was about to take fifteen of Annette's tight-fisted dollars when your stinking ball almost rolled right between my legs. Lucky for you if I had putted then there's no way I'd get her money. You'd just better pray that when I get back up on that green that I make this putt, or Reverend, you're meat. Ya hear me? Meat."

"Jill, Jill. It really was a mistake. I'm a crummy golfer, a hacker. It took the shot of a lifetime for me to do that. I couldn't do that again in a million years. I'm sorry. Smitty knew I couldn't hit a ball that well which is why he told me to hit away. I'm sorry. But while I'm sorry, I don't think that calls for threats. I can assure you it will never happen again."

With that and as rapidly as it started, it was over. Without saying a word, Jill Campbell hopped back onto her golf cart and headed back to the Eighteenth Green. As I saw her drive away, as the safety margin increased, I prayed fervently that she made her putt.

"Man, I still got to go," Smitty complained.

Having just avoided my premature death, totally devoid of compassion, my double entendre was intentional, "Put a cork in it, Smitty. We just escaped death."

Surprisingly, a few minutes later, after the green had been cleared, I wandered cautiously onto the green. I had a ten footer for birdie. I looked up toward the clubhouse—The Women were still in session. I guess Jill made her putt. Listening carefully for any hearsay, hoping not only that the worst had passed, but was completely gone, I respectfully missed my birdie putt, and tapped in for a par.

Smitty, parred the hole as well, jumped on the cart, as I recorded our scores. "Let's go, man, I have got to go." But I was going nowhere at least until The Women had moved beyond aftershock range.

"Hold it, Smitty, our lives depend on it. Wet your pants if your must, but I'm not going up to the clubhouse until they're gone."

Then I knew BCCC was a matriarchal establishment. A few unrepentant macho fools refused to acknowledge the apparent truth. But I knew the truth. I learned the truth.

"You think you're gonna join what? Tri-Kappa?" So began the peculiar conversation between Mike and Nikki Rondstat, when she informed him she was joining a women's club in town, Tri-Kappa. "Tri-Kappa. That's K-K-K. Is that the women's auxiliary of the Klan?"

"Mike, now darn it, stop that. You know what Tri-Kappa is. That's what Annie Banks, Nina McLean, Carla Wheeler, a whole bunch of women in town belong to. You know, Nancy Rayburn is President. And you know darn well it doesn't have anything to do with the Klan," Nikki rebutted.

"Well, maybe. But it seems like a peculiar coincidence that it goes by those same three letters. And if it wasn't part of the Klan, don't you think they'd know that such a choice of letters would cause such suspicions. Surely they'd change their name to avoid the problem, unless they really are a Klan front organization."

Nikki had had enough. "Mike, now that's enough. Tri-Kappa, I think even your mother may have gone to a few meetings up there in Rochester at their chapter meetings. Tri-Kappa's like the Junior League; it's a women's club, a sorority that gives scholarships to assist outstanding young women in the community. They have emergency funds to assist those in need in the community. Those are all good things, good causes, and certainly nothing whatsoever to do with that darned Ku Klux Klan. Anyway, I have been invited to join, and I told them I would. So I'm joining next Monday night."

Mike's harassment and playing dumb finally proved boring for him so he conceded, "Well, that's okay with me, I just didn't want you joining the Klan."

Next Monday night, at the Ida Lawson Community Center, the Tri-Kappa sorority convened for its monthly meeting; this meeting featuring the initiation of new members. Nikki Rondstat, and a half dozen others were about to pass through the initiation rites. The women, the town's finest, civic leaders, church leaders, and a few gadabouts, convened with the calling of the rolls. I overheard this calling of the rolls one time, and when your name was called, you didn't say something as common as "Present," or, "Here," but you said, "Kappa." So the rolls were called, not up yonder, but at the Ida Lawson Center. "Rachel Adams," was answered with Rachel saying, "Kappa." And with the entire roll called, they proceeded to sing a few of their sorority songs. One of the members accompanied at the spinet piano to a rousing rendition of "We are ever loyal Kappa Girls." Of course, sopranos and altos forged the choral symphony. A few more sorority songs, and the President of Tri-Kappa, Nancy Rayburn, stood to greet everyone, and begin the initiation rite.

Candles were lighted, promises were made by the about-to-be-initiated, and current members. Hugs and kisses exchanged; a pin was presented to each, and the new members of Tri-Kappa were in. The next item on the docket was the reminder of an upcoming big event. Nancy spoke up, "Girls, girls, pipe down now. Please quiet down for just a minute. I just want to remind you that our candy-making day is this Saturday over at the Presbyterian Church. Be there promptly at 8 o'clock, and yes, that's in the morning." Laughter interrupted her, but she persevered. "So, we need all of you there, because we need everyone of you in order to make enough mint candy and fudge." A few more matters were discussed and that evening's Tri-Kappa festivities were over. Amidst a great deal of chatter the sorority went back into the night, and on to their homes.

The siren on the firehouse let loose with its roar about one o'clock that October Saturday afternoon. I was about half napping watching a college football game; I think it was Florida State mauling Puny Tech. A siren at anytime during the day or night was not all that unique. But as I heard the fire trucks race out of the station only to pull up outside of the Presbyterian Church, that was smelling salts to me. It startled me out of my afternoon hazy dream state. I looked out of my window and, sure enough, the firemen were running into the church. Jumping up from the couch, I tossed on a jacket and jogged over to investigate.

Even as I came into the church yard, I heard a few volunteer firemen shouting back and forth, "Yeah, a few women passed out down in the kitchen. Overcome with some sort a fumes."

As I stepped through the front doors, not to be kept out of my own church even by firemen, the cause of the problem became somewhat apparent. Fumes. Fumes indeed. Now in my short life I've been around fumes and toxic gases on a few cases. One time a chlorine tank leaked at my high school swimming pool. Or there was the time I ignored the warning on the box, you know the one, it reads something like, "Provide adequate ventilation when using this product." I was refinishing a rocking chair in the basement, and nearly expired from the solvent's noxious aroma. Yet as my knees buckled and my eyes instantly starting watering, it was not a toxic vapor that attacked me. It was the most powerful smell, the sweetest fragrance my nose had ever whiffed. Peppermint. Sweet, potent, peppermint. Toxic peppermint.

About that time a herd of ever-loyal Tri-Kappa girls stormed up the basement steps and nearly stampeded me. The firemen were evacuating the church. The parade of sorority candymakers accompanied themselves with sneezing, coughing, nose-blowing, eye-wiping, and other lifesaving gestures.

"I told Nancy that Regina put too much peppermint oil in that last batch." By this time few were prepared to argue against this allegation. The evidence even wafted into the fresh autumn air. Since I have learned that it was not just peppermint fumes, but peppermint oil vaporizes and floats into the air until it lands on someone or something. So all the Tri-Kappa girls not only were breathing peppermint fumes in the air, but it had permeated their clothing. They were soaked in peppermint.

After a few minutes of standing out in the yard, an approaching siren foretold the arrival of another emergency vehicle. Sure enough, Dick Dowell and the Benton County Civil Defense force finally had a chance to use their Hazardous Chemical Spill Unit, known as the HCSU. They jumped out of their truck, quickly assessed the situation, and began deploying huge fans throughout the church, and opened every window to its widest.

But then the confrontation began, it was the Fowler Fire Department and the Benton County HCSU vs. Fowler Tri-Kappa. A few of the women decided that the peppermint candy and the fudge still in process demanded their immediate attention. Garnett Phillips reminded Nancy Rayburn with the affirmation of a number of other minty fresh candymakers, "Nancy, if we don't get right back down their those next batches of candy will be a waste, and no telling how that fudge may scorch."

But Fire Chief Bill Robertson would have nothing to do with such folly, "I'm sorry ladies, but you can't go back in there yet. Not until Dowell decides it's safe. Nope, you'll just have to sit tight."

Another not-so-gentle K-K-K confectioner said, "C'mon Bill, you're not gonna stop us. What you gonna do? Arrest us? Arrest us for wanting to make some candy?"

So it happened that even without gasmasks the candymakers of the Fowler Tri-Kappa chapter stormed the kitchen to the most strenuous objections of all the men of the Fowler Fire Department, and the Benton County Civil Defense Unit, HCSU. In spite of the potential conflict with the authorities, despite the hazards of potent peppermint gas, the women of Fowler Tri-Kappa finished their appointed chore. The candy was made, every last pound of peppermint candy, and every delicious slab of rich chocolate fudge.

Early that evening a cold front hit town. So when I opened up for church early the next Sunday morning, though it was a bit nippy in worship with all the windows open, it was the only way the Peppermint Presbyterians could survive that day's worship hour. Actually for the next month or so, every event at The Presbyterian Church was marked by just a touch of mint.

"How much is this mint candy?" asked one of dozens of customers at the big Tri-Kappa Holiday Bazaar and Craft Show held every year the Saturday after Thanksgiving. Nikki Rondstat, now a veteran Tri-Kappa girl answered, "Dick, the peppermint candy is $3.99 a pound, and the fudge is $5.99 a pound."

Dick Dowell said, "I'll have a couple of pounds of the fudge if I can have a small sample?"

Nikki smiled, "Sure, here's a big bite." She handed Civil Defense Unit Supervisor, a savory chunk of Tri-Kappa's fudge. Dick eagerly chewed and swallowed the fudge, "You know, Nikki, is that a little hint of mint in that chocolate?"

Nikki laughed, "Yeah. Everything at this bazaar this year has a hint of mint present. And think, Dick, you weren't going to let us finish that wonderful fudge."

"Pastor, I don't know what's wrong with these young women. Don't they understand commitment? Don't they know that they are part of the Women's Organization?" So went the opening comments when I agreed to come to the Women's Circle Meetings and discuss getting the younger women to join the Women's Organization at The Presbyterian Church. President, Margaret Little continued, "I just don't understand why these young women won't come to our meetings, and join in. They are members of the church. They have responsibilities. Don't they realize that? I mean we're all glad that so many new young families are coming to church; they've been gone for so long. It's great to have young folk and little children back in church. But where are they now? They need to join a circle and be part of the Women's Organization."

Margaret's comment initiated a barrage ventilating frustration from the mostly blue-haired ladies of The Women's Organization of First Presbyterian Church. "And another thing," added Grace Johnson, the oldest active member of the Circles, "they need to get to know us. We need to get to know them. We can help them with our experience being married, raising children and things like that."

"We can still contribute. They don't come because they think we're too old to fuss with. They don't want to be with a bunch of old women. That hurts some of our feelings," said Martha Winton.

Mary Walker chimed in, "Oh, I know they might think we're too old, but I need them to be here, because they make me feel better. They're young; they're doing young things, having babies, getting married, raising children, arguing with their husbands, and when we talk to them about such things it make me feel better … Younger, just being with them, around them. You know?"

"It sure doesn't make me feel younger. I see those pretty young women in their twenties and thirties-well it makes me feel like an old bat," laughed Betty Phillips, and her laughter spawned some chuckling from virtually all of the two dozen or so gathered in The Fellowship Hall, a.k.a. the basement, of The Presbyterian Church.

The Women's Organization, also know as Circle, met on the first Tuesday of the month at two o'clock in the afternoon. It had for years and years. Oh, in past times it met more often, weekly, but then as times change, and the town slowly dwindled, so did the church, and so did the Women's Organization. So with the decline, the numbers became fewer, and as a result older, and they were less inclined to meet weekly. It trailed off to twice a month, and as ailments set in as a function of getting a wee bit older, once a month seemed about all the women could pull off.

Back in the fifties, when the church was at its peak, The Women's Organization was made up of several circles that met at various times. The Rachel Circle met on Thursday mornings once a week or so at Helen Winton's house, usually. The women who lived out on the farms met on Wednesday afternoon's either at the church, or at Mary Walker's house monthly as well; it was the Lydia Circle.

But the Sarah Circle had always met on Tuesday afternoons at the church. Now it was down to once a month, and all the other circles merged into the Sarah Circle.

As I entered the meeting that Tuesday afternoon, and came down the steps into the basement, The Fellowship Hall, I greeted the gathered ladies with, "Is this the Bathsheba Circle meeting today?" They were only mildly offended, but mostly patronizingly giggled at my suggestion that they were part of a circle whose namesake was King David's adulterous consort. After greeting pleasantries, I asked them what they wanted to talk about. And the concern, or gripes began, gripes about the younger women. Hearing them out, I asked, "Why do you think that the younger women, as a rule, do not come to your circle meetings?"

For the most part their reasons amounted to slurs against the character of the subsequent generation. "These women nowadays have no sense of responsibility. All they think of is themselves," said Francis Nicks.

Mabel Holman added, "Oh, they're too busy shopping. All they think of doing is buying antiques and going to the mall. By golly, they never have gone without. They didn't have to live in the depression. Being with the women of the church seldom occurs to them. All they can think of doing is spending their money."

And so it went for some time until I added, "Did it ever occur to you, have you ever considerered ..." I was waffling, trying to be tactful in the selection of my words. "Maybe what you're doing here doesn't meet their needs or their schedule. Have you ever thought like that?"

"What do you mean meet their needs?" a minor firestorm of protest assaulted my thoughtless and foolish words. I was so attacked it was almost as if it were one voice than a dozen or so. "We don't understand what you're talking about. We meet for a snack, a time of singing, a little prayer and some Bible study. Every woman needs that. What's wrong with that, Pastor?"

I realized quickly that my strategy regarding their agenda was fruitless, so I rebroached the other thought, "What about your meeting time?"

"We meet on Tuesdays," said Margaret, "first of every month at two. What's wrong with that?"

"Think with me, Margaret. How many of these young women that we're all so excited about being back here at the church are now in the church ... How many women are we talking about?" With my question, an inventory began.

"There's Lisa, Diane, Fran, Carla, Nikki, Annie, Lisa, Jenny," and so the list was compiled until they arrived at twenty or thirty so-called "young" women.

My probe continued, "And how many of these women would be free to meet this afternoon at two o'clock on any first Tuesday of the month, or for that matter, during any weekday?"

The previous as encouraging as it was, was followed by equally great discouragement. They were uplifted at the thought of more than twenty young women in the church; disheartened when it finally dawned on them that virtually none of them could come to a meeting on any weekday afternoon. Most all of them had a job, a career that prevented them from coming during the day. Time of day, what seemed like a trivial matter, finally appeared a better explanation than the shoddy character of the next generation.

"Well you don't expect us to change our meeting time, do you, Pastor?" asked Carol Fisher.

"Yes, I do, ladies, that is, if you want to reach these women. Or maybe we need to start another group that focuses on a time more convenient for them. And periodically you could meet on Saturdays, maybe for a tea or a brunch, something like that. No, you don't have to stop meeting, but something at the church has to change to meet changing needs, circumstances. Doesn't that make sense to you?"

There was no groundswell of enthusiasm for my radical innovation, but neither was there major protest, just subdued murmuring.

"Ladies, ladies," I tried to subtlety shame them, "What would you prefer? A church with no young folk, no little children, no crying babies, or this problem with busy, young working mothers? How many years was it before a young family was in church? Aren't you glad to have the young families back in church even if it means that somethings around here may have to change a bit? Of course, you don't want to come back to those sad days."

My strategy paid off. A few reluctant nods, concurring with my thesis, and soft smiles returned to their faces. "Ladies, I suggest you continue with your circles just the way you've always liked them, and think with me ways that all the women of the church can meet together. If not at your circle meetings, then how?"

It was that afternoon that the idea to unite the women of the church was born: The Mother-Daughter Banquet. It was only a month or two later that The Presbyterian Women held their first Mother-Daughter Banquet. Actually, it wasn't the first, it was just the first in a long, long time, longer than anyone could remember.

That Saturday morning a few cars began pulling up out front of the church, even before eight, to begin set up. It was to be a brunch, egg casseroles, Danishes, fruit plate, and coffee or punch, to begin promptly at ten o'clock. Audrey Jenkins and Betty Phillips were the first to arrive. Reinforcements arrived shortly thereafter and soon the smell of coffee brewing, the ruffle of table cloths, and glass tea sets were clanking. Preparations transformed the basement of the church quickly into a place of feminine repartee.

Yet it all began in the church sanctuary. The women, fifty or so, gathered in the little sanctuary, and Barbara Christensen accompanied the variety of voices on the piano singing, "Holy, Holy, Holy, Lord God Almighty," which is a great Protestant favorite. The voices were quite a mix. Some had the beauty and melodiousness of an opera's soprano, others were more grating, tinny, as often happens to the vocal cords with the toil of years, but all the voices were touched with the beauty of sincerity. Following the opening hymn, Barbara Christensen accompanied her daughters, Michelle and Heather, as they sang a lovely duet in homage to a mother's love and faithfulness. Then Annie Banks and her daughters, Pepper and Joanie, recited a dramatic reading called, "An Ode to My Mother." By this time tears were readily flowing in the majority of worshippers. President of The Presbyterian Women, Margaret Little, followed with a brief reading from the Bible out of the book of Ruth. Then Margaret offered a sermonette interpreting Ruth's promise to love her mother-in-law no matter what. She ended with a prayer, and the women ended singing in unison another hymn, "Now Thank We All Our God." The sung "Amen," at the end of the song, signaled the time for brunching to begin.

Introductions, which were entirely unnecessary in a town of just over two thousand, followed the serving of the generic egg-cheese-sausage-bacon-onion casserole. Each place setting also had a small corsage, and a little bundle of mints. As the brunch progressed, the prissy neatness gave way to more enthusiastic camaraderie. Mabel Holman, at the time about eighty-seven, introduced her daughter, Cora, a young sixty-seven; they won the "Most Tenured Mother-Daughter Pair." Jackie Sharp won the opposite award; she was twenty-two, and her six month old daughter was still nursing while the rest of the women brunched.

As the social continued throughout the generational mix, The Presbyterian Women's effort to unite was an obvious success. So that when Margaret Little announced that they were all going to cooperate for a clothing and Christmas present drive for a needy family in the community, the murmuring was no longer of complaint, but of enthusiasm, "Oh, now that's a fine idea."

The brunch was a great success, and ended in womanly, sophomoric hilarity when Mabel Holman suggested that the melon balls be replaced at future

Mother-Daughter Banquets, "I move next time we add prunes to the fruit plate." To which Betty Phillips added, "Yes, then I'll be moving too."

"I think it's time we did some exercise. Walking. Aerobics. Maybe even jogging. Boy, I looked at myself coming out of the shower the other day. I almost broke down crying staring in the mirror. It was terrifying. Then I giggled murmuring to myself, 'I didn't know Orca the Whale was made out of cellulite,'" said Annie Banks to the small gathering of coffee drinkers in pow-wow at The Dairy Barn.

Jeanne Lindstrom reluctantly concurred, "Yeah, I've gained more than ten pounds since Van and I got married, and that's only been about ten years. Don't leave me out, I'm gonna go get another donut," and the others, Lisa, Susie, and Audrey, broke out laughing.

"While you're up, Jeanne, get me one of those almond-stuffed bear claws. If I'm gonna trim down, I want to pork out first," shouted Audrey.

So it happened that over coffee and donuts, and a bear claw or two, The Women's Exercise Group was born in Fowler. Exercising women is not the exclusive domain of lithe, lean, hardbodied blondes aerobically-dancing on some black sand beach in Hawaii. No, the exercise movement came to Fowler amidst the slush, ice, snow, and gray cold of mid-January, over a donut chomping and frustrated women, most of whom flirted with something called middle age. But not just middle age, also cellulite.

"What would we do?" asked Susie.

Annie, the instigator of this newly-born fitness craze answered, "Well, we could get one of those fitness videos, you know the ones Jane Fonda sells. We could either bring a TV, or just learn the exercises at home, and then get together...."

"Get together. What do you mean, 'get together'?" said Jeanne.

Again Annie developed the strategy, "Well, if we don't get together, we'll never do it. We'll just sleep in."

"Sleep in? We're gonna do this in the morning, like when it's dark," interrupted Lisa. "The only thing I do in the morning is kiss Dave off to work, shove the boys out to school, and drink me a cup or two of coffee, and smoke a cigarette. That takes me 'til ten."

"No it's not. We're gonna have to get up if we're going to beat cellulite. And I'm ready now." Annie sounded more like Ike before the invasion of Normandy in 1944, than she did the motivator of a small passel of women with poor body-esteem.

Always the practical, Susie asked, "Where? Where would we do something like this? We can't do it in anyone's home. We don't have the room. And there is no fitness center or Y' anywhere's around here. Where?"

Silence ensued until Shorty Shamburger interrupted, "Girls. I couldn't help overhearing. My barn's open anytime you want it. But I don't suppose any of you would want to work out in my dirty old barn. Why don't you use the gym over at the school or Sacred Heart? I bet you could use one a those gyms."

Annie smiled, "Thanks for butting in, Shorty. Good idea. Let's go ask Rex right now."

With that, the girls paid for their coffee and donuts, and adjourned to the parking lot, each pointed toward their own car. Annie shouted over the brisk wind which lowered the wind chill to below zero, "Hey, I'll go get Rex to let us use the gym over to the elementary school, and I'll give you a call. Maybe we can start tomorrow morning; let's say seven o'clock." With that Annie stepped into her car, completely ignoring the complaints of her companions. "Seven o'clock is for only one kind of work: sleep," added Lisa. But she was ignored by all.

A week or so later Shorty stepped in from the frigid blast for a morning cup with Bob Goetz to see the same huddle of women gathered around the table. "You gals don't look any better than farmers. I'm sorry to tell ya. What the hell's the matter with you?" Shorty questioned with a big grin on his fleshly face.

"Oh, shut up, Shorty," muttered Jeanne.

Lisa added, "Yeah, if you hadn't told Annie about the darn school, maybe I'd still be sleeping now instead of sweating, and creaking."

With a huge belly laugh, Shorty ribbed them, "Oh, that's it. You're getting in shape. That's why you've shed your designer garments for those damned ugly sweat outfits. If you don't mind me telling you., you all look better in Laura, what is it Laura Ash-?, Ashbery? Laura Ashton? Ash-something. Well, you all look better in them things than you do wearing them sweat clothes."

"Stop it, Shorty. You're no Vic Tanny, you ol' Tub," Annie wasn't intimidated.

"Girls, no hard feelings. Just to show you how much I love you, let me buy you all a round of donuts," with that Shorty ran out the door laughing, actually, he howled.

Misery found no comfort in company. Lisa, Annie, Susie, Audrey, had also recruited a few more, Barb, once in a while, Nikki Rondstat, and Nancy Rainier also donned sweats and joined in. But their exercise had not improved their spirits.

"I hate this," sobbed Lisa. "This is no good. I'm not gonna lose weight. I still smoke. And I'm losing sleep. Annie, what's the use?"

Annie ignored her. "I read in an exercise book that you got to promise to hang in there for at least six weeks to establish the exercise habit. So let's not quit. Let's not give up. See you tomorrow morning. I've got to go."

Reluctantly, they persevered. Days passed into weeks. Most days following their tortuous ritual, they congregated for a cup of coffee at The Dairy Barn. On one of those mornings, as he was so prone to do, Shorty Shamburger crashed their party, but this time he brought a parcel.

"Get lost, Shorty," snarled Annie. "We don't need your encouragement this morning."

"And to think I've come this morning to bring all my dear, dear girlfriends a gift," Shorty gently placed a bag on the table amidst their coffee, donut crumbs and Lisa's cigarette ashes.

"What'd ya get us, Shorty?" asked Susie.

He answered with a big-proud-of-himself-smile, "Open it and see." They did. They pulled from the bag a stack of bright red, fire engine red, T-shirts. Jeanne held up one, "Look Annie, 'Exercise Babes'." In large white letters across the chest was Shorty's title for the women's exercise group. On the back, just like a football jersey was each lady's name: Lisa, Susie, Annie, and so on in those same white letters. But below, centered across the back was written, "Shedding the Flab!" Shorty hardly knew what to do when Annie jumped up and hugged ol' Shorty, and kissed him on the cheek while she murmured, "You ol' tub, thanks." From then on they were "The Exercise Babes," famous in the town. As the weather moderated, they started exercise at the school, but then took brisk walks through the streets of town. You couldn't miss them. A bright red huddle of women strutting through town.

But they were more than an aerobic exercise group. The Exercise Babes were comrades in arms. When the doctor told one of them they had a nasty pap smear, or a cloud in their mammogram, they huddled around one another to help, lift, support, and share. When one of their kids flunked out of IU, they shared their frustration with their children, and their love of their children together. Audrey was having trouble with Ricky, her husband. She didn't visit her priest, she went to the Babes. When they'd run short of cash, they didn't head to the bank or the ATM (Fowler didn't have an ATM), they turned to their fellow financiers.

"Girls, it's been a year tomorrow since we've been exercising," Annie proudly announced.

Lisa took a hit on her cigarette. Sipped a bit on her coffee and whined, "Yeah. A whole year of exercise. I've only gained three pounds, and gone up one dress size. But you know, I feel better than I did a year ago. How do you figure?"

So it was with The Exercise Babes.

The jury no longer is out. Patriarchy was the great illusion, a helpful illusion, it helped the women dupe the hapless men of town think they ran the show. But the verdict was in, women ran the town. Passing through, you may never know it. Come into town; walk with the babes; eat a donut with them, or park out front of the brokerage in the wrong spot, you'd quickly find out. Not many, man or woman seemed bent on protest.

ENDANGERED PATRIARCHS

Okay, the verdict is in. In the muddle of opinion, the matriarchs seem to have much more sovereignty in life beyond the stoplight than seems apparent at first. But do not think the mantle of leadership has been abandoned by the much-threatened and much-maligned patriarchs. The men of Fowler, taught by their fathers, teaching their sons, are trustees of the crumbling foundation of male hegemony. The apprenticeship of male virtues was on the line, virtues such as getting lost and never asking for directions, the notion that the success or failure of the household rested solely on the man's shoulders, and the unchallenged communication rule: A wife asks her husband if something is troubling him, he's been awfully quiet lately; he responds, "Oh, nothing. Nothing's wrong." Which may be true, or they may be about to be foreclosed.

The men of Fowler are a strong lot. They still may change their oil; they may work in the garden. Never will they hire a lawn service to tend to the cutting of the lawn or trimming of the hedges. Certainly, they might pay the neighbor boy to do that, but no lawn service. You might find them cooking burgers on the grill, but as a rule, the men of Fowler will not be wearing an apron and cooking some haute cuisine in a designer kitchen. They were men, like men used to be. Men like their grandfathers were.

The town worked well, the society functioned reliably with the given role expectations. Admittedly, not everyone liked it this way, but things seemed to get along just fine. The women of the county may be more gregarious, easier to get to know, but the men need to be known in order truly to appreciate life beyond the stoplight.

The well-used Ford pick-up must have been doing 60 MPH as it raced up 5th Street. The blue light flashing on the dash board was a feeble indication that a fire call was underway. Every member of the Fowler Volunteer Fire Department got three things: a beeper, a new ring, and a blue light. The beeper was to be worn on all occasions away from their home to be summoned to the next fire call. The new ring was not worn on the finger, but their home telephone had an additional ring. As opposed to the normal bbbbrrrrriiiinnnnggg, repeated in a deliberate three ring rhythm, the ring would change, if a fire call, to a rapidly repeating, continuous ring. This indicated that a fire call was in progress. The blue light was that portable device similar to a regular red police light, except this one had a magnetic base, and when the light was plugged into the car or truck's cigarette lighter, it would be placed on the roof of the vehicle or the dashboard, and the cool blue light would flash.

What was to happen next, as if a well-oiled machine, the volunteers would proceed in an expeditious manner to the firehouse in downtown Fowler, and following a drilled procedure, the firefighters would fulfill their assigned duties until the firetrucks were on the way to the fire call. That's what was supposed to happen. And it usually did.

The first volunteer firefighter was to jump from his car, run into the firehouse garage, and right next to the garage door, flip the switch on the siren which prompted the wailing bringing the fire call to the town's attention. When the last of the assigned crew arrived, he was to turn the switch off on the siren as the trucks rolled out of the station. But sometimes, not often, but sometimes, this task was forgotten. On several occasions, the siren would be blaring for fifteen minutes or longer after all the trucks and volunteers had left. At three o'clock in the morning, a sleepy-eyed neighbor would have to walk over to the firehouse and turn off the siren. I had to do it myself on several occasions, as I only lived a block away from the siren switch.

To witness Kenny Johnson race up 5th Street, blue light flashing for a fire call, was not unprecedented. On several occasions I had broached my concern to Fire Chief, Bill Robertson, "You know, Bill, I've been out on the front porch on several occasions. It's pretty scary to see Kenny race up 5th Street to a fire call. There's a lot of little kids along that street. It doesn't make much sense to kill someone by driving like a maniac to a fire call, in order to, perhaps, save someone in a burning house. I know he wants to get there quickly, but certainly it shouldn't be done recklessly."

The Fire Chief concurred, "Dale, you're right, I'll have a word with him 'bout being more careful."

As the beat-up Ford pickup roared up 5th, that conversation with Bill, and his conversation with Kenny both came to mind. Perhaps, they had been in vain. Per chance I was lounging in a chair on the porch of our house. Thirty to thirty-five was the more common speed back and forth on the main drag through town. The roar of Kenny's motor awakened me from my daydreams. The blue light was flashing. In an instant I knew it was Kenny trying to be the first one to the firehouse. I guess he wanted to flip the switch on the siren. But about the moment

Firefighter Johnson roared like a bullet before my porch, was the same moment that Eleanor Davidson pulled her new Cadillac deVille out of the library parking space, about fifty yards in front of Kenny, one hundred yards from the firehouse.

Ms. Davidson never saw what happened. She simply continued on across 5th Street oblivious to the near-disaster, and what would be infamous hilarity. The screech of Kenny's Johnson's tires on the old pickup brought focus on the few bystanders who were in the vicinity on a drowsy Saturday afternoon. Kenny locked up the brakes just past my house, but the screech was just the beginning. The truck went into a slide, turning a quarter turn to the left, as if pointing right at my house. But by now he'd passed my house and was in front of the American Legion. Yet as he slid sideways up 5th, the rotation of the beat-up, pickup continued so the truck skidded backwards on up the street and crossed the oncoming lane, until finally it crashed into the opposite curb coming to a stop, neatly parked, perfectly parallel to the curb, but now facing the opposite direction in which he had begun. Kenny parked across the street from the firehouse. Fire Chief Bill had witnessed it all. His truck pulled up at the fire house as the volunteers gathered almost simultaneously, not to laugh, scold or mock Kenny Johnson, but to race out to the grass fire west of town. As the siren blared, Kenny finally composed himself sufficiently, to jog across the street, pull on his boots and firecoat and ride out to be one of the angels of mercy, a.k.a. smokeeaters. The mocking, scolding and laughing would come, but it would be delayed.

"Bill, I've learned my lesson. Really, I'm really careful now, you can ask everyone in town. I don't even care to be the first one anymore; I don't need to turn on that darn siren." So began Kenny Johnson's plea more than a year after that dangerously funny Saturday afternoon spin. "But seeing as I've learned my lesson, and I'm doing a good job, could I be one of the pumper drivers?"

"Kenny," the Fire Chief hesitated, "well, I don't know. Let me think about it a bit." Kenny reluctantly submitted to Bill Robertson's caution, and delay tactic. Evidently, the Fire Chief was going to approach a step by step strategy to orient Kenny Johnson in the fine art of firetruck driving. A week or so later, Bill, smile on his face, offered Kenny Johnson a stroke of encouragement, "Hey, Kenny, why don't you pull Pumper #2 out in the back lot, so we can wash it?" In a flash, Kenny was in the driver's seat and the motor was running.

It was a workday for the volunteers. Sweeping the firehouse, washing the trucks, general tidying up were the chores of the quiet Saturday afternoon. Kenny put Pumper #2 in gear and cautiously pulled out onto 5th Street headed around the block to pull into the lot behind the fire house. By the time Kenny, on his maiden voyage, pulled onto the back lot, his caution had given way to the confidence of a veteran firetruck driver. The goal was to have the firetruck centered on the lot, so the two hoses could easily reach the extremities of the truck. His first attempt at centering was off just a bit. So he backed up, but with his waning caution, and increasing audacity, he backed up a bit too fast. He realized that he couldn't see well enough out the right-side rearview mirror. It was while he switched his field of vision that it happened.

The time it took to turn his head from the right rearview mirror to the left, all the time the truck was backing up at a pretty good clip, this was the time to spell Kenny's doom. By the time his eyes focused on the left mirror, simultaneously, he knew he was going to have a wreck. There in his mirror he saw the tower.

The tower was a thirty foot derrick-type tower that supported at its top, the Fowler town siren. The notorious siren that chimed noon, curfew, tornado watches, pending nuclear attack, and of course, fire calls, was about to be attacked again. Yes, it had known its share of collisions, but a small car, even a Cadillac, though it could dent the tower, rattle it a bit, it could not threaten the tower much. But a many-ton firetruck, that was another matter.

The reverse running red firetruck was wide enough, and fast enough that the force of the blow destroyed two of the four legs of the tower. The siren and the tower, as in Newton's Law, "every action must have an equal and opposite reaction," responded to the laws of physics. The tower collapsed falling as if a giant redwood in a California forest. Fireman Smitty, just filling a bucket with soapy water saw it all, and he shouted out most appropriately, "Timber." The collapsing siren tower fell almost harmlessly. It completely missed the firetruck. The tower could have fallen on the library. But it missed that too. Didn't hit a soul, in fact. But it creamed the Fire Chief's brand new Chrysler New Yorker. It was a fatal blow, dead-center.

When the Fire Chief appraised the situation, he didn't say a word. But to this date, Kenny Johnson has yet to drive a firetruck again.

Profit margins on the farm are narrow. The difference between a comfortable year, a handsome profit, and taking a bath in red ink sometimes comes down to a rainfall on just the right day, or choosing the proper time to apply an herbicide. The application of an herbicide may cost the farmer hundreds of dollars, but to fail to do so, may shrink the yield so that the farmer loses dollars either way. So every opportunity to cut expenses is seriously pursued. When the roof leaks, the farmer doesn't call a roofer or a carpenter to repair it. He does it himself. Or when a retainer bracket breaks on a plow assembly, the farmer doesn't take it to a welder, he welds it himself. Anything to trim costs. But as the song goes, "The times they are a changin'." Technology has come to the farm. And while the demand to cut costs is as critical as ever, technology, the complication of the farmer's hardware, makes it ever harder to service and repair one's own equipment. Such a dilemma prompted Terry Myers to get in a bit over his head, when it came to technology.

I giggled as I read the Saturday morning Lafayette *Journal and Courier* newspaper. The caption beneath the photo read, "Fowler Debacle: Benton County Farmer, Terry Myers stands before his barn, after the accident that destroyed" So as we expected, Terry's embarrassing harassment had begun.

"I suppose you oughta come on up here if you don't have too much to do. I might need your support on this, and you really need to see it," greeted Terry Myers on the phone to me.

"Terry, is everything all right?"

"Oh, sure, nobody's hurt or nothin', but, just c'mon up here if you can," and Terry hung up on me.

Now the Myers place was only five or six miles north of the stoplight, and a bit east. Some years before, as I prepared to make my first trip out to Dena and Terry's farm, I learned that people in the country don't give directions the same way that city folk do. "Okay, buddy, you just go ten or fifteen blocks North, that a way, 'til youz come to Pulaski Avenue, then youz hang a right on 63rd street. And there it is. Ya can't miss it." That's how city folk give directions. Street names, street numbers, and addresses are the hallmark of urban directions. Not so rural directions.

"Myers's place. Hmmm. Myers's place. Oh yea. You go up Highway Fifty-Five maybe four, five miles, you know, on up and beyond the Walker' farm. Then when you get to Eblings' place go right on the Wadena blacktop, you can't miss that. It's the first blacktop up that way. Then you go a couple a miles or so, on the blacktop 'til you come to old man Henry's farm. Go a little north on that gravel road, and you'll come to a brand new farmhouse. That's Myers's place." So went the directions I was given by a couple of guys hanging out one afternoon there at The Dairy Barn.

"Okay, thanks, I think I got it, but just one question. How will I know which one is old man Henry's farm?"

The other oldtimer interrupted, "Hell, that house ain't been in the Henry family since back in the fifties. Remember? Who owns that place now? Who was that?" So began a several minute title and deed search that would rival any title company, but as they argued with who owned the old Henry farm, I was growing just a bit perturbed, so I interrupted them.

"Fellas, I'm not sure it matters who owns it now. But if you could just describe it for me, maybe I'd recognize it, and then I could get on out there." And so they did, and sure enough I made it to Dena's and Terry's. But I learned a valuable lesson. City folk want a street address, "435 Elmwood Road." Such directions are worthless in the country. What you need is a quick lesson in history, and a good sense of dead reckoning.

But by that Friday, it was old hat to get out to Myers's. Just shoot up Fifty-Five, right on the Wadena blacktop, 'til you get to old man Henry's place, and sharp left, over the hill, and there was the Myers place. As I pulled into the graveled area out front of his barn, there were already two pickups paying Terry a social call.

Terry, covered with a big sheepish grim, ambled over to my car, and as I stepped out, he said, "There it is, over there at the pole barn."

Pole barns are another relatively recent innovation to modern farming. For those of you who recall those architectural masterpieces, a lovely white clapboard old barn, those rapidly are becoming a relic of the past. They are cost-prohibitive to build and to maintain. Few are being built these days. Pole barns are the way. Admittedly, they lack all of the charm of the individually-designed country barn, but what they lack in aesthetics and landscape enhancement, they make up for in the cost of construction, maintenance, utility, and ease of construction. A pole barn gets its name for the series of 4x4 or 6x6 timbers that are anchored in concrete around the barn's perimeter. In between the poles are fastened corrugated aluminum or vinyl sheeting, whatever color you like. Then install pre-fabricated roofing joists, nail on the corrugated, galvanized roofing sheets, and voila, you got a brand new barn: cheap, quick, and nothing to maintain. Terry's pole barn was where he stored all of his machinery: plows, tractors, lawnmower, trucks, and planters. The planter was the center of this story.

Brian Christensen and Sam Jenkins butted in on Terry's narrative as to what really happened. "Reverend," Sam gloated, "I'd like you to meet Mr. Techno-Wizard Farmer, Terry Myers here. He really screwed up this time." As Terry continued to eat crow, he then told me how it all happened.

The previous spring Terry splurged. He bought a technological wonder, a brand new John Deere Corn Planter. It was a marvel of modern technology: a twelve row digital, computer-assisted planter. It was mammoth, so gigantic that six of the planters were connected to a central assembly that trailed behind the tractor. But to each side, three additional planters were attached to hydraulic folding arms, like wings on a fighter jet. These arms after use, folded out of the way so that the planter could be more readily stored, or pulled down narrow country roads. The planter executed its described task just as advertised. In just a few days that first season, Terry planted nearly a thousand acres of corn, all by himself. So when he was finished, he trailed the planter back to his pole barn, and with the wings retracted, he backed it neatly into its assigned space, not to be disturbed until the next spring.

Prior to using his planter again in the subsequent planting season, this spring, Terry consulted his Owner's Manual for routine maintenance, wherein he read that he should first, clean and inspect the planter thoroughly for signs of problem, or improper wear. Second, he should thoroughly lubricate all the serviceable lubrication joints. And third, he read an ominous warning:

WARNING!

Prior to using your John Deere Series 6350 Multi-Gang, Pneumatic Digital Planter, a factory technician should recalibrate the microprocessor-CPU interlink with the appropriate towing/tractor device. Failure to comply with this may result in inaccurate application of seed. It is highly recommended that this procedure be performed ONLY by a factory-trained technician. Other attempts to recalibrate may severely damage the microprocessor and void existing warranty provisions.

With perusal of the instructions, Terry set out to service his planter. The inspection revealed no problems, after all prior to putting his planter away the past spring, Terry power-sprayed the dust and crud off the planter, so it looked shiny like a Mercedes. Next, he picked up his grease gun, and explored the various grease fittings, giving each a shot of lubricant. As Terry contemplated the third step, he threw caution to the wind. "Heck, I can't afford to take this thing into the shop. Let me just see if I can do this." He pulled his electric tester out of his tool chest and sauntered over to the planter. No sooner had he touched the probes to the interface connector, a strange and horrible thing began. One of the hydraulic planter wings began to open.

Now the corn planter, even in its folded and stored state stood probably six, maybe seven feet tall. And the roof on Terry's pole barn maybe was ten to twelve feet high. As that hydraulic wing began to unfold, it quickly traveled through an arc that brought it crashing into the barn's roof. Frantically, Terry fumbled with the tester, the wires, and the interface connector, but to no avail. After all, he didn't know what caused it to begin opening in the first place, and he certainly didn't have the foggiest idea of how to stop it and save his roof.

Christensen's and Jenkins' harassment only intensified as I walked from my car to inspect the damage. Terry said, "Well, there it is." There it was indeed. Sticking up out of the roof of Terry's handsome pole barn, through about a ten by ten jagged hole ripped in the roof, stood about five or six feet of Terry's John Deere Series 6350 Multi-Gang, Pneumatic Digital Planter, bright green and yellow, dazzling in the Hoosier afternoon sun, sparking like a Mercedes. "I told you, Dale, I'm really gonna get razzed for this. Can't believe I did such a stupid thing. The dern Owner's Manual warned me. I figured I could do it myself."

To which Jenkins added, "Ya figured wrong, bub."

So the next morning as I read the story in the *Journal and Courier*, the big city paper, I had little idea that the picture would be picked up by the wire services and Terry's story would spread across the Midwest. I slurped my coffee, giggled, and mumbled to myself, "Terry, you're right. You're gonna really get it from the boys for this." And he did.

To get to know those who live beyond the stoplight is to see the independent, self-determined virtues and vices of our American breed. Panache marks these people, not in the sense of the opulence and splendor of a party held in Monte Carlo, people in Fowler could care less about such goings on. No, the panache, the flair lies in how they got things done.

"What you doin' today? Got a bunch a chores?" so inquired Shorty Shamburger of his best buddy, Henry McElroy. McElroy and Shamburger were to Fowler and Benton County society as Laurel and Hardy or Burns and Allen were to comedy. It was hard to think of the one without the other. Sure, both were married, good wives, fairly large families to boot, being Catholics, you know. There is no disrespect intended, but McElroy and Shamburger were just thought of as a pair. To greet them in public without the other in their company, they would always hear, "Where's Shorty?" or, "Where's McElroy?" respectively. It had to occur to others why they each had their own vehicle. Why drive two cars when you're always together? Shorty Shamburger lived south of town and had a beat-up robin's egg blue Chevy half ton pick-up. McElroy on the other hand drove an unexpected car, at least for a farmer, an equally-beat-up metallic gold Volkswagen Rabbit. But like Shamburger and McElroy were always together, so were the cars. It was almost as if the cars were melded at the axles.

In truth they spent plenty of time apart, caring for their separate farms, families and wives. But out in public, whether it be at The Dairy Barn, the club, or over to the bank, Shorty and McElroy were together. And so it was that they sipped hot coffee one spring morning at one of their frequent rendezvous, The Dairy Barn. They were fixtures to this watering hole, expected to be there almost as certain as the proprietor, Kay, or the tables and chairs.

McElroy answered his buddy's query, "Well, I'd like to start planting, but it's still too dern wet. Don't expect I'll be plantin' for a week or so, and that's if it don't rain no more."

"You mean you've got nuthin' to do?" asked Shorty.

"I guess not."

So with a big smile on his face, Shorty proposed a solution to their inactivity. "You know how a couple of us have kept talkin' 'bout puttin' in a new sand trap alongside Number Two?"

"Yeah. Go on," McElroy encouraged Shorty's thinking-out-loud.

"Well, I was figuring, 'What if a bunch of us guys get our trucks and a tractor and put a new sandtrap in over there today?' Hell, I bet we could do it in a day, two tops."

About that time Chuck and Smitty came in for their morning cup. As Smitty poured his cup into the Styrofoam from the Bunn Coffee machine with a depth of sensitivity seldom heard, he gazed over at the scheming Shamburger and McElroy and said, "What are you two bumps on a log up to?"

"Git over here. I've got a great idea," shouted Shorty, totally ignoring the insult, knowing he'd have plenty of time to defend his character and reputation in the future.

"Smitty, Chuck. McElroy and I been figuring on putting that new sandtrap in on Number Two. If a few of us get at it, I bet you we can have that thing done in a couple hours."

Chuck, the most concerned and law-abiding of the four, brought up the propriety of such an initiative. "Who are we to do such a thing? The Golf and Grounds Committee hasn't approved it."

To which McElroy with annoyance retorted, "Hell, if we wait for them, we'll never get that trap. Everybody's been talkin' 'bout it. I haven't heard anybody say we ought not to do it. So, by God, let's do it now."

So in just a manner of minutes, the impulsive foursome set about to go into the golf course landscape and design business.

"I'll put one of my tractors and a bobcat on my lowboy trailer. We can use those for digging and movin' dirt," said McElroy. "Chuck, can you bring us a load of that fine torpedo sand from over there at the lumber yard?"

Chuck answered positively, but somewhat reluctantly. "Smitty, you go over to the CO-OP and get Dienhart. We'll need his help, and tell him to bring a couple of other guys. If we get at it, we'll have this thing done in a flash," Shorty's enthusiasm grew as the conspiracy to modify Benton County Country Club proceeded.

In a flurry, they were out the door, and within about an hour a group of workers stood beside Hole #2, at BCCC.

It is true that one of the chronic conversations at The Horseshoe Bar at the club, was putting in a new sandtrap to the right side of Hole #2. Oh, it had been talked about for years. Yet it never was too seriously discussed, and it was no more expected to take place than if hell were really to freeze over. In fact, the resistance was two-fold. There was never enough money in the club's facilities and grounds budget to install the new feature, and some of the members, in truth, did not want to make the course more of a challenge. They liked the hole the way it was, member-friendly. So while scuttlebutt often discussed the proposed addition as a unanimously-supported idea, the fact that it actually never had seriously been considered belied the fact, a given number really did not want the added challenge.

Hole Number Two was a straight Par Four, long, four hundred and fifty yards. The green was shaped a bit like a kidney. To the lower left of the kidney, the green, there already was a small sandtrap that was no great problem. But to the right side of the green, or the inner curve of the kidney, was just open rough. The idea was to place a long sandtrap all along that inside curve of the kidney which would penalize a shot that went too far right in approaching the green. It would have the effect of making the hole considerably more of a challenge.

No sooner had Henry McElroy driven his tractor off the trailer, and he started cutting along the right side of the green with his lowered bucket. Such aggressiveness alarmed Chuck, and he shouted out above the humm of the tractor's motor, "Hey, hold the phone. What are you doin'? What are we gonna do here? Don't ya think we oughta do a little planning first?"

McElroy was annoyed by the delay and the doubt, "C'mon Allen. We been planning this thing in our heads for twenty years. You know. We're gonna cut a long shallow pit along the right side contour. Fill it with sand and voila, a new sandtrap." With little more debate, his digging and plowing continued, and in just over fifteen minutes or so, an ugly black scar marred the rich green to the side of Hole Number Two at Benton County Country Club.

They dug three narrow and fairly shallow trenches leading away from the trap in which they placed draining tile to help the traps drain after a downpour. After the sculpting was completed, and the landscape architect-farmers agreed in principle that they had what they wanted, Chuck Allen backed a small dump truck up beside the pit and dumped a load of golden sand into the hole. Moments later McElroy drove his bobcat, a mini-bulldozer, and began to spread evenly the sand. Better than their word, while they didn't start until about eleven that morning, they worked right through lunch, and by three that afternoon, the much-discussed sandtrap at Hole Number Two was a reality.

The unapproved modification of Hole Number Two took place on Monday, convenient. Convenient, because the club is closed on Mondays, so only a few knew what had transpired. Evidently the fear of repercussions from this vigilante modification hushed the normal gossip channels. By Tuesday afternoon, the weekly occasion for the Men's Twilight golf event, came around, few yet knew of the change. The foursomes began teeing off right at four for the nine hole competition. But trouble didn't happen, in fact, most hardly seemed even to notice, until Whiff, a.k.a. Dick Rayburn, BCCC Club President, and his foursome approached Hole Number Two. Actually, Whiff really was one of the first to enjoy the challenge of the newly-modified hole. Whiff let a Seven Wood leak just a bit to the right from about one hundred eighty-five yards out. His ball plopped neatly and snugly in the golden torpedo sand, neatly-raked along Hole Number Two. To which Dick Rayburn hollered across the fairway to his partner, "Where the hell did that trap come from? When did we approve that? Who in the world put that in? When did they ..." The flurry of invectives, and rhetorical questions from Whiff's mouth didn't abate for the rest of his round.

As Dick stormed into The Horseshoe Bar, McElroy and Shorty were parked in their favorite stools, having nursed a couple of Bud's to exhaustion already. Rayburn charged the bar as a man on a crusade. "McElroy, Shamburger," began Whiff's interrogation. "I hear you two are behind all this sandtrap crap. What's the idea? Who do you think you are to just go out there and plow up our beautiful course? You had no right. Boy, a lot a people are really gonna be ticked 'bout this."

Shamburger interrupted Rayburn's assault, "Who's ticked? I only see one ticked person. And the only reason you're mad is that you're gonna be bogeying Number Two a lot more than you used to due to your slice."

But Rayburn was not finished, or appeased by such conflict management techniques. Yet after the bulging veins subsided a bit, McElroy ended it all with, "C'mon, Whiff. Everybody's been talkin' about putting that trap in for years. We just finally did what we always intended. In fact, we did a darn good job too."

Still, even after McElroy and Shamburger bought the Club President a double scotch, Dick Rayburn added, "We can't have it. We just can't have it. We just can't have everybody going on doin' their own thing."

Shamburger with a disbelieving look answered, "Why not?"

"R-O-T-A-R-Y, that spells Rotary ..." the chorus chanted, and so began the weekly meeting of the Fowler Rotary Club. President Ted Ryan with the accompaniment of the town dentist on a spinet, led the Rotarians in a ritual that was necessary, at least to Rotarians. No singing, no supper. As the local Rotarians gathered in the basement of the local commodities brokerage, said basement also doubled as the town community center, each picked their official nametag which registered their attendance, a songbook, and picked up in whatever ditty the President, and Songleader chose at the moment. Upon the conclusion of the club's rendition of "R-O-T-A-R-Y," Rotarian Junior Mason shouted out, "Hey, school marm, let's sing "Oh, Susanna." And so they did. Apart from a few of the official Rotary songs, none of the songs had much to do with the events of the evening, year, or life in general. The songs sounded more appropriate to sing at Summer Camp, than a gathering of mostly middle-aged community mohoffs: "I love to go a wandering along the mountain paths ... Valeri, Valerii, Valeraha-ha-ha-ha-ha-ha, my knapsack on my back." Evidently the purpose was as a tenderizer for the meal to come, and to grease the wheels for the evening's agenda.

As there were organizations in town for women other than Tri Kappa, so it was true for men as well, but The Rotary was a mainstay of local male civic involvement in Fowler. The membership list was as diverse as a tiny community could boast. Yes, there was a minister in membership, insurance agents, real estate brokers, lumberyard bosses, farmers, bankers, lawyers, gas station owners, gigolo golfers, farm implement dealers, school administrators, teachers, and so it went. It is true, there were not many factory workers in membership, or grease monkeys from down at the Amoco, but they must have had their clubs as well. I suppose their club was the stool at one of the local taps.

The songs finally ceased with an impassioned refrain of "My Country 'Tis of Thee." Ted nodded to the Rotary Chaplain. Shortly, thereafter, following a few antiphonal clearings of the throat, the chaplain began, "Gray-shus Gawd, we thank thee for the food of which we are about to partake. And we thank you for the loving hands that prepared it. Add it to the nourishment of our bodies, and may we ever be thankful. A-a-a-men."

Amidst a few echoed, softly-voiced, "Amens," Junior Mason shouted, "Let's eat the mystery meat boys." Buddy Dent was the caterer under contract to provide the Wednesday evening grub for the Rotary crowd. While Buddy was the county's caterer, it must be also noted he was the county's only caterer. Many who partook of Buddy's fare hoped he would take up some other vocation like brick-laying or custodial work. Oh, it wasn't that the food was so bad. It wasn't bad. Nobody, in fact, had ever heard of anyone dying or even getting ptomaine from one of Buddy's meals. Nope, it was just so nothing, mediocre, forgettable. Tonight was Buddy Dent's *piece de resistance*: nobody knew what it was called, it was just contemptuously labeled, "mystery meat." Those of us who have experienced institutional dining in the service, or a college dorm, probably have encountered this generic meat. It was some sort of meat pieces that when cooked was a white meat, yet always those pieces, little chunks were skewered on one of those push-up sticks. You know, the sticks in the summer kiddy ice cream treat? The stick holds the chunks together, plus the meat is dunked in a little batter, flower and egg, or something like that and then fried. Add a dose of mashed potatoes and gravy, some Indiana succotash, and a dollop of congealed salad, and that was the evening's entrée.

As Smitty stood in line for his serving, he harassed Buddy. Buddy stood behind a serving table with a few of his helpers, each of whom plopped the various menu items on the Rotarian's plates with all the panache of a cook in boot camp. "Buddy, what the hell is that mystery meat?"

Obscure, as unhelpful as ever, and most unaffected by Smitty's needling, without ever looking up, Buddy muttered, "It's a mystery." And he continued slinging the hash.

Served, the forty or so Rotarians spread out amidst the tables of eight each, and in spite of the whining, ate with a passion. Conversation amounted to an assortment of notes about the price of corn, the latest sports gossip, how the Republicans or Democrats were leading us all to hell, or some other superficial conversation. After what seemed only a few minutes, Ted finished his eating and turned to announcements.

"Okay, next week, Harold (the town dentist), you're in charge of program. What have you got for us?"

"He's gonna fit us all with dentures and give Smitty a root canal while we all watch," interrupted Junior Mason.

Harold was only somewhat offended by this ribbing, and mocking of his professionalism. "No, no freebies. I've invited the A Cappella Choir from the high school to come a sing a spell for us. They'll be good."

"Yeah, and it will sure beat our singin'," an anonymous voice shouted.

Ted tried to restore order, "Okay, guys, next week we'll have a bunch of our own kids here, so try to behave yourselves." He continued, "And Rob, then the next week, that's two weeks from now, you'll be in charge. What'll be your program?"

"A professor from the School of Pharmacy at Purdue will be with us to talk about what's going on down there."

Ted continued, "Okay, that's enough about program. What announcements do we have to deal with?"

A more serious Junior Mason rose to speak this time, "Fellas, Harold Wilson's wife, Ruth, took a bad turn for the worse this week, and Harold's had to put her in the nursing home. Nobody knows for how long. I hope you'd all keep Ruth and Harold in your thoughts, I know Harold'd appreciate it." He sat again, and there was a spontaneous quiet that stopped the activity.

"I've got something to remind us," Steve Stokely stood up to command the floor's attention. "The Scholarship Committee's meeting over at my place tomorrow night, and we're gonna go over the applications, and we've gotta bunch of 'em, maybe thirty or so. We'll pick the top five, and schedule interviews here in a week with each of those kids in order to select the best girl and boy to win our annual scholarship. So if you're on the committee, and you know who you are, guys, be there on time tomorrow night, I mean it, and don't forget fellas, be careful out there." He giggled, sat down, and a few of the Rotarians murmured, "What the hell did that mean?" Still a few others smiled knowing it was a veiled reference to a routine comment on a discontinued television series then showing in syndication.

"Anymore announcements?" asked Ted. After a brief pause, Ted nodded to Rotarian Van Lindstrom and directed him, "Okay, Van, you want to introduce our guest tonight?"

Van quickly stood up and stepped before the assembly. The fact that what was to follow may represent a slight self-interest need not be commented upon here, "Guys, you know I'm in the insurance business. And I go to training and education events to stay up on things in the business. A few weeks ago I went to a seminar taught by a professor. Rob, you're not the only one who hangs around with professors, but at this seminar, a professor from Purdue-What is it that you're a professor of, Chuck?" He glanced over at the somewhat embarrassed guest, and without even listening to the answer to the question, Van continued, "Oh, yeah, he's a Professor of Banking and Insurance there at Purdue in the School of Business. He's going to talk to us about setting up 401Ks, and how helpful they can be for our retirement, and for some of you, this is too late. I give you Dr. Charles Brockwell. Chuck!"

With that Dr. Brockwell spoke for about twenty minutes on how to set up a special retirement savings tool, and why every Rotarian ought to do it for, as he described it, "The best bang for your retirement buck!" After a few questions from the listening assembly, Dr. Brockwell was completed.

"Okay, guys, that's it for tonight," said Ted Ryan, Rotary President and School Principal. "Please stick around to help a bit cleaning and straightening up. Oh, yeah. Compliments of Rob's Pharmacy, we've got a humongous bottle of Tums up here that may help any of you strugglin' a bit with Buddy's Mystery Meat. See you next week, Rotarians."

"Audrey, do you know where Sam is? I've been trying to get hold of him all morning. He's not at home. The furnace has gone out again over at the church. Audrey, where can I find him?" I called Audrey Jenkins at her bookkeeping office just off the courthouse square.

"Dale, I'm not sure. He said something about goin' up to Goodland, and he and Jack'd be helpin' Ed remodel some house up there."

"Thanks, Audrey, sorry to interrupt."

"No problem. That's where I think they are. Bye." As Audrey hung up to return to bookkeeping, I hung up and headed to the door. This encounter with Ed Ownby Construction was to be enlightening. After years filling my drowsy afternoons with the Cubs by watching TV commercials on WGN, in between the innings, I became familiar with the home remodeling business. Grade B television spots boasted of turning a tar paper shack into the Taj Mahal, and of course, FHA financing was always available. But these TV shysters had never met Ed Ownby Construction; he was in the same business.

Farmers during the off season, after harvest until preparation for planting in early spring, aside from tinkering and busy work, farmers don't have all that much to do, neither do they make all that much money. Therefore, odd jobs, part-time work, are common, if not a necessity. Ed Ownby Construction wasn't much more than Ed himself during the farming months. But during the winter, often, he would press his buddies, Sam Jenkins, his son, Jack, and even Phil Jenkins, Sam's Uncle into the construction crew. Sometimes another farmer, Brian Christensen, would also be part of the construction crew.

Finding them in Goodland would be no great quest. Goodland is only about seven or eight miles North of Fowler, and there are only forty or fifty houses in the whole town, so I just cruised up and down a few streets until I saw Ed's beat-up pale blue Chevy pickup, and the other armada of trucks out in front of the house. This was my introduction to Ed Ownby Construction. They were fixing a little two bedroom bungalow: remodel the bathroom, and put new cabinets and countertops in the kitchen. I was to learn that remodeling looks more like demolition.

The front door stood wide open, and a wafting cloud of dust slowly filtered out the opening. "Hi, there, Dale. Did ya bring a hammer or a crowbar? Just find any spot along this wall and start whacking' and tearing' apart." So greeted Ed to my invasion into their workplace. I was to learn that while Ed Ownby Construction usually did good work on what they were actually hired to do, neatness, and protecting the rest of the work site from devastation was not one of their long suits.

Tearing through the sheetrock walls was fairly fast work, but the dust was thick. And Ed Ownby Construction did not own a drop cloth. Now this two bedroom bungalow did not contain precious furniture or heirlooms, but what was there was left naked to be engulfed in the soot of remodeling. Besides flying shrapnel coming off the ripping crowbars and smashing hammers, the furniture and carpet were already immersed in construction dust and debris. This did not include the marks of workboots throughout the house. Allegedly the mess of destroying would be replaced with something much better. But it didn't look like there was any bright future for the living room and kitchen, so I ventured toward the bathroom to see what transpired there.

In the tiny bathroom, Jack Jenkins was working with his father, Sam. Sam tossed aside a crowbar, tearing out much-mildewed bathtub tile, and then he turned his attention to the tub. Jack was fast attacking the walls, ripping the sheetrock, wallboard, with the hopes of replacing it all in a day or so. Yet, at this point there was no sign of construction, only destruction: dust, devastation, and making a horrible mess. This was a lesser-advertised trademark associated with the work of Ed Ownby Construction.

"Jack, get me that pipewrench, over there," his dad asked. "You know, if we just bust a hole in the floor, I think I can get at the plumbing, and get this monster out of here." Looking up from the plumbing, Sam finally noticed me, "Well, hello, Reverend. Any ideas on how to get this out of here?"

"Not a one."

It was really a rhetorical question which he followed with, "What brings you up here anyway?"

"Well, I thought you oughta know that the furnace is out again at the church, and when you get a bit of time, I wonder if you could check it out," I answered.

"We'll be up here today, and a few more, but maybe I could stop by late this afternoon, until then, wanna help?" Sam asked. And so began my brief employment with Ownby Construction, but actually, while I shared a bit in the demolition phase of the remodeling project, what I really did was marvel at their work.

"There, Jack, I told you if we cut a hole here in the floor, we'd get this sucker out of here. Now we've gotta get it out of this bathroom and into the junk heap out back," Sam said.

The bathroom, the only one in this bungalow, could barely accommodate the three of us standing therein. But when Sam and Jack lifted the tub, and rotated it ninety degrees in the attempt to squeeze it out through the bathroom door, there was no room left for me. I exited, but continued my observation. Jack told his father, "Okay, Dad, let's be careful, and I think we'll get it out of here." Yet Jack's hopes were in vain.

The bathtub was about three inches wider, no matter how you twisted it, than the door opening. Grunting and snorting, and an occasional muttered curse could not expand the opening. Three minutes of manipulation prompted Sam to gasp with no small frustration, "Oh, put the damn thing back over there. I'll guess we're gonna have to widen the opening a bit." As they put the tub back down, Sam, now thoroughly exasperated, was not quite as careful as he ought, and he crashed into the lavatory, which shattered. The right front corner of the porcelain sink, no longer was connected to the rest. "Darn it. Now we're gonna have to replace the sink too. We weren't supposed to do that," Sam muttered. But he quickly turned his attention back to the bathroom doorsill. He reached into the nearby toolbox, and removed a crowbar. "Maybe if I pull this molding off the sill we can get that tub out."

Molding that has been in place for more than thirty years, and covered with more coats of enamel than can be remembered, resists being carefully pulled. Sam tried to ease the crowbar under the molding and tried to pry the molding free. But nothing budged. So he applied a bit more persuasion to the crowbar which succeeded in getting him a bit more leverage, but as he pried the molding snapped. Sam is a Presbyterian elder, and while the circumstance may cause one to be empathetic to his frustration, empathy did not entirely explain the monologue of expletives that followed. Any gentleness and care in the removal of more molding were forgotten. Hammer and crowbar immediately ripped away the remaining molding, and father and son returned to the tub. Again they lifted it up toward the now slightly larger doorsill. But still after several angles and manipulations, the tub would not fit through the opening.

What followed next became etched forever in my memory of the trademark of Ownby Construction: demolition is as much a part of their method as construction. Again they tossed the tub back out of the way, but this time with even less care than after the prior defeat.

Sam stared at the sill for a few more moments, fuming, fermenting until he grumbled, "Gimme that crowbar and hammer. I guess we're gonna have to bust this darn sill out of here itself." With no time to debate his decision, Sam starting prying and whacking the door sill assembly, which was about the exact moment that bossman, Ed, checked out all the cursing.

Ed stood for a moment in the gathering dust when Sam shouted at Ed. It must be kept in mind that in better moments that Sam Jenkins and Ed Ownby are best friends, in fact, they were each other's Best Men in their weddings now more than twenty-five years ago. For the moment, however, friendship was forgotten. Ed asked, "Hey, partner, what in the world are you doin'? We're supposed to be remodeling, not destroying."

Sam was in no mood to be second guessed, even by his boss, and best friend. "Shut up, and get out of here. I've tried everything, and you're not payin' me enough to put up with this, so just get out."

Ed was no hypocrite. His handling of the kitchen, while not quite the debacle as the bathroom, still looked as no small devastation, so he thought it prudent to comply with his buddy's suggestion. He went back to the kitchen. I thought it safer, as well, to retreat to destroying the kitchen with Ed, than stay to endure Sam's solution to exiting the tub.

I helped Ed pull a decrepit dishwasher out of the kitchen and dump it in the trash dumpster. And after an hour or so, we left Sam and Jack to their plan, Sam hovered in the kitchen announcing he'd finally won the war of attrition with the tub, "It's out. You got me. But I don't know how there was any other way of doing it, but it's out. Hole in the floor. Broken sink. And we'll have to replace that bathroom doorsill, but by God, the tub is gone, and the hole in that doorway is big enough now that we could put a pool in that bathroom."

At which time I announced, "Well, guys, it's been good, but I've gotta go do a funeral for a dead poodle, Bye!" And so I left. Sam's holler followed me,

"See ya, Reverend. I'll be by this afternoon, and check out the furnace. Don't you worry 'bout it."

I didn't. And true to Sam's word, he fixed the furnace as well. A few days passed before I saw the crew grabbing an early morning coffee at The Dairy Barn, when I inquired, "How you doing with that house up in Goodland?"

Big smiles painted their faces. All frustration had disappeared from Sam's face, as he spoke for the others, "We're almost done. We're going up there now. C'mon up with us. You won't believe it. It looks great. You and the wife would love to live there yourselves."

A few minutes later, and a few miles, we stepped through the front door, and in truth, I did not believe it. The kitchen was beautiful. Julia Child would long to cook and wile away her life in such a kitchen. And as I headed down the short hallway to the bathroom, I tried to picture what transformation would have been necessary to make anything redemptive of the destruction that was required just to remove an old tub. But they had pulled it off. A sparkling tub and lavatory were the keynotes of a beautiful new bathroom. The two rooms were right out of *House Beautiful*. Yet one question remained.

"Guys, this looks great. You've done some wonderful work here. I never thought I'd see anything look this good after it looked so bad a few days ago." I paused before I asked what was really on my mind. "But what about the rest of the house. There's dust and junk, a horrible mess throughout the house. Don't you clean that up?"

Ed laughed, "Naw, that's not our job ... not part of the deal. We remodel. We don't clean." I shuddered at the heartlessness.

It was several months later when I came home from a meeting of the Board of Elders of the church when I told my wife the good news and the bad news. "Hon', I've got some good news, and some bad news. The church is going to put all new windows in the manse, our house."

"Gee, Dale, that's terrific. What's the bad news?"

I paused a moment. I always pause a moment before I'm going to lie. "The bad news is that Ownby Construction's going to do the work. Oh, hon', they do good work, but it may mean us doing a little clean up when the job's done."

The men in Fowler have big hands. One of the necessities of my calling is shaking hands and maybe giving the occasional hug with the folk as they leave church on Sunday which means I do a lot of handshaking. Shaking hands with city folk is a necessary formality. We teach our children the proper etiquette of handshaking. Right hand to right hand, make sure the hands are well-intertwined, then a modestly firm grip is to be reciprocated. I suppose I've shaken thousands of city hands. Petite hands. Bigger hands, but I never remember big hands.

I'm a man of somewhat above average stature, and while I am used to being bigger than most adult males, occasionally I encounter a man who towers above me. But that is the exception. I am not used to being engulfed when shaking hands, however. But that was before I shook a few hands in Fowler.

The first time I shook the hands of a few of my farmer-members, I encountered my first truly big hand. Willard McKay has big hands. He also had a fine wife and three lovely daughters. In the five years I was Willard's pastor, I don't suppose he said twenty words to me. Reticent to speak, he was not shy to shake my hand. The first time Willard wrapped his paw around mine I felt like a leaf must feel in the fall when it is caught up in a large leaf rake. His hand consumed me. Willard was big all over, big through and through. His handshake was his affirmation, and friendship all in one gesture. Because he'd never use enough words to say what he felt, he let his grip do his talking.

Jim Banks Jr. had big hands as well. Jim talked a bit more than his big-handed counterpart, Willard. So I got to know a bit more about the man through conversation, coffee-drinking, golfing, and scotch-drinking than I ever did with Mr. McKay. But both of their grips betrayed men of substance, and character. The first time I pulled my little mitt from the grasp of Jim Banks, I was so startled, I gaped at this hand. Hands! My what hands. Each of his fingers looked the thickness of bratwurst linked to the palm the size of a pancake. But the more I knew Jim, the more I knew his grip paled in comparison to the size of his soul.

But it was Alex's grip that brought my grip-fixation to my awareness. It was Alex Myer's handshake that cautioned me that this was no perfunctory human with whom I grappled. Alex was the best of the farmers, the best of the good people, the good men with whom I was privileged to mingle. His handshake preached to me that the people who lived beyond the stoplight are people of substance. I was shaking a heavy-weight's hand. Oh, not heavy-weight in mass, not in that sense of proportion, but heavy-weight in terms of this person knows how to love, to live, to be honest, strong. His grip on me was such that it was not easy to let go. So it is with people of substance, integrity and character. Funny, that we'd learn that just shaking a hand.

It was handshaking that taught me that any poll between matriarchs and patriarchs determining who was in charge of town was largely a pedantic exercise. The town worked well regardless of who ran it, regardless of sex. It wasn't the gender, it was the substance. One will never know such truth by just driving through. You have to stop, turn and drive in. Doing so, you get to know the hand that's shaking yours.

WORSHIPPING COMMUNITY

Church-going was a big part of life beyond the stoplight. Regardless of where one worshipped, one's church put a framework, a boundary of understanding around much that was hard to understand, painful, disappointing, or, wonderful, the surprise of joy. The church helped the folk deal with disillusionment, and the grief of disease and death, whether natural or unnatural, those in which we are victim, and that self-inflicted grief. People showed up in their church to drink from the wells of courage to persevere, not just in the challenges of marriage, or child-rearing. No, they went to church to be revived when grappling with the unknowns of too much rain that floods the crops, or too little rain that desiccates them.

People's church helps them have another context in which to raise their children, learn how to be married, learn how to give birth, how to love, and how to die. Life in the worshipping community afforded revelatory glimpses into the people who lived beyond the stoplight. Much is said of never really knowing someone until you stand in their shoes. But the thought of wearing another's shoe made such a metaphor a bit troubling, if not offensive, to me. I say, it's awfully hard to think you can know anyone, or what's going on in the lives of a town just by driving by in your car, making ignorant assumptions, and never turning and driving into town, and finally, sitting next to them in the pew. You never really know someone until you sit in life next to him in the pew. Could that be true?

It came as a shock to me when I learned that the county and the town were half Catholic. So much for stereotypes. Many assume that rural America is dominated by people who take their religion in Protestant flavors. Catholics dominated the sanctuaries of the large industrial and urban sprawls of Cincinnati, St. Louis, Milwaukee and Chicago, whereas Protestants emerge in the 'burbs, and rural landscapes. While the assumption is largely true of the urban Midwest, there is a band across the rural grainbelt, in which the Catholic missionaries claimed as "theirs" in the nineteenth century. Fowler was such a town, Benton, such a county. Less than ten thousand residents in the entire county, and half of them Catholics. Only about twenty-five hundred in the town, and half of them followers of Rome. That left twelve hundred or so folk for the five Protestant churches in town: Baptist, Methodist, Wesleyans, Christian, and the Presbyterians. As a result the community was largely colored by Roman Catholic hegemony.

In the town's more prosperous days, there was two of everything: two banks, two pharmacies, two groceries, and so forth. But with the shrinking prosperity, Darwinian survivalist patterns eliminated this inefficiency, and this ghetto mentality. While the Catholic Church was still the big show in town, as the years wore on, the bigoted competition, Catholic vs. Protestant lessened, which was good for all. The town learned to live together in religious peace.

"Hellfire, it's almost four. We gotta get to church," said Henry McElroy. Actually it was ten till four. Four of us sat together on a weekday afternoon at a table adjacent to The Horseshoe Bar at Benton County Country Club. We had just completed an afternoon round of golf together: Henry McElroy, Shorty Shamburger, Junior Mallioux, and me. My three Catholic golfing companions were about to give me a lesson in the theology of the worshipping community, ecclesiology, theologians call it. Real people simply call it: what do we believe about the church?

"To church? At four in the afternoon? Why?" I asked.

"We gotta go to a funeral," answered McElroy.

My incredulity grew rapidly, even as they made ready for their hasty departure. "Funeral? Who died?"

McElroy turned somewhat unknowingly to his partner in crime, Shorty, "Who was it again, Shorty?"

"Dern it," muttered Shamburger. "What was his name? It was Myrtle Deno's boy. You know the one who was never just quite right. What was his name?"

McElroy interrupted his partner's reflection, "I don't remember his name. Anyway we gotta go. We'll be late and I promised my wife I'd be there in time to sit next to her. See ya, Reverend." And just that quick, they were off to the funeral.

Their three Buds sat about half-empty there on the table. I was left to contemplate their lesson to me. "Compliantly going to a funeral of a man they didn't even know. Hmmm," I said to myself. "Those Catholics are different than us Protestants. I like that they went to the funeral." But why? Why did I like their devotion?

Nobody likes the setbacks that life deals us, but it's good knowing what to do, having something to do when tragedy and grief bring their unwelcome kiss. When death hits a house, or some other grief, many of us mutter, "What am I gonna do?" But these Catholics knew what to do. They had something to do. Morrow, Shorty and McElroy took off for church.

This may be the shortcoming of the Protestant flocks. We're long on thinking about our problems, reluctant to do much about them. Protestants analyze, and then determine what they believe about the situation. Then they integrate their feelings with their thoughts. God forbid do anything that you don't feel good about, and haven't thought through. Pray, if you want, for example, but golly, don't pray if you don't feel like praying, and if you don't understand prayer. Such is Protestant thinking. And such thinking often ridicules Catholic piety as mindless devotion to the commands of the priest, even the pope. The criticism goes like this: You only go to a funeral if you know why you are going to the funeral. Protestants, supposedly, only do what they comprehend. Catholics are mindless zombies of episcopal bondage—goes the thinking.

But that thought seemed less justified when my golfing buddies jilted me at The Horseshoe Bar. When a Protestant dies a two-step process commences: first, there is a viewing at the funeral home, second, there is some sort of a commemoration in a worship service, either at the funeral home, or at the deceased's church.

The Viewing is the primary level of community support. Usually it is a night or so before the funeral or memorial service. The family of the deceased gathers at the funeral home, Windler's Funeral Home.

In Fowler, Windler's used to be the Catholic funeral home, as the Windlers are Catholic. But when the Protestant funeral home suffered its own demise, Windlers became THE funeral home, take it or leave it, Protestant or Catholic. Pam and Bobby Windler ran a nice enough funeral business. The business was attached to their split-level home. So they didn't have a long commute to go to work, just a walk down the hall. But as the business was adjacent to the home, there was some inevitable blurring of the boundaries between business and family business. The Windlers had three little boys. Shorty Shamburger called them, "The Hell on Wheels Gang." And there was some empirical evidence to support their nickname. I think it was during my sermon upon the death of Omer LaGue that one of the boys rode his big wheel through the chapel with his mother whisper-shouting, "Get out of here, your daddy's gonna kill you." So the Windler boys added color to the grief process.

When the family gathered on the evening of the Viewing, Bobby greeted them into a lounge area, offered them a cup of coffee, or a soft drink. Then he explained the evening, an explanation that usually was redundant. In a small town with an aged population, most people were well-versed in the appropriate protocol, and what to do upon the death of a loved one in anyone's family. "Okay, the people should begin arriving here in about fifteen minutes, and we have a three hour scheduled visitation. What I suggest is that you plan on standing over there by the casket for fifteen minutes, maybe a half hour at most, you know, sort of do it in shifts. If you don't pace yourself, I'm afraid you're gonna get worn out. It isn't rude to sit down and have a refreshment every now and again. Any questions?" There were none.

So he went on. "About nine, I expect, most everybody will be gone. Then you people need to get on home, and try to get a good night's sleep. The funeral tomorrow is at eleven, so you need to be back here by no later than ten-thirty. Questions?" Seldom were there any questions. Usually people were so unresponsive, the presence of grief being as it was, there was no time or need to be too fussy about very many details. By the time Bobby finished, the first friends, and acquaintances began to arrive. It would be a steady procession for the next three hours.

In the case of the more typical deaths, the death of an elderly woman or man, the picture would look something like this. The casket was placed at one extreme of the chapel area, where a few focused lights drew attention to the deceased. Most normally, the casket was open, and the mortician's art was on display. Such attempts at comfort, and expressions rationalizing the onset of grief most normally are uttered, "My, doesn't grandpa look nice?" When in truth grandpa just looked dead. Nevertheless, understanding that grandpa no longer needed compliments, but those grieving utter such phrases to ease into the grief process, or to attempt to comfort the grieving. Surrounding the casket was a florist's dream: probably the deceased had more flowers upon the occasion of death, than he or she ever knew in their entire life combined. The flowers came from closest family members, fraternal organizations, friends across the county and across the country, and on and on. Perhaps there would be an American flag placed folded on the casket in the event that the loved one was a veteran.

The family formed a line flowing away from the casket. Nearest to the casket would stand the surviving spouse, then next to the spouse, would be the children of the deceased. Usually, the most caring or authoritative of the children would be the head greeter of the clan, also doubling to help the mom or dad cope with the many expressions of comfort and sympathy that would lavish the family.

Continuing in the line would be the next closest or nearest of kin. Sometimes it would be grandkids, or sisters and brothers of the departed. So as the visitors came along the procession, the receiving line, the greetings tended to escalate in importance, significance until one came to the end of the line, the spouse of the now departed loved one. At the beginning of the line, the comments often went something like, "Well, I haven't seen you in years. By golly, the last time I seen you, you was 'bout this high. Geesh, you've grown." The ten year old grandson was to endure three hours of such well-meaning torture. But as the visitors proceeded along the line, the voices became more subdued, as a rule, and more focused on saying such affirmations as, "I'm so sorry. Is there anything we can do? Your husband, Harold, was one of the kindest men I ever knew." And so it went for three hours.

In a town the size of Fowler, if the departed were one of the more well-known, and well-loved, the procession could easily number three or four hundred people. That's more than ten percent of the town. Seldom would there be fewer than fifty for any deceased.

Most normally on the day of the funeral, if you were a Protestant, the funeral would be held in the chapel at the funeral home. People would gather again for the service, but the attendance normally was less than for the viewing. A worship service of about a half hour or so would be held for the departed by that person's pastor, and lacking one, the funeral director would call the pastors in town and ask which of them would be willing to officiate at a funeral for an "unaffiliated."

The services varied somewhat from tradition to tradition, but there was some commonality to the basic elements of the Protestant funeral. The minister begins reading a few passages from the Bible about death, grief and the hope of resurrection, blended in with a few psalms here and there. Then there would be a sermon of sorts, interpreting the passages to the listeners, lifting up such themes as grief, hope, and what lessons we survivors can learn from this passing of life from our midst. The conclusion of this would end with a prayer acknowledging grief and affirming our hope in a new life in a better world apart from this veil of tears. Options to these basics would include musical interludes composed of some dreadful selections played through the funeral chapel tape cartridge of "Funeral Favorites." This greatest hits CD or tape included such funeral favorites as "How Great Thou Art," "Amazing Grace," and the most beloved, "In the Garden." For the more resource-rich, a family member could solo any one of these "Funeral Favorites" accompanied to tape tracks, or someone's Aunt Rose on the spinet piano that Windler Funeral Home provided at "no extra charge," as Bob Windler was pleased to announce. Some funerals added eulogies, good words, about the loved one now gone. These eulogies, often, poignant, though too often, tended to be a bit hyperbolic in the now departed's virtues, and completely ignoring their now-forgotten vices.

When the service was over, Bobby would stand in front of the casket, and suggest that everyone but the family now exit to make ready to proceed to the cemetery. Obediently those present complied. The family then made one last pause gazing into the casket for the last time. Crying, sobbing, even wailing, were not uncommon at this point, and the family would bind closest together at this sacred moment. Then Bobby and Pam would close the casket, and if a flag were present, it would serve as the drape for it all. Old Glory was the banner over it all, as they wheeled the casket to the hearse which would proceed out to the Benton County Cemetery.

Art, the town sheriff, would already be positioned in front of the funeral home to escort the procession the two miles out to the cemetery. Following Art in the police car with every light flashing would come Bobby driving the hearse, then the cars of the family, closest to the deceased first, and so on in accord with dignified processional protocol. Upon the arrival of the hearse near the gravesite, Bobby Windler would summon the six pallbearers, and they would first, carry the casket to the gravesite, then place it on the stand over the already-dug grave. Almost always, the funeral director had provided a tent-like shelter around the gravesite to shelter from the cold wind of the winter, the searing sun of the summer, or the rain possible most anytime.

At the graveside, fewer people than even at the service now were in attendance, and the minister called the gathered around the grave and the family, the closest sitting in folding chairs immediately in front of the casket. The minister read a little more scripture, said a prayer or two, and ended with something like, "Ashes to ashes, and dust to dust ..." and finished with an "Amen." It was over. Laced with the words, continued various gestures of grief again, but the family pulled together, and after more words of comfort, graveside pleasantries, the funeral was over. A few handshakes, kisses, and the family, most normally, headed back home for sandwiches provided by friends, or maybe the women of their church would host a luncheon or reception for everyone at their church.

And so it went. So it went, at least if one were a Protestant. But if you were a Catholic, there were a few modifications of the above. It was the modifications, and the most significant of these, that caught my attention when Shamburger, Morrow, and McElroy took off for church for a funeral of an almost-stranger.

The Roman Catholic modifications were only variations on the same theme, but the changes were significant. The flow of events was remarkably similar. Usually a viewing initiated the community's active involvement in assisting the surviving family. Viewing then funeral. But the funeral was always done at the church. Even though it was a funeral home run by a Catholic, the actual Mass commemorating the dead would only be in one place: the church. The priest would never have permitted it to be held any other place. So this was the first variation. Protestant funerals more than likely would not take place at the church, but at the funeral home.

The worship service, which would be a standard Catholic mass, focusing on the life and death of the departed, and the Christian hope in light of death, like the Protestant, may have a few eulogies, and perhaps, a few family members or friends would be invited to assist, perhaps, even read a few favorite and relevant scripture passages. Likewise, following the worship, there would be the interment at the cemetery, the Catholic side. Then all may be invited to a reception of sorts at the church or at someone's home, for a luncheon, or snack.

So the differences were not so obvious, but still significant. The worship service took place at the church in the Catholic context, always. But the Protestants often funeraled at the funeral home. The funeral took place at the church for Protestants only if the deceased was a matriarch or patriarch of that particular church, was particularly committed in their piety, or the minister of that particular Protestant church was fussy, adamant, "Funerals must take place at the church." While funeral homes and directors are honorable enough institutions, they are entirely too sterile and removed from real life, the real life of the now-departed member of the church. Funeral homes aren't designed to accommodate the life of the church. Nothing against the morticians' trade, but they don't know worship, and the importance of the church to the worshipping life of the community of faith. Catholic priests know this, that's why they do the funerals in the church. Protestants would do well to take a lesson from my Fowler Roman Catholic friends.

But school doesn't end there. The next lesson my golfing companions taught me, me, a Protestant clergyman. They hopped up and hurriedly ran off to a funeral for a person they didn't even know. Why? Because that's what the church does when death happens. What a contrast to us Protestants. Protestants who lived around the stoplight followed an entirely different funeral protocol, one less informed by healthy community life. When someone dies in our churches, if they are an acquaintance, and if we have nothing else to do, we'll visit the family and offer our condolences upon the death of that church member. If the member who died is a fairly close acquaintance, a relative, then it is proper to go to the funeral. But we would never go to a funeral of a stranger, someone we don't even know his name. Never.

But Shorty, McElroy and Morrow did. Not even knowing the dead person's name, they went not just to the viewing, but to the funeral. Why? Because that is what the church does when death happens.

Is such piety mindless devotion? Does this amount to lemmings running off the edge of a cliff? No, on both counts. It's what the church does when death happens, and it prepares us all for death as it creeps ever closer to each of us. My golfing companions charged off to a funeral mass, because it was good and proper to do so. It gave them something to do when death lurks its ugliness in our presence.

My Catholic compadres taught me a valuable lesson about the funeral and the ugliness of death. Many of us cry out in crisis, grief, even death, "What am I gonna do?" Shorty, Morrow and McElroy had no in depth philosophical retorts, but they knew what to do. They went to church. They knew what to do. And knowing what to do in the face of crisis puts limits, boundaries on the heartache and terror of living under this veil of tears.

Such observation left me enriched, a tad bit more knowledgeable, and with three tepid beers.

The cross of Jesus Christ may have atoned for the sins of the world, but it didn't appear to help Christians cooperate all that well. Sure, the Christians in town, Protestant Christians, they liked one another enough. That is, the Baptists, the Methodists, the Christians, the Wesleyans, and the Presbyterians, they had mutual respect, if not love for one another. Fowler was not Belfast. While there were some deep-seated differences in the various fellowships, it would not lead to terrorism or car-bombings. It did lead to The Good Friday Service.

The Wesleyans and the Baptists probably were the staunchest of the lot, in terms of defending orthodoxy; they were the stalwarts of religion the way grandpa would have wanted it. On the other hand, the Methodists and the Presbyterians, may have been the most tolerant, most open to theological accommodation. Women, for example, didn't just cook pot-luck fare, but could teach a Sunday School class, maybe even go to seminary. The Christian Church was caught somewhere between the polarities of these not-too-wide extremes. Theological spectrum, after all, is a relative matter. All the churches in Fowler, in truth, on both a theological and a political continuum, may have found Barry Goldwater a bit too liberal when they voted in 1964.

Nevertheless, to cooperate and plan a Good Friday Service together, which was done every year, was to test the feeble ecumenical spirits in the best of the groups. At one o'clock that Good Friday afternoon, the service began. This year it was at the Baptist church. "Good afternoon, sisters and brothers. We've just come to praise the Lord," so began the greeting of the host pastor, Brother Tiny Hilton. He wasn't all that tiny. He got the name because years before, he played on the high school basketball team, and while he was a bit of a runt, he had a mean two-hand set shot. Basketball being the idol it was in Indiana, the nickname, Tiny, was never intended to be an insult, but an affirmation, and a term of endearment. Yet when Tiny grew up, he found the Lord, and became a Baptist preacher. "We just wanna worship the Lord, have some sweet fellowship here together-all the churches-and praise the Lord on this special day."

To call Good Friday merely a "special" day, for the more liturgically-minded Methodists or Presbyterians is like calling the day President Kennedy was shot, a bit of a disappointment to many Americans. While both are true, the understatement also misses the point. But Tiny meant well, though his greeting did not bespeak theological sophistication or insight. And everybody there that hour meant well. Good intentions, in fact, were the highlight of such services. Theological reflection, intentional planning of the service, these fell to the wayside in the flood of good intentions.

"Let us sing hymn #223, 'Beneath the Cross of Jesus,' and when you do, don't forget the blood Jesus shed for you." We sang. The accompanist pounded out the melody and the rhythm, and we were off in ecumenical worship, Benton County style. After the hymn, Tiny led the folk in a prayer. Tiny would have made a great television game show host. He was smooth. Yet when he prayed, his voice acquired a quiver, a vibrato. Evidently the quiver was his way of demonstrating his sincerity, and ardor. "Faw-ahh-thur, We-uh jessst a-door you-ooo. And we-uh jesst want to thaa-yank you—" Two repeated antiphons marked Tiny's prayers: the words, "Father," and "just." This was not unique to Tiny, but many of that wing of Christendom add to the grammar of prayer these interjections. "Father," precedes every, second or third sentence or so. I'm not sure why, perhaps, a continued restatement of the focus of the prayer is helpful, yet it surely is an observable syntax. Likewise, "just" is inserted after almost every utterance of the subject of the sentence. "We just—" or, "I just—" and then comes the predicate of the sentence. I have less understanding of the purpose of this interjection, perhaps, it functions like a breath mark in a score of music. He ended, "Aaaa-men and Aaaa-men." Tiny's prayer was finished, and he transitioned as well as Pat Sajak ever did on Wheel of Fortune. "Now some ladies from over to the

Christian Church, a quartet, I guess, are gonna sing, 'Precious Love'." Now why they were to sing a hymn normally associated with syrupy weddings, no one knew. But it had been a while since they had sung, so they told their pastor, "Darrell, we'd love to sing 'Precious Love,' so in the planning meeting for that service, Darrell was quite assertive in getting the quartet to sing at least somewhere during the service.

The quartet was lovely, and certainly well-intentioned. Following it came the reading of scripture. The texts were Psalm 22, where first is spoken, "My God, my God, why have you forsaken me?" followed by the reading from the gospels about Jesus being crucified, and he too uttering, "My God, my God, why—". There was no small irony, or perhaps, coincidence that the service took a dramatic turn about this time.

Thunderstorms in the middle of April in Indiana are as common as flies at a picnic. About the time the service began, the cold drafts coming from the gathering thunderhead foretold some inconvenience, but no one anticipated such an interruption. No sooner had the Methodist pastor begun to read the gospel passage, and the thunder and lightning began. With the first crack of lightning the lights at the Baptist church flickered just a wee bit, which served as a minor distraction, but a few more cracks, and that was all she wrote. Everything went black. Darkness at noon was recreated, though it was one o'clock. Such atmosphere happened quite beyond any plans in the ministers' script or the printed Order of Worship. As the thunderstorm hovered overhead, and the torrents of rain pounded down upon the gathered congregation, everything came to a halt. It was too dark to read. Had we been in the Methodist or Presbyterian Church, we could have lighted some candles. But Baptists have little use for candles, evidently too much of a connection with Catholicism, so we sat in the dark. Pete Carter, the Methodist minister, tried to read on, but he gave up. He peered back at the gathered officiants, his fellow ministers as if to ask, "What now?" Realizing quickly that we would be no help, he ad libbed. "Sisters and brothers, let us pray." And so we prayed. Pete prayed and prayed. He prayed for the cessation of the storm, for our protection, for the protection of the crops. Petitions were offered to the Almighty that his followers would be obedient, faithful witnesses, and that all in Christ in Benton Country would dwell in unity.

When Pete finally muttered, "Amen," the next distraction occurred. At first the splat sound was infrequent, irregular, and unidentified. But as the rain continued, even intensified, the occasional splat, turned into a splat with a pause, two-three-four, splat, two-three-four." The dim light caused the ears to locate the place of the increasing drip. While it was hard to see, it was less and less hard to hear. The increasing drip, increased in frequency, volume, and prominence in the interrupted service, which caused Tiny Hilton to search out the leak in the dike, or roof. The sound confirmed that it was not far away. There were several wooden pews just behind where the ministers were seated. Normally occupied by the choir, they sat empty for this service. Yet upon Tiny's investigation, it was clear that at least one of the pews was filling fast. The drip from the ceiling sounded more and more like a drum roll every time the next splat hit the hard wood. All could hear. Tiny slipped into the kitchen and returned with a plastic bucket lined with kitchen towels. He hadn't entirely solved the problem, but the volume was less distracting, even though the flaw in the roof was unchecked. And it was still nearly dark.

It was Rev. Darrell Smith, the Christian Church minister's time to preach. Darkness served as no hindrance to the Rev. Smith. He was not as structured in his preaching technique so as to be dependent on notes or a manuscript. So in darkness or light, he began to preach on the meaning of the cross of Christ in spite of the drip and the darkness. Occasionally his proclamation would resonate with one of the other preachers or gathered ecumenical congregation, and from the near darkness would be heard a "that's right," or, "Uh-huh," or an emphatic and affirming, "A-a-a-a-men." It took him fifteen minutes, maybe twenty to speak the Word of God and to bring the light into our very present darkness. When Darrell finished, the closing prayer was offered by the Wesleyan pastor. His "Amen," ushered in the last crisis.

The closing hymn, #402, "When I Survey the Wondrous Cross," required lights. But it was still mostly dark, and the storm carried on unabated. So, Tiny, ad libbed a solution. He asked his pianist, knowing that we all really didn't know the words to "Wondrous Cross," to play "Amazing Grace." As he said, "Ever' body knows and loves 'Amazing Grace,' even his accompanist-in the dark. As the last of five stanzas was sung, in the dark, to the out-of-rhythm-drip in the bucket, "When we've been there ten thousand years, Bright shining as the sun, We've no less days to sing God's praise, Than when we've first begun," I am sure I caught Tiny gazing in the dimness hoping for a miracle, the bright shining of the sun. But it wasn't to be. The miracle, to be sure, was that we were there at all, being the community of faith. The miracle in the gathering reaffirmed that what divided us was really much less than what united us. Such actions brought light to the whole town, even in the darkness of the Good Friday thunderstorm.

"No, no more balloons. Not next year, not any year. It's been decided. No balloons. I don't care about the symbolism or anything else. No balloons." It had been nearly ten months since the last Easter Sunrise Service. A few of the concerned parties from the Methodist Church were meeting with their counterparts from the Presbyterian Church. The Easter Sunrise Service, therefore, was a joint venture. The ministers of the two churches, and a few leaders of each congregation were gathered in a Sunday School classroom at First Methodist Church to plan that year's cooperative Sunrise Service. And for the first time in memory, the planning session was marked by controversy, dissention, and no small emotion, at least from one of the planners present. So the planning session began as last year's Sunrise Service ended … in some controversy.

Dorothy Harold was emphatic. "No balloons. Not after that disgrace of last year. Well, I never—at a church service, on the day, the holiest day of the year, our Lord's resurrection. I was appalled. Appalled. Do you understand? Appalled. No balloons."

Pete, Dorothy Harold's pastor, tried all of his pastoral skills to lance the emotional boil of festering rage trapped inside poor Dorothy. And while eventually, he succeeded, it was only after she said, "No balloons," twenty or more so times. He finally turned the road to the future, and Dorothy's emotional well-being by promising, Dorothy, there'll be no balloons. I promise you. And while I am sure that no one intended to offend you, or anyone else last Easter with the balloons, I guess the guys were just having a little sophomoric fun, and things just got out of hand. And I can see it offended you and others, but there'll be no balloons this year." With that, and a promise based upon Mrs. Harold's last protest, "Or in the future?" Pete added, "Right. Never, never again will we use balloons at the Easter Service." With that, Pete contracted into eternity that balloons would never again be part of the liturgy of the Presbyterian-Methodist Sunrise Service. Yet more importantly, he placated Dorothy Harold, so we could begin planning the current year's celebration, albeit, without balloons.

The cause of the controversy, and the eternal ban on balloons as liturgical aids, actually was not central to the previous year's Sunrise Service, but more a matter that raised its ugly head as an aftermath of that delightful joint worship time. Sunrise, that year, dawned about 7:03. And for even the most dedicated of church folk, this represented a great challenge not only to a timely arrival, but to being present at all. Conceding the need to be realistic, and assuming the sinful habits of the irresponsible members of each congregation, 7:30 was the time of the service, though this meant it was somewhat of a post-Sunrise Service. And this year it was to be held in the church yard at The Methodist Church, it was their turn as the Presbyterians had hosted it in their yard the year before. And that year, it hadn't really been in the Presbyterian yard, what with the rain and all. But that was the intention.

The people started pulling up to the Methodist church by about 7:15, though the kitchen crew had been cooking since about six. The agenda for the morning was Sunrise Service followed by a pancake breakfast, then cleanup. And many of the folk then would head home for a short while, freshen up, and venture to their respective church for the regular worship service at eleven. It was a full morning. That year's was fuller than most, but it started as all the others had.

The people gathered in the church yard almost as in a huddle. The two choirs combined to form a mass choir, the prime feature of this service. Singing the great Easter hymns was what this was all about with a few touches of drama thrown in. The ministers were just minor bit players in the Sunrise Service.

About 7:30, the service began. Two high school boys came out of the bushes not far from the gathered congregation. They were dressed in white robes that looked suspiciously reminiscent of the robes that the shepherds wore in a previous Christmas pageant. The angel effect was accomplished with the addition of wings on each of the guys. They were splendid wings shaped from baling wire to outline the supposed look of angel wings, and stretched across the wire was white yarn sprayed with Christmas tree flock and scattered with gold glitter. Ray Phillips' whispered slur was ignored by most, "By God, they look like flyin' shepherds." Nevertheless, the drama continued as the angels asked the Easter query to the entire congregation standing in the grass, "Why do you look for the living amongst the dead? He is not here, but he is risen."

From the other side of the yard, another voice attracted the worshipper's attention. Pointing to a flower trellis that had been covered with paper mache to look like the opening of a burial tomb, a non-descript girl spoke, "See here. The tomb where they laid him is empty. He is risen." And with that the congregation on cue-the cue learned from years of experience, having repeated the ritual for generations-shouted with smiles coming from the hearts, "He is risen indeed. Christ is risen. He is risen indeed!" To which the choir promptly began to sing to the accompaniment of a spinet rolled out onto the church sidewalk, "Jesus Christ is risen today! Alleluia!" What followed was a flurry of resurrection songs which ended with the most triumphalistic of the lot, "Up from the grave he arose with a mighty triumph o'er his foes."

Upon the conclusion of this last hymn, it was time for the grand finale: balloons. As part of the preparations for this climax of the Easter Sunrise Service, three or four Methodist men had purchased a small bottle of helium, and several gross of balloons. The fellows inflated the balloons, and stored them in large garbage bags. Those bags had to be tied down, or given some ballast, to prevent them from floating away prior to their proper cue. Well, the time had come.

The guys who blew up the four or five hundred balloons, began to release them now into the bright, blue, Easter Sunday Sunrise sky. The multi-colored balloons were gorgeous in contrast to the sky, like jellybeans or M&Ms in the heavens. All observing enjoyed the spectacle, but the theologically-inquisitive, pondered, "Why balloons? What does it mean to release balloons on the morning that we celebrate Jesus' victory over death?" One response to such contemplative thought was, "Oh, what difference does it make? They're neat. They're pretty. The kids love 'em. Shut up and enjoy 'em." And they were pretty regardless of the ill-defined symbolism.

Then host pastor, Pete Carter, prayed a brief prayer offering thanksgiving for the victory of resurrection, and all the implications deriving from believing in a risen Savior. The "Amen," of Pete's prayer marked the transition to the pancake breakfast. Still, though, the controversy had not begun.

The pancake crew, that had been busy in preparation since long before sunrise, was ready for the Methodist-Presbyterian famished breakfast hoards. Going down the steps into the basement, Wesley Fellowship Hall, everyone was directed to the serving windows where Styrofoam plates had two pancakes, and two sausage links for all. Next came the table with tubs of margarine and warmed syrup. Pickup a napkin roll containing knife and fork and one was ready to head to the paper-covered dining tables. After one chose a spot to eat, most headed back to the large coffee pots and drew off a cup of hot brew, or grabbed up a cup of orange juice; some drank both.

Within fifteen minutes or so, most everybody had been served, and were licking their chops on "the fruit of the griddle," as Ray Phillips called pancakes and sausage. It was about then that a few of the servers came downstairs, having been outside as part of the clean-up crew. Grown men in their thirties and forties, three or four of them, afflicted with the giggles-actually it went far beyond the giggles: tears poured down each of their cheeks as their sides split with hilarity-they stumbled down the steps for their own pancakes.

At first nobody had a clue as to what was the provocation of their mirth. While they were the designated yard cleanup crew, they stumbled onto the bottle of helium that they had failed to exhaust as they blew up all the balloons which prompted in them an idea. They also represented a few of the male voices in the Methodist choir. They picked up a few of the unused balloons, and filled them with the helium, but instead of tying them up and releasing them to float away over Indiana, they inhaled the entire contents of the balloon, the helium, and instead of just exhaling, being in the spirit of Easter, they began once more to sing those great old hymns. They had heard the rumor that helium inhaled affects the vocal chords by giving even the deepest basso profundo, a shrill voice reminiscent of a cross between Munchkins and the Chipmunks. So they started singing, "Up from the grave he arose, with a mighty triumph o'er his foes." But this time it was in the voice of Chip and Dale. This prompted the laughter, and even euphoria. So they did it again and again. Laughing, giggling, harder and harder. No longer did they take the time to fill up the balloons, now they just inhaled a drag right off the helium bottle. Never had "Jesus Christ is risen today" been sung as it was in the church yard of The Methodist Church.

It was about the time that they all were falling over in the grass outside the church, still hitting the bottle, the helium bottle, time and again, howling like drunken fraternity brothers on a sordid Friday night buzz—it was about then that Dorothy Harold pulled up in the parking lot in the alley behind The Methodist Church. She saw it all. She drank in the spectacle of debauchery. To Dorothy's eyes, had they been smoking opium from a water pipe, it could have been no more decadent.

Dorothy stormed into the Wesley Fellowship Hall and called a meeting of the ad hoc committee for the prevention of Drug Addiction at Methodist-Presbyterian Easter Sunrise Services. And she stirred up quite a hornet's nest of helium temperance enthusiasm. The hornet's nest had not even calmed as late as ten months later when Dorothy insisted, "No balloons."

If you asked the people who lived beyond the stoplight, why they went to church, I suspect that a few could speak with theological acumen reflecting on the significance of the church and why the Lordship of Christ summons people into his church. But only a few. Most would speak a few words, and with no great precision they would vaguely describe the church, the worshipping community as a place of comfort and hope, a locus of meaning in a world ever more troubling to understand. Souls intermingle there, and it's that intermingling that brings the hassles, the petty conflicts in churches. But at the intersection of the souls, that place called the church, they also find their humanity.

OLYMPIANS

A town of just more than two thousand, a county of less than ten thousand, cannot boast an NFL football team; you'll never watch an NBA game in Fowler—at least live; once in a great while some sect of the Harlem Globetrotters may pass through, but big time professional sports is a major void in Benton County. But the other side of that coin is that the voters will never have to pass a bond issue to build a multi-million dollar coliseum, and the businesses will never have to amortize luxury boxes to entertain clients. The town and the county avoided such complications. Still Benton County was as addicted to America's obsession with sports as any other location. No, the Dallas Cowboy Cheerleaders did not decorate the sidelines of the high school football games, and the sporting events missed some of the glitz of the big city, but they also missed the pretense. Yet as one perused the calendars hanging on the refrigerators throughout the county, sporting events dictated much of the social calendar. Watching an event, be it basketball or baseball, or anything else, was like going to the Olympics, but sports beyond the stoplight afforded you the treat of knowing first-hand all the Olympians by name, or at least their kin, and sometimes you were an Olympian yourself.

"Ma'am, I'm gonna have to ask you to sit down, and be quiet, or the sheriff is gonna have to remove you from the arena."

"What do you mean, 'remove me,' I'd like to see the army it'd take to pry me outa here. I'll sit down and shut up when you start callin' this game like you deserve to wear those black and white stripes. My goodness, you're lettin' those boys from Frankfort stand in the paint so long I thought they were buying real estate." This conversation was not at all unique for a Friday night in the winter in Benton County. What made it unique was who was doing the talking.

Grace Johnson, the late 80s Hoosier B-ball fan, the part-time cook at the old folks' home, the crochet queen of bread wrappers, was also a rabid fan of Hoosier Hysteria, Indiana High School basketball. She had owned a season ticket as long as anyone in the county, even before there was such a thing as season tickets. Every home game, Grace sat about four or five rows behind the scorers' tables,

142

not far from the school superintendent. She also sat well within earshot of the officials, "zebras," as she so disrespectfully called them.

On this particular night the zebras were not "homers," by no means could they be accused of being partial to the home team. Quite the opposite. And she meant to let the referees know it was on record that they were obviously partial to the visitors, the Frankfort "Hot Dogs." Yes, that's right, hot dogs, a not-too-veiled reference to the frankfurter, I assume. Grace, however, was no surprise to the officials; she was famous in the conference, and how, in truth, could an official eject a nearly ninety year old from the arena, a truth, that the elderly Mrs. Johnson knew all too well. So the ref's continued to warn her, and she continued to warn them that they were in jeopardy of losing their official's licenses if they kept up their incompetent and blundering ways.

Indiana basketball has some notoriety nationally when it comes to a phenomenon known as "Hoosier Hysteria." What makes Indiana basketball so famous is not so much the quality of the game. I guess the caliber or skills of its players aren't all that exceptional, nor is it mediocre, for that matter. The hysteria takes place in the stands, as Grace Johnson illustrates every game. What makes it a phenomenon is the enthusiasm, interest, and support of the adoring fans, who also know the game, and have extraordinarily high expectations. If the Chicago Bulls had come to play the BC boys, it would be expected the hoopers would give Jordan and Pippen a run for their money. Hoosier hysteria is about the fans.

The love affair with Indiana High School basketball begins way back in grade school, fifth and sixth grade games in tiny gyms that smell a lot like cafeterias. The passion for the game begins there. But it also connects to driveways of the state. When Hoosiers buy a new home, they say, "We want a four bedroom home, two and a half baths, a couple living areas, and oh, it has to have a flat driveway." The real estate agents don't even ask why a flat driveway, because they know why. The flat driveway is necessary to put up a hoop and have a decent place to nurture the state's obsession. Hoosiers shoot baskets in the drippy sweat of a July evening, and when they have to shovel the driveway and maybe wear gloves in a late February thaw.

Benton County's population hardly numbered nine thousand, but the arena could seat thousands. There were only a dozen on the varsity team, but three or four thousand showed up every Friday or Saturday night to watch their team.

It began about six-thirty with the Junior Varsity game. The fans continued to trickle in throughout that game, growing in anticipation of the main event, the Varsity game. About eight o'clock the folk prepared. The smell of popcorn filled your nostrils as you entered the main gates of the arena. The pep band played a medley of pop songs, and golden oldies while pompom girls did high kick routines mid court. A band version of Credence Clearwater Revival's "Proud Mary" filled the ears of all as the pompom girls strutted their stuff, and Grace Johnson carefully made her way to her seat in the bleachers. As "Proud Mary" came to a cease, the BC boys team, clad in their green and gold warm-up uniforms proudly jogged into the arena to the adoring hoots, hollers, cheers, and applause of their adoring and faithful fans. The boys took a quick lap around the arena and proceeded into their "get ready for the game drills." Shortly thereafter, the Hot Dogs made a similar entrance to the boos and guffaws of the home crowd.

Following the warm-ups, came the introductions of the starting lineups. For most of these fellows, this was as close as they would ever make it to being worshipped or treated as gods. To be a starter on an Indiana high school team was high veneration in any culture, and these boys knew it. Each team then lined up along the line in front of their bench, and the announcement came through the P.A. system, "Please let us all rise for the singing of our National Anthem." The cheerleaders of both teams, in a moment of non-partisanship, circled around the BC logo in the middle of the court and with a few peculiar gestures, finally placed their hands over their hearts, and joined with all, "O say can you see …"

When the singing was over, it was time to begin: what everyone had come for, the main event, The Benton Central High School Bison versus the Frankfort High School Hot Dogs. It mattered little what the standings were in the conference, or the significance of this particular game. The reason it is called Hoosier Hysteria is all games, early in the season or during the state tournament, the fans treat them all like it was the most important and last game of the season. Normally, as a result, the players submitted to the intensity of the fans, and played like it was their last game.

The Pep Band played an occasional fight song, or a pop song to fire up the crowd, but in truth, once the first tip put the round ball into action, the fans knew what to do. Seldom was there any need to badger the masses to frenzy; it came naturally. The first tip was also Grace's cue to get intense, and make sure the Zebras were doing their job.

BC slipped behind early in the first quarter under an onslaught of Hot Dog long range artillery, so that they trailed 22-16 at the first break. Grace's strategy the first period had been to holler and whoop it up to support the boys to do their best. But it became clear that as the second quarter began, she adopted a more interventionist strategy. As one of the referees approached the scorer's table, just prior to the start of stanza two, Grace began, "Hey, young man, yeah, you, when you gonna start callin' 'em both ways? Does your kid play for Frankfort?

Or does Frankfort pay your salary for road games too?" For the most part he ignored her badgering, but the allegation against his impartiality and lack of integrity, being on the take, that did raise his eyebrow, and he made his first eye contact with the octogenarian rabble-rouser. But he went about his business most professionally.

For those of you who are basketball aficionados, you are familiar with the three second rule. It was midway through the third quarter when the score was getting a bit more tight, 41 to 38, with BC closing the gap; that also marked the sweet little ol' great grandmother received her first warning. Again, Grace's seat behind the scorer's bench was close enough that it was hard to ignore her berating of the officials. "Hey Zebra, yeah, you again, that was a good call, our boy did hack that Hot Dog, but have you ever heard of three seconds. That big oaf for the other team must run a parking lot down there in the paint. When you gonna call him for three seconds. Do you wanna give me your whistle? I know when to call it, and it's sure clear you don't know when." That was enough. He walked over to the BC bench, and summoned the ear of the BC coach. As the ref whispered into the coach's ear he kept gesturing up in to the stands, up in the exact direction of Grace. A few moments later the young coach nodded his head and he walked to the scorer's table, but without stopping he made his way through the several rows of bleachers until he asked the person sitting next to Mrs. Johnson to edge aside, and he sat next to her. And in a kind, but condescending manner he spoke to her, "Mrs. Johnson, you know we really appreciate your support all these years for our boys, our team. We really do. But, please, could you stop hassling the refs? And you really cannot make insulting comments about the other team's players. It's very unsportsmanlike. If you don't, and you know we're in a close game here, we might win it. But if you keep it up, that ref is going to call a technical on our bench. Those two points might just be the difference in the game. Worse yet, they may have to ask you to leave; they can eject you from the game."

Grace politely heard every word the well-intentioned coach said, and equally politely she answered his counsel. "Son, they are not going to throw an old lady out of this gym. And besides that, these zebras are atrocious. But I will try to control myself a bit, still if they blow it, Grace Johnson is gonna let 'em know it." The coach did not say another word. He rubbed his forehead with his hands, shook his head, and went back about his business. The action continued, but not for long. About a minute later, a whistle stopped the action again. The referee in question stepped a few steps toward the scorer's table and shouted, "Three seconds, Two-Four Red." Grace was vindicated. And she shouted as if to "Amen," the infraction, "It's about time you called that big lout for illegal parking." He would get called two more times, the last with just about a minute to play.

It was 58-57, still Frankfort leading, and hardly any harassment could have affected the players or the referees. The din of hollering, cheering, and whistling made any possibility of conversation, or even strategic verbal abuse of the officials impossible. Still Grace persevered. The third three second call meant that BC had the ball with its first chance to take the lead. Frenzy seemed a more appropriate description than even hysteria, but the point guard for the Bison was a bit too aggressive on an attempted drive into the paint. The whistle stopped play with forty-seven seconds on the clock. "Charging. One-One, Green." This was too much for Grace. "Charging? Charging," she screamed, "He was getting slapped more than the day he was born. Are you watching the same game we are?" That was it. The referee turned toward the BC bench and motioned with his hands making a sign like a "T", twice. The technical foul against BC was really against a nearly ninety year old woman. She hardly even weighed her age. With that, Dick Atterly, the BC Athletic Director made a trip up to Grace. But he didn't say a word; he just sat next to her, and she didn't say another word.

It was the big lout, the big oaf for the Frankfort Hot Dogs who was to take the two technical foul shots, however, he squandered his one opportunity to quiet once and for all the insults of the little old lady; he missed them both. No sooner had the visiting team put the ball back on the floor, and with a jab at the ball, the Bison, the home team, had possession of the ball and their chance to make their own destiny.

They passed the ball around a few times, and with seventeen seconds they called their last time out. This was Hoosier Hysteria at its best. But this time, Grace sat silently, as if muzzled by her monitor, the Athletic Director. It took just a moment once the ball was in play. A jump shot from fifteen feet sealed the victory for BC, and somehow Grace Johnson left justified. BC won 59-58.

In the full flush of victory, as Grace was helped by her junior escort, Dick Atterly, she spoke to the much maligned referee. With a grin of unmeasurable proportions painted on her face, and questionable sincerity, she told the zebra, "Good game, young man." Such is the way of Hoosier Hysteria, even for a little old lady who cooks for the old folk at the nursing home on Sunday nights.

Golf. It's a rich man's sport, or at least such is the stereotype. From the Masters Tournament, Augusta National Country Club, to the local snobbishness of the landed urban gentry, golf is not associated with the rural lifestyle. Certainly there is something to those stereotypes, but there are exceptions too. If you drove to the stoplight, and turned west, it was just a quarter of a mile until you came to the exception. You'd never see Ben Crenshaw, Jack Nicklaus or Tiger Woods frequenting the greens of BCCC, but the champions, the local lords of the fairways were there nevertheless. And this was no rich man's game. Lawyers, farmers, bankers, retirees, they were all there, and no gentry.

"We're gettin' together a foursome for Diddle Day. How 'bout you playin' with us. The lumber yard'll pay for it," so asked Chuck Allen of one of the local farmers, Jimbo Sharp, if he'd fill out the last slot in the Diddle Day foursome.

Jimbo asked, "What in the world is Diddle Day?"

"Oh, hell, I don't know. Diddle? George Diddle. I think he was some guy who designed a bunch of golf courses around here, and he designed our club. But it doesn't make any difference. It's a scramble with a bunch of guys. We'll drink some beers, play us some golf, then that night we'll have us a good steak dinner, give out some prizes, drink us some more beers … it'll be a good ol' time. How 'bout it?"

"When is it?" Jimbo asked.

"It's next Thursday," Chuck informed him.

"Well, I don't know. I think the wife wanted me to take her to Indianapolis to go shopping …"

"Shopping? Forget it. You can take her shopping anytime. But Diddle Day is only once a year. You're goin'."

So it was that Jimbo Sharp got bullied into his first Diddle Day.

The beer had already been flowing for a good while as the foursomes took off for the tees. Eighteen foursomes were all that was allowed to compete in the Diddle Day competition. By 11:30 that Thursday morning, most all were ready to get with it. Their golf carts congregated outside the Horseshoe Bar, near the Number One Tee. It was a shotgun start.

Now a shotgun start is not a literalism. There were no guns. But precisely at noon all the teams were at one of the eighteen tees, as they had been respectively assigned. When a loud boat horn was blown (the substitute for a shotgun), sufficiently obnoxious, sufficiently loud so that all the golfers could hear, and most of town as well, they were to begin play. So a team starting, for example, on the Seventh Hole, would play eighteen holes, thereby finishing on the Sixth Hole, and so forth.

As the foursomes gathered outside the Horseshoe Bar, they looked at eighteen pieces of paper posted on a large bulletin board. On those pieces of paper, each about one foot by two, listed the four golfers in that particular foursome. Below their names were boxes with holes one through eighteen listed. The rules for this raucous event called for a scramble. Simply put, each team was to be composed of one really good player, the "A" player, and one really bad player, the "D" player, and two in-between players, the "B" and "C" players. The rules called for all four players to hit a ball from the tee on each hole. But the team could pick from those four balls, the best ball, and from that best ball's approximate location each of the players would hit again the next shot. This process would be repeated until the ball was in the hole. Oh, actually it was slightly more complicated than that, but that suffices to speak of the gist of a scramble.

The horn blew, and Smitty, the "A" player for this foursome hit a crunching drive about 240 yards, just to the left of a large oak tree on Hole Number Seven. The "B" player, Chuck Allen, hit one into the corn field on the left side of the fairway, so his shot was of little help. Chuck invited a vendor buddy of his, Louie, a paint salesman for Sherwin-Williams, to be the "C" player, and he hit a decent drive just a little short and to the left of Smitty's. Jimbo gripped his driver, but swung so hard the ball took off hard to the right of the tee and hit a small oak tree square and ricocheted back, and nearly knocked Smitty of the seat of his golf cart. Smitty sarcastically encouraged Jimbo, "Swing harder next time Sharp; we'll use my drive." And so they did, and so began that year's Diddle Day.

No sooner had they started rolling their carts up the golf path, and the "Beer Wench," as Smitty so irreverently nicknamed her, brought her rolling saloon to ply her wares upon these eager patrons. "Hey, honey. Give us each two beers to start, and put it on my tab." Smitty was leading his partners into a blue alcohol haze, but he was generous, buying, and what all.

Diddle Day, after all, was less about golf, and more about fun, and in this case, fun meant a more than average dose of bawdy behavior, and way too much beer drinking. This foursome was simply an example of the behavior and activity of the other seventeen foursomes.

The rhythm of the day proceeded much as the first hole. Every once in a while, the C and D players would contribute to the betterment of the team's cause, but for the most part it was the A and B players, Smitty and Chuck, who toted the load.

On Number 6, a long par four paralleling a soybean field, there was a prize on the line, the long drive competition. There was a white stripe painted right up the middle of the fairway. Being in August, and that summer was a bit drier than normal, and the fairways at BCCC were not watered, the fairways still had a hint of green left in them, but it was a burnt green at best. Still there was a nice contrast between the white stripe up the middle and the tinderbox green turf. The object of this special competition within the larger competition was to cream the ball as far as one could up the fairway. However, you had to hit it straight, too.

By the time the motley crew of Smitty, Chuck, Louie and Jimbo came to Number 6, a number of foursomes had already played, and there was a little flag stuck in the ground with a name on it; written in barely legible pencil was, "Whiff." Dick Rayburn had hit one about 250 yards. A noble effort. Louie hit first with no consequence, and Chuck did not threaten Whiff's accomplishment either. Smitty was next, and he ripped one down the left side which clearly was farther than Rayburn, but it would remain to be seen, if it was farther "net." More about that in a moment. It was Jimbo though, who hit his second best shot of the day. "Holy smokes, you crunched that one," shouted Smitty, "Hell, if you hadn't hit it in the soybeans you might just have won the prize. You still might. Let's go measure."

As the golf carts pulled up to the marker sign, Smitty amused himself still further when he saw "Whiff" written on the card. "Whiff, I beat you, you wimp," Smitty speaking to the wind, but still he was not quite sure if he was longer. There on the ground next to the sign was a huge surveyor's tape measure. You had to subtract the distance off center from the total length. So Smitty's ball to the eye was fifteen, twenty yards beyond Whiff's, it was a bit off center to the left. So he measured. He was twelve yards left of center, and with some quick math, he had driven the ball about five yards longer, "net," than Dick Rayburn. "I did beat the wimp."

But Jimbo shouted from the soybeans, "Not so fast." Sure enough, Jimbo had crunched it. He must have hit it over 300 hundred yards, but was probably 20 yards into the soybeans. So Smitty took the tape over to Jimbo and measured. "Hell fire, you're wearing me out. I came to play golf, not go hiking … You're 73 yards off center, but you're 319 yards off the tee. Sharp, you can't hit a golf ball that far and lose, that makes you 246 yards net, about 10 yards short of me. Good try. Now carry me back to my cart." Although he was in the beans, that was Jimbo's second best shot.

Beer, golf and playful harassment continued throughout the afternoon. Smitty saw another foursome about ready to tee it up on an adjacent hole which merited his mischief. "Chuck, gimme that old ball there in the cart, yeah, that one." Moments later he threw the refuse ball about the time Dick Rayburn was taking his backswing. Whiff looked up annoyed, but Smitty was unrelentless and unrepentant, "Sure Whiff, so you can hit it when everyone's quiet. It takes a real man to hit the ball during incoming artillery." Diddle Day mischief, Smitty style, or lack of style for that matter.

The team was doing pretty well, what with the beer, the sophomoric behavior, but the greatest drama of the day came on Number 14, a par three, across the pond in the park, about 150 yards. Jimbo was the last to hit. Smitty had hit a good eight iron onto the green, Chuck hit his just short and a little to the right of the putting surface, and Louie dumped it into the pond. So Jimbo asked, "A six or seven iron?" And, "Hey, what's that car doing parked here?" Smitty answered both questions in order. "The way you been hittin' 'em I'd say a six iron; just swing easy and keep your head down. And the car, if you put that ball in the hole on this shot, you win that brand new Chrysler New Yorker."

Jimbo modestly responded, "I guess I will put it in the cup, I need a new car." On the new car was a sign, "Car courtesy of McCreary Chevrolet, Geo, Dodge, Chrysler, Plymouth." Actually, the dealer didn't give away the car. But the dealer bought an insurance policy from Lloyd's of London in the amount of the cost of the new car. Lloyd's figured the odds, and charged according. But Lloyd's had failed to figure on a D player, Jimbo Sharp, playing on that day.

With a herky jerky swing that had paid him little pleasure or reward all day, he flailed at the white sphere with his six iron war club. He didn't hit it all that well. It was kind of a screaming line drive over pond, bounced about twenty yards in front of the trap, hopped over the sand trap and started to skip over the green, still racing way too fast to come to a stop for any sort of a decent putt. But then the miracle occurred. It just so happened that the ball still rocketing across the green hit the shaft of the flag on the pin squarely. Upon hitting the flag stick, it caromed straight up into the air about a foot or so, and fell cleanly into the cup. Hole in one. Chrysler New Yorker for Jimbo.

"I can't believe it, Geesh. You won the damn car. The car. Louie, Chuck, just gaped dumbfounded. Smitty mumbled repeated blasphemies at the miracle. Jimbo just over and over again asked, "Is it in? Did I make it? Is it in? Did I win the car? The car is mine? Is it in? Did I make a hole in one."

The long and short of it was simple. Yes, he had won, the car was his. Even a crummy shot can sometimes pay off. This time it did for a farmer. His shot probably was more effective than any Arnold Palmer would have hit.

By the time the awards were passed out, more beer and whiskey were drunk, nobody really cared all that much what foursome was third, second or had won that year's Diddle Day Tournament. The club, and then the town was abuzz. "Did you hear that Jimbo won the car, that Chrysler, with a hole in one?" For years a car had been sitting next to the fourteenth hole, and never claimed. Diddle Day would never be the same, never the same after Jimbo Sharp won the New Yorker. Much like the state lottery frenzy, Jimbo's good fortune stirred interest throughout the community. The next Diddle Day there was so much interest, not so much in the golf, the harassment and the beer, but in the chance to win a car, that a decision was made to expand the field to thirty six foursomes, two would start on each of the eighteen shotgun start holes. It was suspected that few cared all that much about the golf. Heck, you can drink beer golf, cuss, and act like a fool on any day, but Diddle Day, you just might win a car, and as the saying goes, "You can't win unless you play."

But there were easier ways to make a killing playing golf beyond the stoplight than making a hole in one. Calcutta, as I was to learn, was more than a city in India. The Olympian golfers gathered, one will learn, for a variety of incentives.

"Hey, Reverend, do you wanna play in a Calcutta? It's the last Saturday and Sunday of June ..." Bub Grantland asked me.

"What's a Calcutta?"

"Calcutta? Calcutta?," my ignorance seemed to stupefy Bub. "Oh yeah. A Calcutta is just a special kind of golf tournament. You'd be in a foursome, a handicapped foursome made of A, B, C, and D players, like you're used to. You'd probably be the C or D player."

Interrupting I asked, "Okay, that's fine, but what is a Calcutta? Why do they call it a Calcutta?"

"Oh yeah. It's gambling. Pari-mutuel betting on each foursome. Meaning on Friday night before the tournament there's what's called an auction. All the foursomes are posted on a board with the team players' names, and people start bidding on buying part or all of various teams. The team with the most money bet on it, if it would win, would pay the lowest odds in return, and the team with the least bid on it would be the long shot and have to pay the highest odds if it wins, places or shows, you know, just like a horse race. Well, what do you think, wanna play in my foursome?"

After a silence of ten seconds or so, I answered, "You know Bub, I'm not sure what the folk would think about me gambling and stuff, and you know I don't have any extra money to be wagering and buying part of our team."

"No, no, no. You don't have to gamble at all," this time it was his turn to interrupt me. "No, all you have to do is play golf on our team. I mean, if you wanna buy in to our team or any other team, you can, but all you do is golf. No money is involved on your part, unless you want. You just play golf. You in?"

"One more question," I had one contingency left that may prohibit my participation. "You said the Calcutta is on Saturday and Sunday. When on Sunday?"

"Reverend, it's Saturday and Sunday afternoon. You'll have afternoon tee times both days, so it should be no problem. You can preach all morning if you want to, and still play in the Calcutta. You don't want to preach all morning do you?" Bub grinned sarcastically.

And so it was that I played in my one and only Calcutta, and got caught up in the unintentional half truth of Bub's explanation of just what a Calcutta was.

"Budweiser sponsors this summer's BCCC Calcutta," this was an added feature, a white plastic banner draped over the Horseshoe Bar, with the red Bud logo, and navy blue bold letters encouraged the participants not only to join in the festivities, but specifically, to belly up to the bar, and announce, "Hey, get me a Bud." Yet in truth it was almost impossible to belly up to the bar; there were too many gamblers, golfers, and beer drinkers in the room. The Horseshoe Bar easily accommodates thirty or forty guys, but there must have been nearly eighty squeezed in for the Calcutta auction.

Taped on most of the available wall space were the eighteen pairings, foursomes, or teams available. Each team had to pay $200 to enter the event, which a small portion of that paid for the post-tournament dinner, but most of it was the initial money in the gambling pot, somewhere near $3000. BCCC President, Dick Rayburn spoke through a tinny PA system that rang with hollow sounding feedback after every phrase. "Okay, guys, it's about time to begin the auction. Let me tell everybody how we're gonna do it." And he proceeded to do so, though many ignored him, a few heckled him, and after about three minutes of what some thought was gibberish, if not legalese, Smitty shouted above the PA feedback, and the general din of table muttering, "Hell, Whiff, let's get on with it. I bid one hundred bucks on Team #6," which by the way, was the team for whom Smitty would play.

But Rayburn would have nothing to do with Smitty's impropriety, "Shut up, Smith, if we don't do the rules, some of you will start whining about getting ripped off. When I've finished, and there are no questions, then we'll start the bidding. Until then, keep a lid on it." And so Smitty did, but Rayburn went on and on, while Smitty drank another beer or two. Finally, bids for the various teams began. Dick Rayburn would recognize the bidders, and shout, "Team Two, $350." Someone else, "Team Seven, $150." "I'll give two hundred seventy five bucks for Number 11." The better teams attracted the higher prices, and lesser or unknown teams sold for a deflated value. By the time the bidding was over Team Number Six sold for $950, and Number Two went for $1100. On the other hand, Team Number 14 sold for only $150. The auction concluded with Rayburn's announcement, "Okay, guys, the odds for the teams will be calculated tonight, posted tomorrow morning, please note your tee times and be here on time. May the best team win." And so the evening slowly wound down.

Yet the activity picked up by lunch time. There in The Horseshoe Bar were all the postings, plus the tee times, and above all, the calculated odds. Team Number Two, the favorite was only going to pay 3-2 odds, meaning for every two dollars bet, it would pay three. Smitty's team, Number Six, paid even money, or for every dollar bet, it would double the money. The longshot, Team Number 14, paid 12-1. My team, Number 11, paid 4-1. That may make it worthwhile. Yet for the first time, I sensed a pain in my gut, though I owned no part of my team, or any team, it first dawned on me that at some time in this event, how I hit the ball may cause someone to win some money, or lose some. I didn't like that feeling, but it was too late to back out. Yet the gnawing in my stomach, golf-pressure anxiety, didn't really hit me until late in our second round of golf, Sunday afternoon.

Yes, the Saturday eighteen holes went as well for our team as could be expected. We played to our potential which means we were in the middle of the pack. But by the sixteenth hole late Sunday afternoon, things were tightening up. We were in position for second or third place. In other words, we were in the running for big money, at least for our team owners.

Still, I was only the C or D player on my team, so no one could expect me to add much to our team's chance of cashing in on the big bucks. I'd just keep my nose clean, do my best, and relax. But it wasn't to be. By the time we came to the eighteenth green on Sunday afternoon, we were the only team left with a shot at third place. The gallery, the gathered fans, let us know as we stood over our putts on the last hole of competition.

I had hit a fairly good approach shot into the last hole but was barely on the green. Yet when it came time to putt, I was the farthest away, so golf etiquette dictates that I putt first. It was about a 35 foot putt down hill. I was a bit too aggressive, and the ball picked up more speed than I anticipated. My initial putt just missed the cup, and its momentum carried it seven or eight feet below the hole. For a person of my skill, it was considerably less than a 50-50 chance that I would sink the putt. But it probably would be no big deal in any case. Or so I thought.

After waiting a few minutes, my partners informed me that I was the last to putt out. But it was an irritating voice from the gallery that caused me to nearly toss my cookies. "Hey Patterson," a gravelly, raspy and annoying voice announced to me and the rest of the world, "Patterson, you make this putt, and you earn your team $850 ... Miss it and you get squat." I tried to ignore this information. I came to golf, not earn money. Yet for the first time in my undistinguished amateur golf career, putting for a beer was about the greatest stakes I had ever endured. $850? $850, that changed everything.

"$850, that's a mortgage payment," I thought to myself. It was more than I wanted to play for. It was more than I wanted to putt for. There must have been forty people huddled around the edge of the green as I looked over the putt. Speaking of squat, I squatted down near my ball, and eyeballed the putt. "I'll have to hit it pretty firm, but it looks straight as an arrow." As I came up out of my squat making ready to putt, Smitty again reminded me, "Yep, Patterson, this putt's worth $850."

Here I am, a minister of the gospel, not interested in gambling all that much, and certainly with no competence in golf to justify putting for nearly one thousand dollars, but nevertheless, I was forced to do so. I stood over the ball, lined up the face of my putter, and felt mentally how hard I needed to strike the ball. About that time, though it occurred to me, if I made the putt, I would make $850 for my owners, and if I missed it, which is only what was to be expected, I would blow 850 smackeroos.

Almost as if pulling back a sledgehammer of solid lead, I pulled back my putter. Then came the downswing. The ball clicked on the face of my putter, and clearly I was right. Not only had I hit the ball straight as I wanted, the putt was indeed straight. The ball took off headed square for the center of the hole. But would the putt have enough, enough speed, enough momentum to fall in the hole? The ball quickly traversed the first six of the eight foot trip, but it suddenly hit the brakes. It was quite literally like a car coasting out of gas. As the ball came within six inches of the cup, paydirt, it rolled so slowly I remember being able to read the logo on the ball, "Titleist." Still it had enough. Not only did the trademark disappear, so did the ball. It fell into the cup. Somebody had earned $850 on a putt I should not have made.

That was my last Calcutta. I was a professional minister of the gospel, not a golfer. I am committed to the pressures of the pastorate, of the pulpit, but not of the professional golf tour. Someone was happy I had made the putt. On the other hand, my making the putt, cost someone else a chance at the money as well. As an Olympian, an athlete, I enjoyed the joy of the thrill of victory, but the potential of the agony of defeat was more than I could bear.

While the population around the stoplight was small, the athletes, the Olympians abounded. The golf course entertained some, the basketball courts and arenas quartered still others, but one of the more populated venues of Olympic competition was the Little League baseball diamond. After all, there would be no Little League Parade, Festival or Queen, without Little League, and Favorite Fan Ernie would have no place to cheer on his host of favorite teams, if it weren't for the Little League competitors.

"Hey, George, what am I doing hanging here from this fence?" asked Billy Brown of his Assistant Coach, George Taylor. The position and situation merit further explanation. Billy and George with a few of their Little League Team were in the major league quality dugouts at the Fowler Little League Ball Park. The dugouts were nothing but class. Concrete block construction, only the finest corrugated, galvanized steel roof sheeting, and neatly-carpentered lumber finished the roof. In front, protecting the inhabitants from errant foul balls, was a chain link fence that ran to the roof line, probably about eight feet from floor to ceiling. Usually the coach and players in the dugout would either pace like a caged lion inside the confines during the game, or they would be seated on the bench that runs along the back wall, the closed portion of the dugout. But Billy was neither seated nor standing. Instead he was hanging, hanging six to ten inches off the concrete floor of the dugout. His two hands clawed at the fence not far from the roof, and the toes of his faded and well-worn green canvas Converse All Stars were sort of stuck, sort of dangling in mid-air. The position: Billy somehow came to be dangling from the fence. "George, what am I doing hanging here from this fence?"

The position is more readily explained than the situation that led to that position. It was the heat of Olympian baseball competition that led to Billy assuming the position. It was the last game of the season. While there were only sixteen games in the season, by early July, many hot and humid nights, the challenge of competition, most parents, fans, players, would readily have sworn that they had played nearly a major league 162 games. And for George and Billy the season was made longer by coaching a less than best team. In fact, when the season started, their team, the Tigers, lost their first four games, and five of the first six. This makes for more wear and tear than winning the first six, be assured. When the season started, it was not so much a less than best team, it was the worst team, with dismal prospects.

But that had all been forgotten. The Tigers were playoff bound, playoff bound, that is, if they won their last game. Of the eight teams in that league, the top two went to the playoffs. By knocking off the Yankees, the Tigers would not only eliminate the Yankees from the playoffs, but secure for themselves the unthinkable at the beginning of the season, second place, and a playoff spot. A miracle had happened, and neither Billy nor George had any great clue as to how it was accomplished. Losing five of their first six ballgames, the winds of fate blew in an entirely new direction. The Tigers had reeled off eight wins in nine contests. This tenth win would clinch a berth in the playoffs.

The Yankees, on the other hand, had nearly a mirror image of the Tiger's season. They were off to a victorious start, but under the siege of the season discovered it evermore difficult to win a game. So as the Olympians gathered prior to the game, all knew it would be a laurel wreath of triumph for one team, and a fall and winter of disappointment, discontent and unrealized dreams for the others.

The game began much like the season. The six inning game saw the Tigers fall behind six to one by the end of the third inning. No one thought this an insurmountable lead, but the gloom of defeat seemed to hang over the Tiger's dugout even after the fourth inning when the Tiger's answered the Yankee's increase of one run with two of their own. Score: 7 to 3. They traded runs in the fifth: 8 to 4. Still the cloud of gloom and defeat fogged the optimism of coaches Billy and George, even though they managed to hold the Yankees scoreless in the top of the sixth, what could be the last inning.

The gloom failed to lift when Chucky Bishop whiffed on three pitches to make it one out with only two outs left. The hope for a miracle nearly was extinguished. Kelly Thompson's walk seemed noneventful, at the time, but consecutive walks, the second to Jimmy Reston breathed the first waft of hope into the sad confines of the Tiger's dugout. A wild pitch, and a passed ball next, scored one run, and the remaining runner came to third base. Score: 8 to 5, one out.

Billy's son hit an anemic first pitch pop-up that proved effective enough to score another run and leave him, Clay, on first. Another walk moved him to second and two runners on, which resulted in a timeout. The Yankees changed pitchers. The pressure seemed too much. The next pitcher fared no better in finding the strike zone; he walked the first batter he faced, Tim Gillis, on four pitches, bases now loaded. Still the score was 8 to 6 with one out.

The surprise of the hoped-for-miracle was that the best player on the team, Lenny Vaughn, who hit anything thrown in his zip code did just that, but with a most surprising result. The first pitch to Lenny with bases loaded, was smacked like a rocket right at the pitcher's face. Nine out of ten times this would have been a single at worst, and probably a double as the fielder bobbled the ball and a crafty aggressive runner like Lenny would stretch his luck for second base. But Lenny's luck would not stretch in anyway. As the pitcher ducked from the concussion-potential projectile, he held his glove in front of his face. That glove was opened just enough that he trapped the ball. Two outs, he did not deliver the goods, and he almost helped the Tiger's commit suicide, and in doing so, Lenny Vaughn's line drive produced the situation.

What followed took place in an elapsed time of about four or five seconds. Those seconds could have provided the third out for the Yankees, thus securing for them playoff glory, or accomplish the comeback miracle of a comeback season for the Tigers.

Upon catching the ball, a series of events and explosion of noise interrupted the quiet tension of the Tiger's attempting to come back for the win. The noise started as cheering for a great catch by the Tiger's pitcher. Yet as Little League Olympians are prone to do, they react more than think. The runner at first, Tim, took off for second base. Without getting too muddled in the intricacies of baseball rules, that was not a good thing to do. And the pitcher knew it. His coaches, still amidst the cheering of the crowd for the great catch, hollered to the pitcher to throw the ball to first to get the third out. About that time Billy and George hollered for Tim to get back to first. The problem for Tim was the first baseman was still cheering in glory for the pitcher, and was ill-prepared to participate in the game saving put-out at first base.

The shouting only grew in intensity as the pitcher ran off the mound toward first base to either step on first or put the tag on Tim. It was not at all certain whether Tim or the pitcher would make it to back to the base first. Yet as soon as the pitcher stepped toward first, Billy and George hollered for the runner on third, Clay, Billy's son, to run for home.

At this point about two seconds had elapsed, and the noise rivaled any riots in any place, any time. But the pitcher remained relatively calm, even though all else seemed to be falling apart at the seams. In the next second a chain reaction of events provided the miracle, at least a miracle from the Tiger's perspective. First, the pitcher, with the encouragement of his coaches' shouts realized that the problem of his team's destiny was no longer at first base, but was somewhere headed from third to home. Second, he wheeled and fired to the catcher standing on homeplate. If Clay were to continue his attempt to score he would be easy pickings. So within a step, third, Clay turned about and headed back to safety at third base. Now if the fourth step had not been taken, the outcome would have been still largely in doubt. It would have been 8 to 6, two outs, and bases loaded.

But such is history that there was a fourth step. The catcher noticed that the runner at second was almost to third, Clay was headed back to third and the third baseman stood ready with glove open to tag either runner out and win the game for the Yankees. Fourth, the catcher fired the ball into the growing congestion at third. But his ball, thrown amidst the shouts, the adrenaline of the moment, had just the slightest rise on it as it traversed the distance from the catcher to the third baseman's glove. That rise proved fatal. It just nipped the top of the third baseman's glove and caromed into left field.

With the error Billy and George shouted new instructions and Clay and the other runner scampered home. Two outs, bottom of the sixth. Score: 8 to 8. Fifth, Billy turned to George and asked, "What am I doing hanging here from this fence?" About the time the ball caromed into left field, Billy launched himself off the concrete with a shout, "Run, Clay, run, run, run." As he shouted he launched off that concrete to roost with his claws in the chain link fence in some vicarious running of his own as he watched the two runners cross home plate. Score: 8 to 8.

When the noise abated, and the dust cleared, and with some embarrassment, Billy pulled his claws, his fingers, out of the fence to light again on terra firma, the score was 8 to 8, two outs, and Tim Gillis was at third base, posing as the potential winning run. Billy called timeout and gave instructions to Tim, and to the next batter, Patrick Thompson. But it seemed somewhat anticlimactic as Patrick hit a grounder between first and second and Tim Gillis stomped on home plate. Miracle accomplished. The comeback game capped off the comeback season.

The Olympians all, winners and losers, seemed numb to it all. There were no laurel wreaths handed to anyone. The Yankees had nothing but the disappointment of squandering a victory for a loss, and the enjoyment of another season of playing what is known as our nation's pastime. The Tiger's only had the joy of the comeback, the thrill of accomplishment of what for any number of times seemed impossible. Still they had another game to play, another opportunity for joy, or the same heartache that they currently were watching the Yankee's bitterly endure.

It was not that many moments later, after the game, after the shouting, after the running, hitting and catching, after Ernie had packed up his folding chair gathered up his boombox, to return to "the home" just up the block, after the last crushed snow cone cup had been tossed in the trash can-after all this, and you gazed across the diamond, glad the season was over, but looked forward to the Olympians' return again in the spring.

The torch came thousands of miles. From the eternal flame in Athens it was lighted, and traversed the globe in its path to Los Angeles, to the next Olympic Games in the City of Angels. Nobody in Fowler ever expected it to come there, to the stoplight. Life bypassed Fowler just like the interstate highway did. So what a surprise as the torch came up the highway headed for our town, pointed right for the stoplight.

As in my days in college, usually the highway was a seldom traversed thoroughfare, the road that led to some other place. As the Olympic Torch came north up Highway 52, up from Indianapolis, up from Athens, it was headed to Chicago and other parts destined to ignite the torch for the games in California. But the Torch Lighting Committee chose a route that by good fortune brought it right up to the stoplight, and then on north, on to Chicago. But for several minutes that torch would illuminate the day of the folk there in the county, most notably Fowler.

The estimated time of arrival was 1 PM on that certain summer Friday. Yet by noon, the highway found itself bordered by hundreds, if not thousands of Olympic fans, and torch voyeurs. Starting as far as a mile south of town the gallery gathered to watch a Grecian flame bisect through town. That gallery proved to be a representative sampling of the town and county itself, and most were Olympians themselves. To be sure they had never hurled a javelin in Rome, or skated in Helsinki, but many in their day, and in their way, had competed in the local Olympiad. Some at the bowling alley, some on the gridiron of yesteryear, others shot baskets, women and men in a grade school gym. Then the more famous, the Diddle Day champions at BCCC, they lined the highway too, gaping, maneuvering for the best platform from which to gaze upon the international flame. A few who watched had the mark of Olympians, callused thumb and index fingers from pitching horseshoes. A number bore the scars of being wounded in the heat of competition, stung by the horn of a Channel Catfish caught in a nearby creek, or up to Willow Slough; they gazed on as well. The Friday afternoon Bridge Club suspended their heated competition not wanting to miss this chance of a lifetime. The county Olympians were there, the baseball teams and the Little League Queen too.

It was more exciting than the Wells Fargo Wagon. The murmuring built as the runner neared. At first it was hard to make out the runner, let alone the torch. The runner was preceded by a state trooper on a cycle ahead of the flame by as much as one hundred yards. Following the runner carrying the torch was a press and camera truck, and a van with some of the other runners. The runners rotated, each running several miles at a time, and periodically they rendezvoused with a new load of runners honored to carry the torch. But as the torch came to the city limits of Fowler, it was the Lieutenant Governor doing the honor. He was running at a modest clip, and in his outstretched hand was the Torch with flame from Ancient Greece.

Most along the route applauded, others added cheers, and many had glistening eyes as the torch of all that is good about athletic competition, all that binds humanity together in goodness, rather than bickering, passed the spectators. The sun was bright enough that the mostly blue flame was hard to make out, but an occasional trail of black sooty smoke evidenced the Grecian flame.

"Well, mommy, there it goes. Will that be the same flame that lights the fire in Los Angeles at the Olympics?" a youngster asked. The mommy answered, "Yes, honey, that's the one, that's the flame. And yes, there it goes."

And so it did. As the runner pushed on north, it was almost impossible to track the egress as one could monitor the inbound access, what with the press and van blocking the view. So quickly after the Lieutenant Governor passed, the crowd disbursed, but there was a pride in the eyes of the citizens, the Olympian spectators. It was a two-fold pride: pride in the reality that they can tell their offspring, "Yep, I saw the Olympic torch when it came to Fowler." And pride that for once their town, the place in the sun, this time had not been bypassed.

The Olympians were as much a part of the town as the farmers, the Steel Magnolias, and the Endangered Patriarchs. In truth there was much overlap and duplication among them all. Only basketball required a season ticket. Usually the only requirement to participate or spectate was the desire to show up, and the willingness to holler a bit, to whoop it up, and join in the fun, the chaos, and the living out of life in the community, the community there beyond the stoplight.

LAST WORD

The years growing up, I never turned to enter, to go beyond the stoplight. Like thousands of others, I simply waited for the light to turn green, and race on north or south back to the big city. Never would I have guessed that a call from God to ministry would lead me to such a place, and pursue a parish ministry in that little town. But so it did, it led to the snare. So when I came to the stoplight, when the light was red, rather than heading on with the green to the city, I turned in and brought my family with me, and my life is richer for it. Prior to my life in the fowler's snare, I may have been guilty of urban ignorance, not knowing the goodness of life, the richness of small town America's people. I had to turn in, enter, go beyond the stoplight to fall in love with a part of this great land that prior I had ignorantly avoided.

To be caught in the fowler's snare must in the norm of things be a dreadful place to be. Surely it was for David, time again captured in the snare of ugly circumstance. But not so for me, or the many people who have the privilege to live there, there in the Fowler's snare.

"Surely he will save you from the fowler's snare …"

—Psalm 91:3

I trust, I hope, I will never escape.

POST-DEDICATION and ACKNOWLEDGEMENTS

To the people of rural and small town USA, to all the people of Benton County, Indiana, and the people of Fowler, Indiana, I dedicate this work. I am forever indebted to the friends I made through the county, in particular, Benton County Country Club, the Dairy Barn, and First Presbyterian Church, Fowler. You made my life forever richer.

Also thank you for the local help of The Reverend Ann Williams, and Mrs. Sandy Sylvester. I am indebted to the creative ideas of my son, Andrew, and family friend, Brenden Macaluso. For the labor of love in reading my manuscript, my good friend, Karen Carson, and daughter-in-law, Lara Patterson, and the best wife in the world, Pat, thank you.

978-0-595-45381-8
0-595-45381-3

Printed in the United States
87963LV00005B/140/A